George Rawlinson

The Story of Ancient Egypt

George Rawlinson

The Story of Ancient Egypt

ISBN/EAN: 9783337241506

Printed in Europe, USA, Canada, Australia, Japan

Cover: Foto ©ninafisch / pixelio.de

More available books at **www.hansebooks.com**

The Story of the Nations

THE STORY OF
ANCIENT EGYPT

BY

GEORGE RAWLINSON, M.A.

CAMDEN PROFESSOR OF ANCIENT HISTORY IN THE UNIVERSITY OF OXFORD,
AND CORRESPONDING MEMBER OF THE ROYAL ACADEMY OF TURIN;
AUTHOR OF "THE FIVE GREAT MONARCHIES OF THE ANCIENT
EASTERN WORLD," ETC. ETC.

WITH THE COLLABORATION OF

ARTHUR GILMAN, M.A.

AUTHOR OF "A HISTORY OF THE AMERICAN PEOPLE," "THE STORY OF ROME," "THE
STORY OF THE SARACENS," ETC.

NEW YORK AND LONDON
G. P. PUTNAM'S SONS
The Knickerbocker Press
1888

COPYRIGHT
BY G. P PUTNAM'S SONS
1887
Entered at Stationers' Hall, London
BY T. FISHER UNWIN

To
REGINALD STUART POOLE,

KEEPER OF COINS IN THE BRITISH MUSEUM,

AND CORRESPONDENT OF THE INSTITUTE OF FRANCE,

IN ACKNOWLEDGMENT OF

MUCH HELP AND MUCH PLEASURE

DERIVED FROM

HIS EGYPTIAN LABOURS.

CONTENTS.

I.

THE LAND OF EGYPT 1-22

General shape of Egypt, 1 — Chief divisions: twofold division, 2: threefold division, 3—The Egypt of the maps unreal, 4—Egypt, "the gift of the river," in what sense, 5, 6—The Fayoum, 7—Egyptian speculations concerning the Nile, 7, 8—The Nile not beautiful, 8—Size of Egypt, 9—Fertility, 10—Geographical situation, 11, 12—The Nile, as a means of communication, 12, 13—Phenomena of the inundation, 13, 14—Climate of Egypt, 14—Geology, 15—Flora and Fauna, 16, 17—General monotony, 19—Exceptions, 20-22.

II.

THE PEOPLE OF EGYPT 23-45

Origin of the Egyptians, 23—Phenomena of their language and type, 24—Two marked varieties of physique, 25—Two types of character: the melancholic, 25, 27 : the gay, 27-29 —Character of the Egyptian religion : polytheism, 30, 31— Animal worship, 31-33—Worship of the monarch, 33— Osirid saga, 34, 35—Evil gods, 36—Local cults, 37—Esoteric religion, 38: how reconciled with the popular belief, 39— Conviction of a life after death, 40, 41—Moral code, 41-43— Actual state of morals, 43—Ranks of society, 44, 45.

III.

THE DAWN OF HISTORY 46-64

Early Egyptian myths: the Seb and Thoth legends, 46, 47—The destruction of mankind by Ra, 48—Traditions concerning M'na, or Menes, 48—Site of Memphis, 49—Great Temple of Phthah at Memphis, 50, 51—Names of Memphis, 51—Question of the existence of M'na, 52, 53—Supposed successors of M'na, 54—First historical Egyptian, Sneferu, 55—The Egypt of his time, 56—Hieroglyphics, 57—Tombs, 58—Incipient pyramids, 59, 60—Social condition of the people, 60—Manners, 61—Position of women, 62-64.

IV.

THE PYRAMID BUILDERS 65-94

Difficult to realize the conception of a great pyramid, 65—Egyptian idea of one, 66—Number of pyramids in Egypt: the Principal Three, 67—Description of the "Third Pyramid," 67-71; of the "Second Pyramid," 72; of the "First" or "Great Pyramid," 75-81—The traditional builders, Khufu, Shafra, and Menkaura, 82; the pyramids their tombs, 82—Grandeur of Khufu's conception, 83—Cruelty involved in it, 84, 85—The builders' hopes not realized, 85, 86—Skill displayed in the construction, 86—Magnificence of the architectural effect, 89—Inferiority of the "Third Pyramid," 90—Continuance of the pyramid period, 91-94.

V.

THE RISE OF THEBES TO POWER, AND THE EARLY THEBAN KINGS 95-112

Shift of the seat of power—site of Thebes, 95—Origin of the name of Thebes, 96—Earliest known Theban king, Antef I., 97—His successors, Mentu-hotep I. and "Antef the Great," 98—Other Antefs and Mentu-hoteps, 98, 99—Sankh-ka-ra and his fleet, 99, 100—Dynasty of Usurtasens and Amenemhats:

CONTENTS.   xi

                                          PAGE
spirit of their civilization, 100, 101—Reign of Amenemhat I.,
102—His wars and hunting expeditions, 103, 104—Usurtasen
I. ; his wars, 105—His sculptures and architectural works,
106—His obelisk, 107-109—Reign of Amenemhat II. : tablet
belonging to his time, 109, 110—Usurtasen II. and his conquests, 111, 112.

VI.

THE GOOD AMENEMHAT AND HIS WORKS . 113-123

Dangers connected with the inundation of the Nile, twofold,
113—An excessive inundation, 114 ; a defective one, 115—
Sufferings from these causes under Amenemhat III., 115, 116—
Possible storage of water, 117—Amenemhat's reservoir, the
"Lake Mœris," 118—Doubts as to its dimensions, 119, 120—
Amenemhat's "Labyrinth," 121—His pyramid, and name of
Ra-n-mat, 122, 123.

VII.

ABRAHAM IN EGYPT 124-131

Wanderings of the Patriarch, 124—Necessity which drove him
into Egypt, 125—Passage of the Desert, 126—A dread anxiety
unfaithfully met, 127—Reception on the frontier, and removal
of Sarah to the court, 128—Abraham's material well-being,
129—The Pharaoh restores Sarah, 130—Probable date of the
visit, 130—Other immigrants, 131.

VIII.

THE GREAT INVASION —THE HYKSOS OR SHEP-
HERD KINGS—JOSEPH AND APEPI . . 132-146

Exemption of Egypt hitherto from foreign attack, 132 —
Threatening movements among the populations of Asia, 133 —
Manetho's tale of the "Shepherd" invasion, 134—The prob-
able reality, 135, 136—Upper Egypt not overrun, 137—The

first Hyksos king, Set, or Saites, 138—Duration of the rule, doubtful, 139—Character of the rule improves with time, 140—Apepi's great works at Tanis, 144—Apepi and Ra-sekenen, 145—Apepi and Joseph, 146.

IX.

HOW THE HYKSOS WERE EXPELLED FROM EGYPT 147–169

Rapid deterioration of conquering races generally, 147, 148—Recovery of the Egyptians from the ill effects of the invasion, 149—Second rise of Thebes to greatness, 150—War of Apepi with Ra-sekenen III., 151—Succession of Aahmes; war continues, 152—The Hyksos quit Egypt, 153—Aahmes perhaps assisted by the Ethiopians, 154–157.

X.

THE FIRST GREAT WARRIOR KING, THOTHMES I. 158–169

Early wars of Thothmes in Ethiopia and Nubia, 158–160—His desire to avenge the Hyksos invasion, 161—Condition of Western Asia at this period, 162, 163—Geographical sketch of the countries to be attacked, 164, 165—Probable information of Thothmes on these matters, 167—His great expedition into Syria and Mesopotamia, 167—His buildings, 168—His greatness insufficiently appreciated, 169.

XI.

QUEEN HATASU AND HER MERCHANT FLEET . 170–188

High estimation of women in Egypt, 170—Early position of Hatasu as joint ruler with Thothmes II., 173 —Her buildings at this period, 173—Her assumption of male attire and titles, 174-177—Her nominal regency for Thothmes III., and real sovereignty, 177, 178—Construction and voyage of her fleet, 178–183—Return of the expedition to Thebes, 184—Construction of a temple to commemorate it, 185 — Joint reign of Hatasu with Thothmes III.—Her obelisks, 186—Her name obliterated by Thothmes, 187.

CONTENTS. xiii

XII.

THOTHMES THE THIRD AND AMENHOTEP THE
SECOND 189-207

First expedition of Thothmes III. into Asia, 189-191—His
second and subsequent campaigns, 191, 192—Great expedition
of his thirty-third year, 192, 193—Adventure with an elephant,
194—Further expeditions: amount of plunder and tribute,
195—Interest in natural history, 196—Employment of a navy,
197—Song of victory on the walls of the Temple of Karnak,
198-199—Architectural works, 199-201—Their present wide
diffusion, 202—Thothmes compared with Alexander, 203—
Description of his person, 204—Position of the Israelites under
Thothmes III., 205—Short reign of Amenhotep II., 206.

XIII.

AMEN-HOTEP III. AND HIS GREAT WORKS—THE
VOCAL MEMNON 208-222

The "Twin Colossi" of Thebes: their impressiveness, 208-
211—The account given of them by their sculptor, 212—The
Eastern Colossus, why called "The Vocal Memnon," 213, 214
—Earliest testimony to its being "vocal," 214—Rational account of the phenomenon, 215-217—Amenhotep's temple at
Luxor, 217, 218—His other buildings, 219—His wars and expeditions, 219, 220—His lion hunts; his physiognomy and
character, 221, 222.

XIV.

KHUENATEN AND THE DISK-WORSHIPPERS . 223-230

Obscure nature of the heresy of the Disk-worshippers, 223-
225—Possible connection of Disk-worship with the Israelites,
226—Hostility of the Disk-worshippers to the old Egyptian
religion, 227—The introduction of the "heresy" traced to
Queen Taia, 228—Great development of the "heresy" under
her son, Amenhotep IV., or Khuenaten, 229—Other changes
introduced by him, 230.

xiv   CONTENTS.

XV.

BEGINNING OF THE DECLINE OF EGYPT . . 231–252

Advance of the Hittite power in Syria, 231 –War of Saplal with Ramesses I., 231—War of Seti I. with Maut-enar, 232 — Great Syrian campaign of Seti, followed by a treaty, 233 235 — Seti's other wars, 236—His great wall, 237—Hittite war of Ramesses II., 238-240—Poem of Pentaour, 241—Results of the battle of Kadesh, a new treaty and an inter marriage, 242, 243—Military decline of Egypt, 244—Egyptian art reaches its highest point : Great Hall of Columns at Karnak, 245— Tomb of Seti, 246, 247—Colossi of Ramesses II., 248— Ramesses II. the great oppressor of the Israelites, 249— Physiognomies of Seti I. and Ramesses II., 250 252.

XVI.

MENEPHTHAH I., THE PHARAOH OF THE EXODUS 253–268

Good prospect of peace on Menephthah's accession, 253— General sketch of his reign, 254—Invasion of the Maxyes, 255 —Their Mediterranean allies, 256,257—Repulse of the invasion, 258-261—Israelite troubles, 262-264—Loss of the Egyptian chariot force in the Red Sea, 265—Internal revolts and difficulties, 265—General review of the civilization of the period, 266-268.

XVII.

THE DECLINE OF EGYPT UNDER THE LATER
    RAMESSIDES 269–287

Temporary disintegration of Egypt, 269—Reign of Setnekht, 270—Reign of Ramesses III., 271—General restlessness of the nations in his time, 272—Libyan invasion of Egypt, 273, 274 – Great invasion of the Tekaru, Tanauna, and others, 275, 276—First naval battle on record, 277, 278 Part taken by Ramesses in the fight, 278 281 –Campaign of revenge, 282 – Later years of Ramesses peaceful, 283 General decline of Egypt, 284—Insignificance of the later Ramessides, 284, 285— Deterioration in art, literature, and morals, 285-287.

CONTENTS.

XVIII.

THE PRIEST-KINGS—PINETEM AND SOLOMON . 288-297

Influence of the priests in Egypt, 288—Ordinary relations between them and the kings, 289—High-priesthood of Ammon becomes hereditary; Herhor, 290—Reign of Pinetem I., 293—Reign of Men-khepr-ra, 294—Rise of the kingdom of the Israelites, 295—Friendly relations established between Pinetem II. and Solomon, 296—Effect on Hebrew art and architecture, 297.

XIX.

SHISHAK AND HIS DYNASTY 298-313

Shishak's family Semitic, but not Assyrian or Babylonian, 298—Connected by marriage with the priest-kings, 299, 300—Reception of Jeroboam by Shishak, 301—Shishak's expedition against Rehoboam, 302—Aid lent to Jeroboam in his own kingdom, 303—Arab conquests, 304—Karnak inscription, 305—Shishak's successors, 306—War of Zerah (Osorkon II.?) with Asa, 308—Effect of Zerah's defeat, 309—Decline of the dynasty, 310—Disintegration of Egypt, 310, 311—Further deterioration in literature and art, 311-313.

XX.

THE LAND SHADOWING WITH WINGS—EGYPT
UNDER THE ETHIOPIANS . . . 314-330

Vague use of the term Ethiopia, 314—Ethiopian kingdom of Napata, 315—Wealth of Napata, 316—Piankhi's rise to power, 317—His protectorate of Egypt, 318—Revolt of Tafnekht and others, 318—Suppression of the revolt, 319-322—Death of Piankhi, and revolt of Bek-en-ranf, 323—Power of Shabak established over Egypt, 324—General character of the Ethiopian rule, 324—Advance of Assyria towards the Egyptian border, 325—Collision between Sargon and Shabak, 326—Reign of Shabatok—Sennacherib threatens Egypt, 327—Reign of Tehrak, 328-330.

xvi   CONTENTS.

XXI.
THE FIGHT OVER THE CARCASE—ETHIOPIA *V*. ASSYRIA 331-341

Egypt attacked by Esarhaddon, 331, 332—Great battle near Memphis, 333—Memphis taken, and flight of Tehrak to Napata, 334—Egypt split up into small states by Esarhaddon, 334, 335—Tehrak renews the struggle, 336—Tehrak driven out by Asshur-bani-pal, 337—His last effort, 337—Attempt made by Rut-Ammon fails, 338—Temporary success of Mi-Ammon-nut, 339—Egypt becomes once more an Assyrian dependency, 340—Her wretched condition, 341.

XXII.
THE CORPSE COMES TO LIFE AGAIN—PSAMATIK I. AND HIS SON, NECO 342-359

Foreign help needed to save a sinking state, 342—Libyan origin of Psamatik I., 344—His revolt connected with the decline of Assyria, 345—Assistance rendered him by Gyges, 345—His struggle with the petty princes, 346—Reign of Psamatik: place assigned by him to the mercenaries, 347—His measures for restoring Egypt to her former prosperity, 348, 349—He encourages intercourse between Egypt and Greece, 350-352—Egypt restored to life: character of the new life, 353—Later years of Psamatik: conquest of Ashdod, 354—Reign of Neco: his two fleets, 355—His circumnavigation of Africa, 356—His conquest of Syria, 357—Jeremiah on the battle of Carchemish, 358—Neco's dream of empire terminates, 359.

XXIII.
THE LATER SAÏTE KINGS—PSAMATIK II., APRIES, AND AMASIS 360-367

The Saïtic revival in art and architecture, 360—Some recovery of military strength, 361—Expedition of Psamatik II. into Ethiopia, 362—Part taken by Apries in the war between

CONTENTS. xvii

PAGE

Nebuchadnezzar and Zedekiah, 363—His Phœnician conquests, 364—His expedition against Cyrene, 364—Invasion of Egypt by Nebuchadnezzar, 365—Quiet reign of Amasis, 366—The Saïtic revival not the recovery of true national life, 367.

XXIV.

THE PERSIAN CONQUEST 368-380

Patient acquiescence of Amasis in his position of tributary to Babylon, 368—Rise of the Persian power under Cyrus, and appeal made by Crœsus to Amasis, League of Egypt, Lydia, and Babylon, 369, 370—Precipitancy of Crœsus, 371—Fall of Babylon, 371—Later wars of Cyrus, 372—Preparations made against Egypt by Cambyses, 373, 374—Great battle of Pelusium, 375—Psamatik III. besieged in Memphis, 376—Fall of Memphis, and cruel treatment of the Egyptians by Cambyses, 377, 378—His iconoclasm checked by some considerations of policy, 379—Conciliatory measures of Darius Hystaspis, 379, 380.

XXV.

THREE DESPERATE REVOLTS 380-386

First revolt, under Khabash, easily suppressed by Xerxes, 381, 382—Second revolt under Inarus and Amyrtæus, assisted by Athens, 382, 383—Suppressed by Megabyzus, 384—Herodotus in Egypt, 385—Third revolt, under Nefaa-rut, attains a certain success; a native monarchy re-established, 386.

XXVI.

NECTANEBO I.—A LAST GLEAM OF SUNSHINE . 387-392

Unquiet time under the earlier successors of Nefaa-rut, 387—Preparations of Nectanebo (Nekht Hor-heb) for the better protection of Egypt against the Persians, 388—Invasion of Egypt by Pharnabazus and Iphicrates, 389—Failure of the expedition, 390—A faint revival of art and architecture, 391.

CONTENTS.

XXVII.

PAGE

THE LIGHT GOES OUT IN DARKNESS . . 393–402

Reign of Te-her (Tacho), 393—Reign of Nectanebo II. (Nekht-nebf), 394—Revolt of Sidon, and great expedition of Ochus, 394, 395—Sidon betrayed by Tennes and Memnon of Rhodes, 396—March upon Egypt: disposition of the Persian forces, 397—Skirmish at Pelusium, and retreat of Nekht-nebf to Memphis, 398, 399—Capture of Pelusium, 399—Surrender of Bubastis, 400—Nehkt-nebf flies to Ethiopia, 401—General reflections, 402.

INDEX 403

LIST OF ILLUSTRATIONS.

	PAGE
PILLARED HALL OF SETI I.	*Frontispiece*
DOM AND DATE PALM TREES	17
FIGURES OF TAOURT	36
FIGURE OF BES	37
TABLET OF SNEFERU AT WADY-MAGHARAH	55
PYRAMID OF MEYDOUM	59
GREAT PYRAMID OF SACCARAH	61
SECTION OF THE SAME	61
GROUP OF STATUARY—HUSBAND AND WIFE	63
SECTION OF THE THIRD PYRAMID	69
TOMB CHAMBER IN THE SAME	69
SARCOPHAGUS OF MYCERINUS	73
SECTION OF THE SECOND PYRAMID	73
SECTION OF THE GREAT PYRAMID	76
KING'S CHAMBER AND CHAMBERS OF CONSTRUCTION IN THE GREAT PYRAMID	77
THE GREAT GALLERY IN THE SAME	79
VIEW OF THE FIRST AND SECOND PYRAMIDS	87

LIST OF ILLUSTRATIONS.

	PAGE
SPEARING THE CROCODILE	103
OBELISK OF USURTASEN I. ON THE SITE OF HELIOPOLIS	107
BUST OF A SHEPHERD KING	141
HEAD OF NEFERTARI-AAHMES	155
BUST OF THOTHMES I.	159
HEAD OF THOTHMES II.	171
HEAD OF QUEEN HATASU	171
GROUND-PLAN OF TEMPLE AT MEDINET-ABOU	175
EGYPTIAN SHIP IN THE TIME OF HATASU	179
HOUSE BUILT ON PILES IN THE LAND OF PUNT	181
THE QUEEN OF PUNT AT THE COURT OF HATASU	183
SECTION OF THE PILLARED HALL OF THOTHMES III. AT KARNAC	201
BUST OF THOTHMES III.	205
TWIN COLOSSI OF AMENHOTEP III. AT THEBES	209
BUST OF AMENHOTEP III.	221
KHUENATEN WORSHIPPING THE SOLAR DISK	225
HEAD OF AMENHOTEP IV. OR KHUENATEN	229
HEAD OF SETI I.	250
BUST OF RAMESSES II.	251
HEAD OF MENEPHTHAH	255
SEA-FIGHT IN THE TIME OF RAMESSES III.	279
CARICATURE OF THE TIME OF THE SAME	286
HEAD OF HER-HOR	291
FIGURE RECORDING THE CONQUEST OF JUDÆA BY SHISHAK	305

LIST OF ILLUSTRATIONS. xxi

	PAGE
HEAD OF SHISHAK	307
PIANKHI RECEIVING THE SUBMISSION OF TAFNEKHT AND OTHERS	320
HEAD OF SHABAK	325
SEAL OF SHABAK	327
HEAD OF TIRHAKAH	329
FIGURE OF ESAR-HADDON AT THE NAHR-EL-KELB	335
HEAD OF PSAMATIK I.	344
BAS-RELIEFS OF THE TIME OF PSAMATIK I.	351
HEAD OF NECO	355

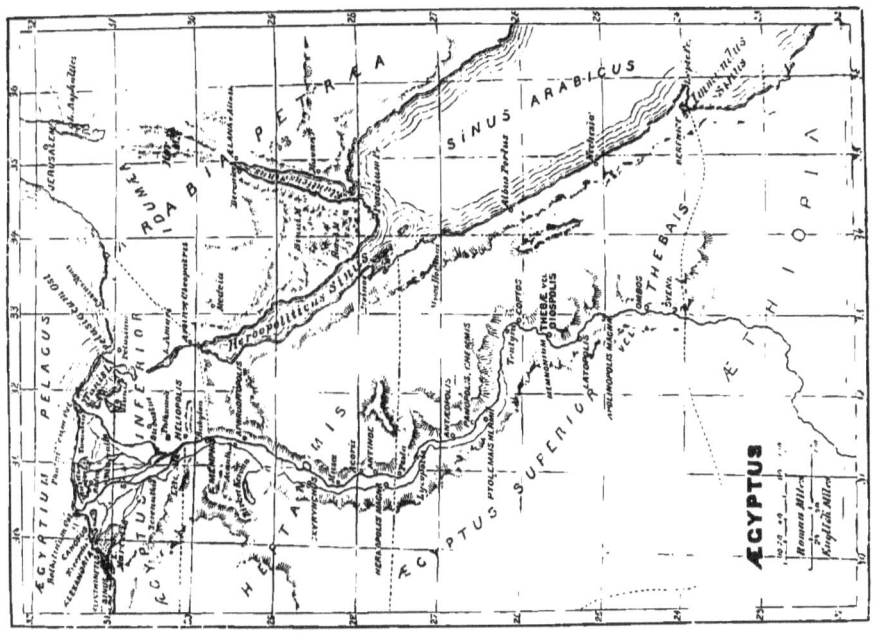

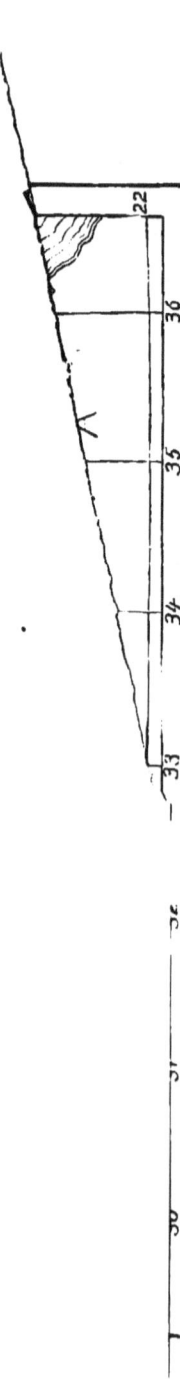

THE STORY OF ANCIENT EGYPT.

I.

THE LAND OF EGYPT.

IN shape Egypt is like a lily with a crooked stem. A broad blossom terminates it at its upper end ; a button of a bud projects from the stalk a little below the blossom, on the left-hand side. The broad blossom is the Delta, extending from Aboosir to Tineh, a direct distance of a hundred and eighty miles, which the projection of the coast—the graceful swell of the petals—enlarges to two hundred and thirty. The bud is the Fayoum, a natural depression in the hills that shut in the Nile valley on the west, which has been rendered cultivable for many thousands of years by the introduction into it of the Nile water, through a canal known as the "Bahr Yousouf." The long stalk of the lily is the Nile valley itself, which is a ravine scooped in the rocky soil for seven hundred miles from the First Cataract to the apex of the Delta, sometimes not more than a mile broad, never more than eight or ten miles. No other country in the world is so strangely shaped, so long compared to its width, so straggling, so hard to govern from a single centre.

At the first glance, the country seems to divide itself into two strongly contrasted regions; and this was the original impression which it made upon its inhabitants. The natives from a very early time designated their land as "the two lands," and represented it by a hieroglyph in which the form used to express "land" was doubled. The kings were called "chiefs of the Two Lands," and wore two crowns, as being kings of two countries. The Hebrews caught up the idea, and though they sometimes called Egypt "Mazor" in the singular number, preferred commonly to designate it by the dual form "Mizraim," which means "the two Mazors." These "two Mazors," "two Egypts," or "two lands," were, of course, the blossom and the stalk, the broad tract upon the Mediterranean known as "Lower Egypt," or "the Delta," and the long narrow valley that lies, like a green snake, to the south, which bears the name of "Upper Egypt," or "the Said." Nothing is more striking than the contrast between these two regions. Entering Egypt from the Mediterranean, or from Asia by the caravan route, the traveller sees stretching before him an apparently boundless plain, wholly unbroken by natural elevations, generally green with crops or with marshy plants, and canopied by a cloudless sky, which rests everywhere on a distant flat horizon. An absolute monotony surrounds him. No alternation of plain and highland, meadow and forest, no slopes of hills, or hanging woods, or dells, or gorges, or cascades, or rushing streams, or babbling rills, meet his gaze on any side; look which way he will, all is sameness, one vast smooth expanse of rich alluvial soil, varying only in being cultivated or else allowed to lie waste. Turning his back with something of weariness on the dull uniformity of this featureless plain, the wayfarer proceeds southwards, and enters, at the distance of a hundred miles from the coast, on an entirely new scene. Instead of an illimitable prospect meeting him on every side, he finds himself in a comparatively narrow vale, up and down which the eye still commands an extensive view, but where the prospect on either side is blocked at the distance of a few miles by rocky ranges of hills, white or yellow or tawny, sometimes drawing so near as to threaten an obstruction of the river course, sometimes receding so far as to leave some miles of cultivable soil on either side of the stream. The rocky ranges, as he approaches them, have a stern and forbidding aspect. They rise for the most part, abruptly in bare grandeur; on their craggy sides grows neither moss nor heather; no trees clothe their steep heights. They seem intended, like the mountains that enclosed the abode of Rasselas, to keep in the inhabitants of the vale within their narrow limits, and bar them out from any commerce or acquaintance with the regions beyond.

Such is the twofold division of the country which impresses the observer strongly at the first. On a longer sojourn and a more intimate familiarity, the twofold division gives place to one which is threefold. The lower differs from the upper valley, it is a sort of debatable region, half plain, half vale; the cultivable surface spreads itself out more widely, the enclosing hills recede into the distance; above all, to the middle tract belongs the open space of the Fayoum, nearly fifty miles across in its greatest diameter, and containing an area of four hundred square miles. Hence, with some of the occupants of Egypt a triple division has been preferred to a twofold one, the Greeks interposing the "Heptanomis" between the Thebais and the Delta, and the Arabs the "Vostani" between the Said and the Bahari, or "country of the sea."

It may be objected to this description, that the Egypt which it presents to the reader is not the Egypt of the maps. Undoubtedly it is not. The maps give the name of Egypt to a broad rectangular space which they mark out in the north-eastern corner of Africa, bounded on two sides by the Mediterranean and the Red Sea, and on the two others by two imaginary lines which the map-makers kindly draw for us across the sands of the desert. But "this Egypt," as has been well observed, " is a fiction of the geographers, as untrue to fact as the island Atlantis of Greek legend, or the Lyonnesse of mediæval romance, both sunk beneath the ocean to explain their disappearance. The true Egypt of the old monuments, of the Hebrews, of the Greeks and Romans, of the Arabs, and of its own people in this day, is a mere fraction of this vast area of the maps, nothing more than the valley and plain watered by the Nile, for nearly seven hundred miles by the river's course from the Mediterranean southwards."[1] The great wastes on either side of the Nile valley are in no sense Egypt, neither the un-

[1] R. Stuart Poole, "Cities of Egypt," p. 4.

dulating sandy desert to the west, nor the rocky and gravelly highland to the east, which rises in terrace after terrace to a height, in some places, of six thousand feet. Both are sparsely inhabited, and by tribes of a different race from the Egyptian—tribes whose allegiance to the rulers of Egypt is in the best times nominal, and who for the most part spurn the very idea of submission to authority.

If, then, the true Egypt be the tract that we have described—the Nile valley, with the Fayoum and the Delta—the lily stalk, the bud, and the blossom—we can well understand how it came to be said of old, that "Egypt was the gift of the river." Not that the lively Greek, who first used the expression, divined exactly the scientific truth of the matter. The fancy of Herodotus saw Africa, originally, *doubly* severed from Asia by two parallel *fjords*, one running inland northwards from the Indian Ocean, as the Red Sea does to this day, and the other penetrating inland southwards from the Mediterranean to an equal or greater distance! The Nile, he said, pouring itself into this latter *fjord*, had by degrees filled it up, and had then gone on and by further deposits turned into land a large piece of the "sea of the Greeks," as was evident from the projection of the shore of the Delta beyond the general coast-line of Africa eastward and westward; and, he added, "I am convinced, for my own part, that if the Nile should please to divert his waters from their present bed into the Red Sea, he would fill it up and turn it into dry land in the space of twenty thousand years, or maybe in half that time—for he is a mighty river and a most energetic one." Here, in this last expression, he is thoroughly right, though the method of the Nile's energy has been other than he supposed. The Nile, working from its immense reservoirs in the equatorial regions, has gradually scooped itself out a deep bed in the sand and rock of the desert, which must have originally extended across the whole of northern Africa from the Atlantic to the Red Sea. Having scooped itself out this bed to a depth, in places, of three hundred feet from the desert level, it has then proceeded partially to fill it up with its own deposits. Occupying, when it is at its height, the entire bed, and presenting at that time the appearance of a vast lake, or succession of lakes, it deposes every day a portion of sediment over the whole space which it covers: then, contracting gradually, it leaves at the base of the hills, on both sides, or at any rate on one, a strip of land fresh dressed with mud, which gets wider daily as the waters still recede, until yards grow into furlongs, and furlongs into miles, and at last the shrunk stream is content with a narrow channel a few hundred yards in width, and leaves the rest of its bed to the embraces of sun and air, and, if he so wills, to the industry of man. The land thus left exposed is Egypt—Egypt is the temporarily uncovered bed of the Nile, which it reclaims and recovers during a portion of each year, when Egypt disappears from view, save where human labour has by mounds and embankments formed artificial islands that raise their heads above the waste of waters, for the most part crowned with buildings.

There is one exception to this broad and sweeping

statement. The Fayoum is no part of the natural bed of the Nile, and has not been scooped out by its energy. It is a natural depression in the western desert, separated off from the Nile valley by a range of limestone hills from two hundred to five hundred feet in height, and, apart from the activity of man, would have been arid, treeless, and waterless. Still, it derives from the Nile all its value, all its richness, all its fertility. Human energy at some remote period introduced into the depressed tract through an artificial channel from the Nile, cut in some places through the rock, the life-giving fluid; and this fluid, bearing the precious Nile sediment, has sufficed to spread fertility over the entire region, and to make the desert blossom like a garden.

The Egyptians were not unaware of the source of their blessings. From a remote date they speculated on their mysterious river. They deified it under the name of Hapi, "the Hidden," they declared that "his abode was not known;" that he was an inscrutable god, that none could tell his origin: they acknowledged him as the giver of all good things, and especially of the fruits of the earth. They said—

> " Hail to thee, O Nile!
> Thou showest thyself in this land,
> Coming in peace, giving life to Egypt;
> O Ammon, thou leadest night unto day,
> A leading that rejoices the heart!
> Overflowing the gardens created by Ra;
> Giving life to all animals;
> Watering the land without ceasing;
> The way of heaven descending:
> Lover of food, bestower of corn,
> Giving life to every home, O Phthah!...

O inundation of Nile, offerings are made to thee;
Oxen are slain to thee;
Great festivals are kept for thee;
Fowls are sacrificed to thee;
Beasts of the field are caught for thee;
Pure flames are offered to thee;
Offerings are made to every god,
As they are made unto Nile.
Incense ascends unto heaven,
Oxen, bulls, fowls are burnt!
Nile makes for himself chasms in the Thebaid;
Unknown is his name in heaven,
He doth not manifest his forms!
Vain are all representations!

Mortals extol him, and the cycle of gods!
Awe is felt by the terrible ones;
His son is made Lord of all,
To enlighten all Egypt.
Shine forth, shine forth, O Nile! shine forth!
Giving life to men by his omen:
Giving life to his oxen by the pastures!
Shine forth in glory, O Nile!"[1]

Though thus useful, beneficent, and indeed essential to the existence of Egypt, the Nile can scarcely be said to add much to the variety of the landscape or to the beauty of the scenery. It is something, no doubt, to have the sight of water in a land where the sun beats down all day long with unremitting force till the earth is like a furnace of iron beneath a sky of molten brass. But the Nile is never clear. During the inundation it is deeply stained with the red argillaceous soil brought down from the Abyssinian highlands. At other seasons it is always more or less tinged with the vegetable matter which it absorbs on its passage from Lake Victoria to Khartoum; and this vegetable

[1] Translation by F. C. Cook.

matter, combined with its depth and volume, gives it a dull deep hue, which prevents it from having the attractiveness of purer and more translucent streams. The Greek name, Neilos, and the Hebrew, Sichor, are thought to embody this attribute of the mighty river, and to mean "dark blue" or "blue-black," terms sufficiently expressive of the stream's ordinary colour. Moreover, the Nile is too wide to be picturesque. It is seldom less than a mile broad from the point where it enters Egypt, and running generally between flat shores it scarcely reflects anything, unless it be the grey-blue sky overhead, or the sails of a passing pleasure boat.

The size of Egypt, within the limits which have been here assigned to it, is about eleven thousand four hundred square miles, or less than that of any European State, except Belgium, Saxony, and Servia. Magnitude is, however, but an insignificant element in the greatness of States—witness Athens, Sparta, Rhodes, Genoa, Florence, Venice. Egypt is the richest and most productive land in the whole world. In its most flourishing age we are told that it contained twenty thousand cities. It deserved to be called, more (probably) than even Belgium, "one great town." But its area was undoubtedly small. Still, as little men have often taken the highest rank among warriors, so little States have filled a most important place in the world's history. Palestine was about the size of Wales; the entire Peloponnese was no larger than New Hampshire; Attica had nearly the same area as Cornwall. Thus the case of Egypt does not stand by itself, but is merely one out of many exceptions to what may perhaps be called the general rule.

If stinted for space, Egypt was happy in her soil and in her situation. The rich alluvium, continually growing deeper and deeper, and top-dressed each year by nature's bountiful hand, was of an inexhaustible fertility, and bore readily year after year a threefold harvest—first a grain crop, and then two crops of grasses or esculent vegetables. The wheat sown returned a hundredfold to the husbandman, and was gathered at harvest-time in prodigal abundance—"as the sand of the sea, very much,"— till men "left numbering" (Gen. xli. 49). Flax and doora were largely cultivated, and enormous quantities were produced of the most nutritive vegetables, such as lentils, garlic, leeks, onions, endive, radishes, melons, cucumbers, lettuces, and the like, which formed a most important element in the food of the people. The vine was also grown in many places, as along the flanks of the hills between Thebes and Memphis, in the basin of the Fayoum, at Anthylla in the Mareotis, at Sebennytus (now Semnood), and at Plisthiné, on the shore of the Mediterranean. The date-palm, springing naturally from the soil in clumps, or groves, or planted in avenues, everywhere offered its golden clusters to the wayfarer, dropping its fruit into his lap. Wheat, however, was throughout antiquity the chief product of Egypt, which was reckoned the granary of the world, the refuge and resource of all the neighbouring nations in time of dearth, and on which in the later republican, and in the imperial times, Rome almost wholly depended for her sustenance.

If the soil was thus all that could be wished, still more

advantageous was the situation. Egypt was the only nation of the ancient world which had ready access to two seas, the Northern Sea, or "Sea of the Greeks," and the Eastern Sea, or "Sea of the Arabians and the Indians." Phœnicia might carry her traffic by the painful travel of caravans across fifteen degrees of desert from her cities on the Levantine coast to the inner recess of the Persian Gulf, and thus get a share in the trade of the East at a vast expenditure of time and trouble. Assyria and Babylonia might for a time, when at the height of their dominion, obtain a temporary hold on lands which were not their own, and boast that they stretched from the "sea of the rising" to "that of the setting sun"—from the Persian Gulf to the Mediterranean; but Egypt, at all times and under all circumstances, commands by her geographic position an access both to the Mediterranean and to the Indian Ocean by way of the Red Sea, whereof nothing can deprive her. Suez must always be hers, for the Isthmus is her natural boundary, and her water-system has been connected with the head of the Arabian Gulf for more than three thousand years; and, in the absence of any strong State in Arabia or Abyssinia, the entire western coast of the Red Sea falls naturally under her influence with its important roadsteads and harbours. Thus Egypt had two great outlets for her productions, and two great inlets by which she received the productions of other countries. Her ships could issue from the Nilotic ports and trade with Phœnicia, or Carthage, or Italy, or Greece, exchanging her corn and wine and glass and furniture and works in metallurgy for

Etruscan vases, or Grecian statues, or purple Tyrian robes, or tin brought by Carthaginian merchantmen from the Scilly islands and from Cornwall; or they could start from Heroopolis, or Myos Hormus, or some port further to the southward, and pass by way of the Red Sea to the spice-region of "Araby the Blest," or to the Abyssinian timber-region, or to the shores of Zanzibar and Mozambique, or round Arabia to Teredon on the Persian Gulf, or possibly to Ceylon or India. The products of the distant east, even of "far Cathay," certainly flowed into the land, for they have been dug out of the ancient tombs; but whether they were obtained by direct or by indirect commerce must be admitted to be doubtful.

The possession of the Nile was of extraordinary advantage to Egypt, not merely as the source of fertility, but as a means of rapid communication. One of the greatest impediments to progress and civilization which Nature offers to man in regions which he has not yet subdued to his will, is the difficulty of locomotion and of transport. Mountains, forests, torrents, marshes, jungles, are the curses of "new countries," forming, until they have been cut through, bridged over, or tunnelled under, insurmountable barriers, hindering commerce and causing hatreds through isolation. Egypt had from the first a broad road driven through it from end to end—a road seven hundred miles long, and seldom much less than a mile wide—which allowed of ready and rapid communication between the remotest parts of the kingdom. Rivers, indeed, are of no use as arteries of commerce or vehicles for locomotion until men have invented ships or boats, or at least rafts, to descend and ascend them ; but the Egyptians were acquainted with the use of boats and rafts from a very remote period, and took to the water like a brood of ducks or a parcel of South Sea Islanders. Thirty-two centuries ago an Egyptian king built a temple on the confines of the Mediterranean entirely of stone which he floated down the Nile for six hundred and fifty miles from the quarries of Assouan (Syêné) ; and the passage up the river is for a considerable portion of the year as easy as the passage down. Northerly winds—the famous " Etesian gales "—prevail in Egypt during the whole of the summer and autumn, and by hoisting a sail it is almost always possible to ascend the stream at a good pace. If the sail be dropped, the current will at all times take a vessel down-stream ; and thus boats, and even vessels of a large size, pass up and down the water-way with equal facility.

Egypt is at all seasons a strange country, but presents the most astonishing appearance at the period of the inundation. At that time not only is the lengthy valley from Assouan to Cairo laid under water, but the Delta itself becomes one vast lake, interspersed with islands, which stud its surface here and there at intervals, and which reminded Herodotus of " the islands of the Ægean." The elevations, which are the work of man, are crowned for the most part with the white walls of towns and villages sparkling in the sunlight, and sometimes glassed in the flood beneath them. The palms and sycamores stand up out of the expanse of waters shortened by some five or six feet of their height. Everywhere, when the inundation begins, the inhabitants are seen hurrying their cattle to the shelter provided in the villages, and, if the rise of the water is more rapid than usual, numbers rescue their beasts with difficulty, causing them to wade or swim, or even saving them by means of boats. An excessive inundation brings not only animal, but human life into peril, endangering the villages themselves, which may be submerged and swept away if the water rises above a certain height. A deficient inundation, on the other hand, brings no immediate danger, but by limiting production may create a dearth that causes incalculable suffering.

Nature's operations are, however, so uniform that these calamities rarely arise. Egypt rejoices, more than almost any other country, in an equable climate, an equable temperature, and an equable productiveness. The summers, no doubt, are hot, especially in the south, and an occasional sirocco produces intense discomfort while it lasts. But the cool Etesian wind, blowing from the north through nearly all the summertime, tempers the ardour of the sun's rays even in the hottest season of the year; and during the remaining months, from October to April, the climate is simply delightful. Egypt has been said to have but two seasons, spring and summer. Spring reigns from October into May—crops spring up, flowers bloom, soft zephyrs fan the cheek, when it is mid-winter in Europe; by February the fruit-trees are in full blossom; the crops begin to ripen in March, and are reaped by the end of April; snow and frost are wholly unknown at any time; storm, fog, and even rain are rare. A bright, lucid atmosphere rests upon

GEOLOGY AND FLORA.

the entire scene. There is no moisture in the air, no cloud in the sky; no mist veils the distance. One day follows another, each the counterpart of the preceding; until at length spring retires to make room for summer, and a fiercer light, a hotter sun, a longer day, show that the most enjoyable part of the year is gone by.

The geology of Egypt is simple. The entire flat country is alluvial. The hills on either side are, in the north, limestone, in the central region sandstone, and in the south granite and syenite. The granitic formation begins between the twenty-fourth and twenty-fifth parallels, but occasional masses of primitive rock are intruded into the secondary regions, and these extend northward as far as lat. 27°10′. Above the rocks are, in many places, deposits of gravel and sand, the former hard, the latter loose and shifting. A portion of the eastern desert is metalliferous. Gold is found even at the present day in small quantities, and seems anciently to have been more abundant. Copper, iron, and lead have been also met with in modern times, and one iron mine shows signs of having been anciently worked. Emeralds abound in the region about Mount Zabara, and the eastern desert further yields jaspers, carnelians, breccia verde, agates, chalcedonies, and rock-crystal.

The flora of the country is not particularly interesting. Dom and date palms are the principal trees, the latter having a single tapering stem, the former dividing into branches. The sycamore (*Ficus sycamorus*) is also tolerably common, as are several species of acacia. The acacia seyal, which furnishes the gum arabic of commerce, is "a gnarled and thorny tree, somewhat like a solitary hawthorn in its habit and manner of growth, but much larger." Its height, when full grown, is from fifteen to twenty feet. The *persea*, a sacred plant among the ancient Egyptians, is a bushy tree or shrub, which attains the height of eighteen or twenty feet under favourable circumstances, and bears a fruit resembling a date, with a subacid flavour. The bark is whitish, the branches gracefully curved, the foliage of an ashy grey, more especially on its under surface. Specially characteristic of Egypt, though not altogether peculiar to it, were the papyrus and the lotus—the *Cyperus papyrus* and *Nymphæa lotus* of botanists. The papyrus was a tall smooth reed, with a large triangular stalk containing a delicate pith, out of which the Egyptians manufactured their paper. The fabric was excellent, as is shown by its continuance to the present day, and by the fact that the Greeks and Romans, after long trial, preferred it to parchment. The lotus was a large white water-lily of exquisite beauty. Kings offered it to the gods; guests wore it at banquets; architectural forms were modelled upon it; it was employed in the ornamentation of thrones. Whether its root had the effect on men ascribed to it by Homer may be doubted; but no one ever saw it without recognizing it instantly as "a thing of beauty," and therefore as "a joy for ever."

Nor can Egypt have afforded in ancient times any very exciting amusement to sportsmen. At the present day gazelles are chased with hawk and hound during the dry season on the broad expanse of the Delta; but anciently the thick population scared off the

DOM AND DATE PALMS.

whole antelope tribe, which was only to be found in the desert region beyond the limits of the alluvium. Nor can Egypt, in the proper sense of the word, have ever been the home of red-deer, roes, or fallow-deer, of lions, bears, hyænas, lynxes, or rabbits. Animals of these classes may occasionally have appeared in the alluvial plain, but they would only be rare visitants driven by hunger from their true habitat in the Libyan or the Arabian uplands. The crocodile, however, and the hippopotamus were actually hunted by the ancient Egyptians; and they further indulged their love of sport in the pursuits of fowling and fishing. All kinds of waterfowl are at all seasons abundant in the Nile waters, and especially frequent the pools left by the retiring river—pelicans, geese, ducks, ibises, cranes, storks, herons, dotterels, kingfishers, and sea-swallows. Quails also arrive in great numbers in the month of March, though there are no pheasants, snipe, woodcocks, nor partridges. Fish are very plentiful in the Nile and the canals derived from it; but there are not many kinds which afford much sport to the fisherman.

Altogether, Egypt is a land of tranquil monotony. The eye commonly travels either over a waste of waters, or over a green plain unbroken by elevations. The hills which inclose the Nile valley have level tops, and sides that are bare of trees, or shrubs, or flowers, or even mosses. The sky is generally cloudless. No fog or mist enwraps the distance in mystery; no rainstorm sweeps across the scene; no rainbow spans the empyrean; no shadows chase each other over the landscape. There is an entire absence of picturesque scenery. A single broad river, unbroken within the limits of Egypt even by a rapid, two flat strips of green plain at its side, two low lines of straight-topped hills beyond them, and a boundless open space where the river divides itself into half a dozen sluggish branches before reaching the sea, constitute Egypt, which is by nature a southern Holland—" weary, stale, flat and unprofitable." The monotony is relieved, however, in two ways, and by two causes. Nature herself does something to relieve it. Twice a day, in the morning and in the evening, the sky and the landscape are lit up by hues so bright yet so delicate, that the homely features of the prospect are at once transformed as by magic, and wear an aspect of exquisite beauty. At dawn long streaks of rosy light stretch themselves across the eastern sky, the haze above the western horizon blushes a deep red ; a ruddy light diffuses itself around, and makes walls and towers and minarets and cupolas to glow like fire ; the long shadows thrown by each tree and building are purple or violet. A glamour is over the scene, which seems transfigured by an enchanter's wand ; but the enchanter is Nature, and the wand she wields is composed of sunrays. Again, at eve, nearly the same effects are produced as in the morning, only with a heightened effect; "the redness of flames" passes into "the redness of roses"—the wavy cloud that fled in the morning comes into sight once more—comes blushing, yet still comes on—comes burning with blushes, and clings to the Sun-god's side.[1]

Night brings a fresh transfiguration. The olive

[1] Adapted from Mr. Kinglake's "Eothen," p. 188.

after-glow gives place to a deep blue-grey. The yellow moon rises into the vast expanse. A softened light diffuses itself over earth and sky. The orb of night walks in brightness through a firmament of sapphire; or, if the moon is below the horizon, then the purple vault is lit up with many-coloured stars. Silence profound reigns around. A phase of beauty wholly different from that of the day-time smites the sense; and the monotony of feature is forgiven to the changefulness of expression, and to the experience of a new delight.

Man has also done his part to overcome the dulness and sameness that brood over the " land of Mizraim." Where nature is most tame and commonplace, man is tempted to his highest flights of audacity. As in the level Babylonia he aspired to build a tower that should " reach to heaven " (Gen. xi. 4), so in Egypt he strove to startle and surprise by gigantic works, enormous undertakings, enterprises that might have seemed wholly beyond his powers. And these have constituted in all ages, except the very earliest, the great attractiveness of Egypt. Men are drawn there, not by the mysteriousness of the Nile, or the mild beauties of orchards and palm-groves, of well-cultivated fields and gardens—no, nor by the loveliness of sunrises and sunsets, of moonlit skies and stars shining with many hues, but by the huge masses of the pyramids, by the colossal statues, the tall obelisks, the enormous temples, the deeply-excavated tombs, the mosques, the castles, and the palaces. The architecture of Egypt is its great glory. It began early, and it has continued late. But for the great works, strewn thickly over the whole valley of the Nile, the land of Egypt would have obtained but a small share of the world's attention; and it is at least doubtful whether its "story" would ever have been thought necessary to complete "the Story of the Nations."

II.

THE PEOPLE OF EGYPT.

WHERE the Egyptians came from, is a difficult question to answer. Ancient speculators, when they could not derive a people definitely from any other, took refuge in the statement, or the figment, that they were the children of the soil which they had always occupied. Modern theorists may say, if it please them, that they were evolved out of the monkeys that had their primitive abode on that particular portion of the earth's surface. Monkeys, however, are not found everywhere; and we have no evidence that in Egypt they were ever indigenous, though, as pets, they were very common, the Egyptians delighting in keeping them. Such evidence as we have reveals to us the man as anterior to the monkey in the land of Mizraim. Thus we are thrown back on the original question— Where did the man, or race of men, that is found in Egypt at the dawn of history come from?

It is generally answered that they came from Asia; but this is not much more than a conjecture. The physical type of the Egyptians is different from that of any known Asiatic nation. The Egyptians had no traditions that at all connected them with Asia. Their language, indeed, in historic times was partially

Semitic, and allied to the Hebrew, the Phœnician, and the Aramaic ; but the relationship was remote, and may be partly accounted for by later intercourse, without involving original derivation. The fundamental character of the Egyptian in respect of physical type, language, and tone of thought, is Nigritic. The Egyptians were not negroes, but they bore a resemblance to the negro which is indisputable. Their type differs from the Caucasian in exactly those respects which when exaggerated produce the negro. They were darker, had thicker lips, lower foreheads, larger heads, more advancing jaws, a flatter foot, and a more attenuated frame. It is quite conceivable that the negro type was produced by a gradual degeneration from that which we find in Egypt. It is even conceivable that the Egyptian type was produced by gradual advance and amelioration from that of the negro.

Still, whencesoever derived, the Egyptian people, as it existed in the flourishing times of Egyptian history, was beyond all question a mixed race, showing diverse affinities. Whatever the people was originally, it received into it from time to time various foreign elements, and those in such quantities as seriously to affect its physique—Ethiopians from the south, Libyans from the west, Semites from the north-east, where Africa adjoined on Asia. There are two quite different types of Egyptian form and feature, blending together in the mass of the nation, but strongly developed, and (so to speak) accentuated in individuals. One is that which we see in portraits of Rameses III., and in some of Rameses II.—a moderately high fore-

EGYPTIAN PHYSIQUE—TWO TYPES. 25

head, a large, well-formed aquiline nose, a well-shaped mouth with lips not over full, and a delicately rounded chin. The other is comparatively coarse—forehead low, nose depressed and short, lower part of the face prognathous and sensual-looking, chin heavy, jaw large, lips thick and projecting. The two types of face are not, however, accompanied by much difference of frame. The Egyptian is always slight in figure, wanting in muscle, flat in foot, with limbs that are too long, too thin, too lady-like. Something more of muscularity appears, perhaps, in the earlier than in the later forms; but this is perhaps attributable to a modification of the artistic ideal.

As Egypt presents us with two types of physique, so it brings before us two strongly different types of character. On the one hand we see, alike in the pictured scenes, in the native literary remains, and in the accounts which foreigners have left us of the people, a grave and dignified race, full of serious and sober thought, given to speculation and reflection, occupied rather with the interests belonging to another world than with those that attach to this present scene of existence, and inclined to indulge in a gentle and dreamy melancholy. The first thought of a king, when he began his reign, was to begin his tomb. The desire of the grandee was similar. It is a trite tale how at feasts a slave carried round to all the guests the representation of a mummied corpse, and showed it to each in turn, with the solemn words—" Look at this, and so eat and drink; for be sure that one day such as this thou shalt be." The favourite song of the Egyptians, according to Herodotus, was a dirge. The " Lay of

Harper," which we subjoin, sounds a key-note that was very familiar, at any rate, to large numbers among the Egyptians.

> The Great One [1] has gone to his rest,
>   Ended his task and his race;
> Thus men are aye passing away,
>   And youths are aye taking their place.
> As Ra rises up every morn,
>   And Tum every evening doth set,
> So women conceive and bring forth,
>   And men without ceasing beget.
> Each soul in its turn draweth breath—
> Each man born of woman sees Death.
>
> Take thy pleasure to-day,
>   Father! Holy One! See,
> Spices and fragrant oils,
>   Father, we bring to thee.
> On thy sister's bosom and arms
>   Wreaths of lotus we place;
> On thy sister, dear to thy heart,
>   Aye sitting before thy face.
> Sound the song; let music be played
> And let cares behind thee be laid.
>
> Take thy pleasure to-day;
>   Mind thee of joy and delight!
> Soon life's pilgrimage ends,
>   And we pass to Silence and Night.
> Patriarch perfect and pure,
>   Nefer-hotep, blessed one! Thou
> Didst finish thy course upon earth,
>   And art with the blessed ones now.
> Men pass to the Silent Shore,
> And their place doth know them no more.
>
> They are as they never had been,
>   Since the sun went forth upon high;
> They sit on the banks of the stream
>   That floweth in stillness by.

[1] Nefer-hotep, a deceased king.

Thy soul is among them ; thou
    Dost drink of the sacred tide,
Having the wish of thy heart—
    At peace ever since thou hast died.
Give bread to the man who is poor,
And thy name shall be blest evermore.

* * * * *

Take thy pleasure to-day,
    Nefer-hotep, blessed and pure.
What availed thee thy other buildings?
    Of thy tomb alone thou art sure.
On the earth thou hast nought beside,
    Nought of thee else is remaining ;
And when thou wentest below,
    Thy last sip of life thou wert draining.
Even they who have millions to spend,
Find that life comes at last to an end.

Let all, then, think of the day
    Of departure without returning—
'Twill then be well to have lived,
    All sin and injustice spurning.
For he who has loved the right,
    In the hour that none can flee,
Enters upon the delight
    Of a glad eternity.
Give freely from out thy store,
And thou shalt be blest evermore.

On the other hand, there is evidence of a lightsome, joyous, and even frolic spirit as pervading numbers, especially among the lower classes of the Egyptians. "Traverse Egypt," says a writer who knows more of the ancient country than almost any other living person, "examine the scenes sculptured or painted on the walls of the chapels attached to tombs, consult the inscriptions graven on the rocks or traced with ink on the papyrus rolls, and you will be compelled to modify your mistaken notion of the Egyptians being a nation of philosophers. I defy you to find anything more gay, more amusing, more freshly simple, than this good-natured Egyptian people, which was fond of life and felt a profound pleasure in its existence. Far from desiring death, they addressed prayers to the gods to preserve them in life, and to give them a happy old age—an old age that should reach, if possible, to the 'perfect term of 110 years.' They gave themselves up to pleasures of every kind; they sang, they drank, they danced, they delighted in making excursions into the country, where hunting and fishing were occupations reserved especially for the nobility. In conformity with this inclination towards pleasure, sportive proposals, a pleasantry that was perhaps over-free, witticisms, raillery, and a mocking spirit, were in vogue among the people, and fun was allowed entrance even into the tombs. In the large schools the masters had a difficulty in training the young and keeping down their passion for amusements. When oral exhortation failed of success, the cane was used pretty smartly in its place; for the wise men of the land had a saying that 'a boy's ears grow on his back.'"[1]

Herodotus tells us how gaily the Egyptians kept their festivals, thousands of the common people—men, women, and children together—crowding into the boats, which at such times covered the Nile, the men piping, and the women clapping their hands or striking their castanets, as they passed from town to town along the banks of the stream, stopping at the various landing-places, and challenging the inhabi-

[1] Brugsch, "Histoire d'Egypte," p. 15.

tants to a contest of good-humoured Billingsgate. From the monuments we see how the men sang at their labours—here as they trod the wine-press or the dough-trough, there as they threshed out the corn by driving the oxen through the golden heaps. In one case the words of a harvest-song have come down to us :

> "Thresh for yourselves," they sang, "thresh for yourselves,
> O oxen, thresh for yourselves, for yourselves—
> Bushels for yourselves, bushels for your masters !"

Their light-hearted drollery sometimes found vent in caricature. The grand sculptures wherewith a king strove to perpetuate the memory of his warlike exploits were travestied by satirists, who reproduced the scenes upon papyrus as combats between cats and rats. The amorous follies of the monarch were held up to derision by sketches of a harem interior, where the kingly wooer was represented by a lion, and his favourites of the softer sex by gazelles. Even in serious scenes depicting the trial of souls in the next world, the sense of humour breaks out, where the bad man, transformed into a pig or a monkey, walks off with a comical air of surprise and discomfiture.

It does not, however, help us much towards the true knowledge of a people to scan their frames or study their facial angle, or even to contemplate the outer aspect of their daily life. We want to know their thoughts, their innermost feelings, their hopes, their fears—in a word, their belief. Nothing tells the character of a people so much as their religion ; and we are only dealing superficially with the outward shows of things until we get down to the root of their being, the conviction, or convictions, held in the recesses of a people's heart. What, then, was the Egyptian religion ? What did they worship ? What did they reverence ? What future did they look forward to ?

Enter the huge courts of an Egyptian temple, or temple-palace, and you will see portrayed upon its lofty walls row upon row of deities. Here the king makes his offering to Ammon, Maut, Khons, Neith, Mentu, Shu, Seb, Nut, Osiris, Set, Horus ; there he pours a libation to Phthah, Sekhet, Tum, Pasht, Anuka, Thoth, Anubis ; elsewhere, it may be, he pays his court to Sati, Khem, Isis, Nephthys, Athor, Harmachis, Nausaas, and Nebhept. One monarch erects an altar to Satemi, Tum, Khepra, Shu, Tefnut, Seb, Netpe, Osiris, Isis, Set, Nephthys, Horus, and Thoth, mentioning on the same monument Phthah, Num, Sabak, Athor, Pasht, Mentu, Neith, Anubis, Nishem, and Kartak. Another represents himself on a similar object as offering adoration to Ammon, Khem, Phthah-Sokari, Seb, Nut, Thoth, Khons, Osiris, Isis, Horus, Athor, Uat (Buto), Neith, Sekhet, Anata, Nuneb, Nebhept, and Hapi. All these deities are represented by distinct forms, and have distinct attributes. Nor do they at all exhaust the Pantheon. One modern writer enumerates seventy-three divinities, and gives their several names and forms. Another has a list of sixty-three "*principal* deities," and notes that there were "others which personified the elements, or presided over the operations of nature, the seasons, and events." The Egyptians themselves speak not unfrequently of "the *thousand gods,*" sometimes further qualifying them, as "the gods male, the gods female, those which belong to the land of Egypt." Practically, there were before the eyes of worshippers some scores, if not some hundreds, of deities, who invited their approach and challenged their affections.

Nor was this the whole, or the worst. The Egyptian was taught to pay a religious regard to animals. In one place goats, in another sheep, in a third hippopotami, in a fourth crocodiles, in a fifth vultures, in a sixth frogs, in a seventh shrew-mice, were sacred creatures, to be treated with respect and honour, and under no circumstances to be slain, under the penalty of death to the slayer. And besides this local animal-cult, there was a cult which was general. Cows, cats, dogs, ibises, hawks, and cynocephalous apes, were sacred throughout the whole of Egypt, and woe to the man who injured them ! A Roman who accidentally caused the death of a cat was immediately "lynched" by the populace. Inhabitants of neighbouring villages would attack each other with the utmost fury if the native of one had killed or eaten an animal held sacred in the other. In any house where a cat or a dog died, the inmates were expected to mourn for them as for a relation. Both these and the other sacred animals were carefully embalmed after death, and their bodies were interred in sacred repositories.

The animal-worship reached its utmost pitch of grossness and absurdity when certain individual brute beasts were declared to be incarnate deities, and treated accordingly. At Memphis, the ordinary capital, there was maintained, at any rate from the time of Aahmes I. (about B.C. 1650), a sacred bull, known as Hapi or Apis, which was believed to be an actual incarnation of the god Phthah, and was an object of the highest veneration. The Apis bull dwelt in a temple of his own near the city, had his train of attendant priests, his harem of cows, his meals of the choicest food, his grooms and currycombers who kept his coat clean and beautiful, his chamberlains who made his bed, his cup-bearers who brought him water, &c., and on fixed days was led in a festive procession through the main streets of the town, so that the inhabitants might see him, and come forth from their dwellings and make obeisance. When he died he was carefully embalmed, and deposited, together with magnificent jewels and statuettes and vases, in a polished granite sarcophagus, cut out of a single block, and weighing between sixty and seventy tons! The cost of an Apis funeral amounted sometimes, as we are told, to as much as £20,000. To contain the sarcophagi, several long galleries were cut in the solid rock near Memphis, from which arched lateral chambers went off on either side, each constructed to hold one sarcophagus. The number of Apis bulls buried in the galleries was found to be sixty-four.

Nor was this the only incarnate god of which Egypt boasted. Another bull, called Mnevis, was maintained in the great temple of the Sun at Heliopolis, and, being regarded as an incarnation of Ra or Tum, was as much reverenced by the Heliopolites as Apis by the Memphites. A third, called Bacis or Pacis, was

THE KING RECKONED A GOD. 33

kept at Hermonthis, which was also an incarnation of Ra. And a white cow at Momemphis was reckoned an incarnation of Athor. Who can wonder that foreign nations ridiculed a religion of this kind—one that "turned the glory" of the Eternal Godhead "into the similitude of a calf that eateth hay"?

The Egyptians had also a further god incarnate, who was not shut up out of sight like the Apis and Mnevis and Bacis bulls and the Athor cow, but was continually before their eyes, the centre of the nation's life, the prime object of attention. This was the monarch, who for the time being occupied the throne. Each king of Egypt claimed not only to be "son of the Sun," but to be an actual incarnation of the sun— "the living Horus." And this claim was, from an early date, received and allowed. "Thy Majesty," says a courtier under the twelfth dynasty, "is the good God ... the great God, the equal of the Sun-God. ... I live from the breath which thou givest." Brought into the king's presence, the courtier "falls on his belly," amazed and confounded. "I was as one brought out of the dark; my tongue was dumb; my lips failed me; my heart was no longer in my body to know whether I was alive or dead;" and this, although "the god" had "addressed him mildly." Another courtier attributes his long life to the king's favour. Ambassadors, when presented to the king, "raised their arms in adoration of the good god," and declared to him—"Thou art like the Sun in all that thou doest: thy heart realizes all its wishes; shouldest thou wish to make it day during the night, it is so forthwith. ... If thou sayest to the water, 'Come from the rock,' it will come in a torrent suddenly at the words of thy mouth. The god Ra is like thee in his limbs, the god Khepra in creative force. Truly thou art the living image of thy father, Tum. . . . All thy words are accomplished daily." Some of the kings set up their statues in the temples by the side of the greatest of the national deities, to be the objects of a similar worship.

Amid this wealth of gods, earthly and heavenly, human, animal, and divine, an Egyptian might well feel puzzled to make a choice. In his hesitation he was apt to turn to that only portion of his religion which had the attraction that myth possesses—the introduction into a supramundane and superhuman world of a quasi-human element. The chief Egyptian myth was the Osirid saga, which ran somewhat as follows: "Once upon a time the gods were tired of ruling in the upper sphere, and resolved to take it in turns to reign over Egypt in the likeness of men. So, after four of them had in succession been kings, each for a long term of years, it happened that Osiris, the son of Seb and Nut, took the throne, and became monarch of the two regions, the Upper and the Lower. Osiris was of a good and bountiful nature, beneficent in will and words : he set himself to civilize the Egyptians, taught them to till the fields and cultivate the vine, gave them law and religion, and instructed them in various useful arts. Unfortunately, he had a wicked brother, called Set or Sutekh, who hated him for his goodness, and resolved to compass his death. This he effected after a while, and, having placed the body in a coffin, he threw it into the Nile, whence it floated down to

LEGEND OF OSIRIS. 35

the sea. Isis, the sister and widow of Osiris, together with her sister Nephthys, vainly sought for a long time her lord's remains, but at last found them on the Syrian shore at Byblus, where they had been cast up by the waves. She was conveying the corpse for embalmment and interment to Memphis, when Set stole it from her, and cut it up into fourteen pieces, which he concealed in various places. The unhappy queen set forth in a light boat made of the papyrus plant, and searched Egypt from end to end, until she had found all the fragments, and buried them with due honours. She then called on her son, Horus, to avenge his father, and Horus engaged him in a long war, wherein he was at last victorious and took Set prisoner. Isis now relented, and released Set, who be it remembered, was her brother; which so enraged Horus that he tore off her crown, or (according to some) struck off her head, which injury Thoth repaired by giving her a cow's head in place of her own. Horus then renewed the war with his uncle, and finally slew him with a long spear, which he drove into his head." The gods and goddesses of the Osirid legend, Seb, Nut or Netpe, Osiris, Isis, Nephthys, Set, and Horus or Harmachis, were those which most drew towards them the thoughts of the Egyptians, the greater number being favourite objects of worship, while Set was held in general detestation.

It was a peculiar feature of the Egyptian religion, that it contained distinctively evil and malignant gods. Set was not, originally, such a deity; but he became such in course of time, and was to the later Egyptians the very principle of evil—Evil personified.

Another evil deity was Taour or Taourt, who is represented as a hippopotamus standing on its hind-legs, with the skin and tail of a crocodile dependent down its back, and a knife or a pair of shears in one hand. Bes seems also to have been a divinity of the same class. He was represented as a hideous dwarf, with large outstanding ears, bald, or with a plume of feathers on his head, and with a lion-skin down his back, often carrying in his two hands two knives.

FIGURES OF TAOURT.

Even more terrible than Bes was Apep, the great serpent, with its huge and many folds, who helped Set against Osiris, and was the adversary and accuser of souls. Savak, a god with the head of a crocodile, seems also to have belonged to the class of malignant beings, though he was a favourite deity with some of the Ramesside kings, and a special object of worship in the Fayoum.

The complex polytheism of the monuments and

the literature was not, however, the practical religion of many Egyptians. Local cults held possession of most of the nomes, and the ordinary Egyptian, instead of dissipating his religious affections by distributing them among the thousand divinities of the Pantheon, concentrated them on those of his nome. If he was a Memphite, he worshipped Phthah Sekhet, and Tum ; if a Theban, Ammon-Ra, Maut,

FIGURE OF BES.

Khons, and Neith ; if a Heliopolite, Tum, Nebhebt and Horus ; if a Elephantinite, Kneph, Sati, Anuka, and Hak ; and so on. The Egyptian Pantheon was a gradual accretion, the result of amalgamating the various local cults ; but these continued predominant in their several localities ; and practically the only deities that obtained anything like a general recognition were Osiris, Isis, Horus, and the Nile-god, Hapi.

Besides the common popular religion, the belief of the masses, there was another which prevailed among the priests and among the educated. The primary doctrine of this esoteric religion was the real essential unity of the Divine Nature. The sacred texts, known only to the priests and to the initiated, taught that there was a single Being, " the sole producer of all things both in heaven and earth, himself not produced of any," " the only true living God, self-originated," " who exists from the beginning," " who has made all things, but has not himself been made." This Being seems never to have been represented by any material, even symbolical, form. It is thought that he had no name, or, if he had, that it must have been unlawful to pronounce or write it. He was a pure spirit, perfect in every respect—all-wise, almighty, supremely good. It is of him that the Egyptian poets use such expressions as the following : " He is not graven in marble ; he is not beheld ; his abode is not known ; no shrine is found with painted figures of him ; there is no building that can contain him ; " and, again : " Unknown is his name in heaven ; he doth not manifest his forms ; vain are all representations ;" and yet again : " His commencement is from the beginning ; he is the God who has existed from old time ; there is no God without him ; no mother bore him ; no father hath begotten him ; he is a god-goddess, created from himself ; all gods came into existence when he began."

The other gods, the gods of the popular mythology,

ESOTERIC RELIGION. 39

were understood in the esoteric religion to be either personified attributes of the Deity, or parts of the nature which he had created, considered as informed and inspired by him. Num or Kneph represented the creative mind, Phthah the creative hand, or act of creating; Maut represented matter, Ra the sun, Khons the moon, Seb the earth, Khem the generative power in nature, Nut the upper hemisphere of the heavens, Athor the lower world or under hemisphere; Thoth personified the Divine Wisdom, Ammon perhaps the Divine mysteriousness or incomprehensibility, Osiris the Divine Goodness. It is difficult in many cases to fix on the exact quality, act, or part of nature intended; but the principle admits of no doubt. No educated Egyptian conceived of the popular gods as really separate and distinct beings. All knew that there was but One God, and understood that, when worship was offered to Khem, or Kneph, or Maut, or Thoth, or Ammon, the One God was worshipped under some one of his forms or in some one of his aspects. He was every god, and thus all the gods' names were interchangeable, and in one and the same hymn we may find a god, say Ammon, addressed also as Ra and Khem and Tum and Horus and Khepra; or Hapi, the Nile-god, invoked as Ammon and Phthah; or Osiris as Ra and Thoth; or, in fact, any god invoked as almost any other. If there be a limit, it is in respect of the evil deities, whose names are not given to the good ones.

Common to all Egyptians seems to have been a belief, if not, strictly speaking, in the immortality of the soul, yet, at any rate, in a life after death, and a judgment of every man according to the deeds which he had done in the body while upon earth. It was universally received, that, immediately after death, the soul descended into the Lower World, and was conducted to the "Hall of Truth," where it was julged in the presence of Osiris and of the forty-two assessors, the "Lords of Truth" and judges of the dead. Anubis, "the director of the weight," brought forth a pair of scales, and, placing in one scale a figure or emblem of Truth, set in the other a vase containing the good actions of the deceased; Thoth standing by the while, with a tablet in his hand, whereon to record the result. According to the side on which the balance inclined, Osiris, the president, delivered sentence. If the good deeds preponderated, the blessed soul was allowed to enter the "boat of the Sun," and was led by good spirits to Aahlu (Elysium), to the "pools of peace" and the dwelling-place of Osiris. If, on the contrary, the good deeds were insufficient, if the ordeal was not passed, then the unhappy soul was sentenced, according to its deserts, to begin a round of transmigrations into the bodies of more or less unclean animals, the number, nature, and duration of the transmigrations depending on the degree of the deceased's demerits, and the consequent length and severity of the punishment which he deserved or the purification which he needed. Ultimately, if after many trials purity was not attained, then the wicked and incurable soul underwent a final sentence at the hands of Osiris, Judge of the Dead, and being condemned to annihilation, was destroyed upon the steps of heaven by Shu, the Lord of Light. The good soul, having first been completely cleansed of its impurities by passing through the basin of purgatorial fire guarded by the four ape-faced genii, was made the companion of Osiris for a period of three thousand years; after which it returned from Amenti, re-entered its former body, and lived once more a human life upon the earth. The process was repeated till a mystic number of years had gone by, when, finally, the blessed attained the crowning joy of union with God, being absorbed into the Divine Essence, from which they had emanated, and thus attaining the true end and full perfection of their being.

Such a belief as this, if earnest and thorough, should be productive of a high standard of moral action; and undoubtedly the Egyptians had a code of morality that will compare favourably with that of most ancient nations. It has been said to have contained "three cardinal requirements—love of God, love of virtue, and love of man." The hymns sufficiently indicate the first; the second may be allowed, if by "virtue" we understand justice and truth; the third is testified by the constant claim of men, in their epitaphs, to have been benefactors of their species. " I was not an idler," says one; " I was no listener to the counsels of sloth; my name was not heard in the place of reproof . . . all men respected me; I gave water to the thirsty; I set the wanderer on his path; I took away the oppressor, and put a stop to violence." " I myself was just and true," writes another : "without malice, having put God in my heart, and being quick to discern His will. I have done good upon earth :

I have harboured no prejudice; I have not been wicked; I have not approved of any offence or iniquity; I have taken pleasure in speaking the truth. . . . Pure is my soul; while living I bore no malice. There are no errors attributable to me; no sins of mine are before the judges. . . . The men of the future, while they live, will be charmed by my remarkable merits." And another: " I have not oppressed any widow; no prisoner languished in my days; no one died of hunger. When there were years of famine, I had my fields ploughed. I gave food to the inhabitants, so that there was no hungry person. I gave the widow an equal portion with the married; I did not prefer the rich to the poor."

The moral standard thus set up, though satisfactory, so far as it went, was in many respects deficient. It did not comprise humility; it scarcely seems to have comprised purity. The religious sculptures of the Egyptians were grossly indecent; their religious festivals were kept in an indecent way; phallic orgies were a part of them, and phallic orgies of a gross kind. The Egyptians tolerated incest, and could defend it by the example of the gods. Osiris had married his sister; Khem was "the Bull of his mother." The Egyptian novelettes are full of indecency and immorality, and Egyptian travellers describe their amours very much in the spirit of Ferdinand, Count Fathom; moreover, the complacency with which each Egyptian declares himself on his tomb to have possessed every virtue, and to have been free from all vices, is most remarkable. "I was a good man before the king; I saved the population in the dire calamity which befell all the land ; I shielded the weak against the strong ; I did all good things when the time came to do them ; I was pious towards my father, and did the will of my mother ; I was kindhearted towards my brethren . . . I made a good sarcophagus for him who had no coffin. When the dire calamity befell the land, I made the children to live, I established the houses, I did for them all such good things as a father does for his sons."

And, notwithstanding all this braggadocio, performance seems to have lagged sadly behind profession. Kings boast of slaying their unresisting prisoners with their own hand, and represent themselves in the act of doing so. They come back from battle with the gory heads of their slain enemies hanging from their chariots. Licentiousness prevailed in the palace, and members of the royal harem intrigued with those who sought the life of the king. A belief in magic was general, and men endeavoured to destroy or injure those whom they hated by wasting their waxen effigies at a slow fire to the accompaniment of incantations. Thieves were numerous, and did not scruple even to violate the sanctity of the tomb in order to obtain a satisfactory booty. A famous "thieves' society," formed for the purpose of opening and plundering the royal tombs, contained among its members persons of the sacerdotal order.

Social ranks in Egypt were divided somewhat sharply. There was a large class of nobles, who were mostly great landed proprietors living on their estates, and having under them a vast body of dependents, servants, labourers, artizans, &c. There was also a numerous official class, partly employed at the court, partly holding government posts throughout the country, which regarded itself as highly dignified, and looked down *de haut en bas* on "the people." Commands in the army seem to have been among the prizes which from time to time fell to the lot of such persons. Further, there was a literary class, which was eminently respectable, and which viewed with contempt those who were engaged in trade or handicrafts.

Below these three classes, and removed from them by a long interval, was the mass of the population— "the multitude" as the Egyptians called them. These persons were engaged in manual labour of different kinds. The greater number were employed on the farms of the nobles, in the cultivation of the soil or in the rearing of cattle. A portion were boatmen, fishermen, or fowlers. Others pursued the various known handicrafts. They were weavers, workers in metal, stone-cutters, masons, potters, carpenters, upholsterers, tailors, shoe-makers, glass-blowers, boat-builders, wig-makers, and embalmers. There were also among them painters and sculptors. But all these employments "stank" in the nostrils of the upper classes, and were regarded as unworthy of any one who wished to be thought respectable.

Still, the line of demarcation, decided as it was, might be crossed. It is an entire mistake to suppose that caste existed in Egypt. Men frequently bred up their sons to their own trade or profession, as they do in all countries, but they were not obliged to do so— there was absolutely no compulsion in the matter.

The "public-schools" of Egypt were open to all comers, and the son of the artizan sat on the same bench with the son of the noble, enjoyed the same education, and had an equal opportunity of distinguishing himself. If he showed sufficient promise, he was recommended to adopt the literary life; and the literary life was the sure passport to State employment. State employment once entered upon, merit secured advancement; and thus there was, in fact, no obstacle to prevent the son of a labouring man from rising to the very highest positions in the administration of the empire. Successful ministers were usually rewarded by large grants of land from the royal domain; and it follows that a clever youth of the labouring class might by good conduct and ability make his way even into the ranks of the landed aristocracy.

On the other hand, practically, the condition of the labouring class was, generally speaking a hard and sad one. The kings were entitled to employ as many of their subjects as they pleased in forced labours, and monarchs often sacrificed to their inordinate vanity the lives and happiness of thousands. Private employers of labour were frequently cruel and exacting; their overseers used the stick, and it was not easy for those who suffered to obtain any redress. Moreover, taxation was heavy, and inability to satisfy the collector subjected the defaulter to the bastinado. Those who have studied the antiquities of Egypt with most care, tell us that there was not much to choose between the condition of the ancient labourers and that of the unhappy *fellahin* [1] of the present day.

[1] A fellah is a peasant, one of the labouring class, just above the slave.

III.

THE DAWN OF HISTORY.

ALL nations, unless they be colonies, have a prehistoric time—a dark period of mist and gloom, before the keen light of history dawns upon them. This period is the favourite playground of the myth-spirits, where they disport themselves freely, or lounge heavily and listlessly, according to their different natures. The Egyptian spirits were of the heavier and duller kind—not light and frolicsome, like the Greek and the Indo-Iranian. It has been said that Egypt never produced more than one myth, the Osirid legend; and this is so far true that in no other case is the story told at any considerable length, or with any considerable number of exciting incidents. There are, however, many short legends in the Egyptian remains, which have more or less of interest, and show that the people was not altogether devoid of imagination, though their imagination was far from lively. Seb, for instance, once upon a time, took the form of a goose, and laid the mundane egg, and hatched it. Thoth once wrote a wonderful book, full of wisdom and science, which told of everything concerning the fowls of the air, and the fishes of the sea, and the four-footed beasts of the earth. He who knew a single page of the book could charm the heaven, the earth, the great abyss, the mountains, and the seas. Thoth took the work and enclosed it in a box of gold, and the box of gold he placed within a box of silver, and the silver box within a box of ivory and ebony, and that again within a box of bronze; and the bronze box he enclosed within a box of brass, and the brass box within a box of iron; and the box, thus guarded, he threw into the Nile at Coptos. But a priest discovered the whereabouts of the book, and sold the knowledge to a young noble for a hundred pieces of silver, and the young noble with great trouble fished the book up. But the possession of the book brought him not good but evil. He lost his wife; he lost his child; he became entangled in a disgraceful intrigue. He was glad to part with the book. But the next possessor was not more fortunate; the book brought him no luck. The quest after unlawful knowledge involved all who sought it in calamity.

Another myth had for its subject the proposed destruction of mankind by Ra, the Sun-god. Ra had succeeded Phthah as king of Egypt, and had reigned for a long term of years in peace, contented with his subjects and they with him. But a time came when they grew headstrong and unruly; they uttered words against Ra; they plotted evil things; they grievously offended him. So Ra called the council of the gods together and asked them to advise him what he should do. They said mankind must be destroyed, and committed the task of destruction to Athor and Sekhet, who proceeded to smite the men over the whole land. But now fear came upon mankind; and the men of Elephantine made haste, and extracted the juice from the best of their fruits, and mingled it with human blood, and filled seven thousand jars, and brought them as an offering to the offended god. Ra drank and was content, and ordered the liquor that remained in the jars to be poured out; and, lo! it was an inundation which covered the whole land of Egypt; and when Athor went forth the next day to destroy, she saw no men in the fields, but only water, which she drank, and it pleased her, and she went away satisfied.

It would require another Euhemerus to find any groundwork of history in these narratives. We must turn away from the "shadow-land" which the Egyptians called the time of the gods on earth, if we would find trace of the real doings of men in the Nile valley, and put before our readers actual human beings in the place of airy phantoms. The Egyptians themselves taught that the first man of whom they had any record was a king called M'na, a name which the Greeks represented by Mên or Menes. M'na was born at Tena (This or Thinis) in Upper Egypt, where his ancestors had borne sway before him. He was the first to master the Lower country, and thus to unite under a single sceptre the "two Egypts"— the long narrow Nile valley and the broad Delta plain. Having placed on his head the double crown which thenceforth symbolized dominion over both tracts, his first thought was that a new capital was needed. Egypt could not, he felt, be ruled conveniently from the latitude of Thebes, or from any site in the Upper country; it required a capital which

SUPPOSED FIRST KING. 49

should abut on both regions, and so command both. Nature pointed out one only fit locality, the junction of the plain with the vale—" the balance of the two regions," as the Egyptians called it ; the place where the narrow " Upper Country " terminates, and Egypt opens out into the wide smiling plain that thence spreads itself on every side to the sea. Hence there would be easy access to both regions ; both would be,.in a way, commanded ; here, too, was a readily defensible position, one assailable only in front. Experience has shown that the instinct of the first founder was right, or that his political and strategic foresight was extraordinary. Though circumstances, once and again, transferred the seat of government to Thebes or Alexandria, yet such removals were short-lived. The force of geographic fact was too strong to be permanently overcome, and after a few centuries power gravitated back to the centre pointed out by nature.

If we may believe the tradition, there was, when the idea of building the new capital arose, a difficulty in obtaining a site in all respects advantageous. The Nile, before debouching upon the plain, hugged for many miles the base of the Libyan hills, and was thus on the wrong side of the valley. It was wanted on the other side, in order to be a water-bulwark against an Asiatic invader. The founder, therefore, before building his city, undertook a gigantic work. He raised a great embankment across the natural course of the river ; and, forcing it from its bed, made it enter a new channel and run midway down the valley or, if anything, rather towards its eastern side. He thus obtained the bulwark against invasion that he required, and he had an ample site for his capital between the new channel of the stream and the foot of the western hills.

It is undoubtedly strange to hear of such a work being constructed at the very dawn of history, by a population that was just becoming a people. But in Egypt precocity is the rule—a Minerva starts full-grown from the head of Jove. The pyramids themselves cannot be placed very long after the supposed reign of Menes; and the engineering skill implied in the pyramids is simply of a piece with that attributed to the founder of Memphis.

In ancient times a city was nothing without a temple; and the capital city of the most religious people in the world could not by any possibility lack that centre of civic life which its chief temple always was to every ancient town. Philosophy must settle the question how it came to pass that religious ideas were in ancient times so universally prevalent and so strongly pronounced. History is only bound to note the fact. Coeval, then, with the foundation of the city of Menes was, according to the tradition, the erection of a great temple to Phthah—"the Revealer," the Divine artificer, by whom the world and man were created, and the hidden thought of the remote Supreme Being was made manifest to His creatures. Phthah's temple lay within the town, and was originally a *naos* or "cell," a single building probably not unlike that between the Sphinx's paws at Ghizeh, situated within a *temenos*, or "sacred enclosure," watered from the river, and no doubt planted with trees. Like the medieval cathedrals, the building grew with the lapse of centuries, great kings continually adding new structures to the main edifice, and enriching it with statuary and painting. Herodotus saw it in its full glory, and calls it "a vast edifice, very worthy of commemoration." Abd-el-Latif saw it in its decline, and notes the beauty of its remains : "the great monolithic shrine of breccia verde, nine cubits high, eight long, and seven broad, the doors which swung on hinges of stone, the well-carven statues, and the lions terrific in their aspect."[1] At the present day scarcely a trace remains. One broken colossus of the Great Ramesses, till very recently prostrate, and a few nondescript fragments, alone continue on the spot, to attest to moderns the position of that antique fane, which the Egyptians themselves regarded as the oldest in their land.

The new city received from its founder the name of Men-nefer — "the Good Abode." It was also known as Ei-Ptah—"the House of Phthah." From the former name came the prevailing appellations— the "Memphis" of the Greeks and Romans, the "Moph" of the Hebrews, the "Mimpi" of the Assyrians, and the name still given to the ruins, "Tel-Monf." It was indeed a "good abode"—watered by an unfailing stream, navigable from the sea, which at once brought it supplies and afforded it a strong protection, surrounded on three sides by the richest and most productive alluvium, close to quarries of excellent stone, warm in winter, fanned by the cool northern breezes in the summer-time, within easy reach of the

[1] R. Stuart Poole, "Cities of Egypt," pp. 24, 25.

sea, yet not so near as to attract the cupidity of pirates. Few capitals have been more favourably placed. It was inevitable that when the old town went to ruins, a new one should spring up in its stead. Memphis still exists, in a certain sense, in the glories of the modern Cairo, which occupies an adjacent site, and is composed largely of the same materials.

The Egyptians knew no more of their first king than that he turned the course of the Nile, founded Memphis, built the nucleus of the great temple of Phthah, and " was devoured by a hippopotamus." This last fact is related with all due gravity by Manetho, notwithstanding that the hippopotamus is a graminivorous animal, one that " eats grass like an ox " (Job xi. 15). Probably the old Egyptian writer whom he followed meant that M'na at last fell a victim to Taourt, the Goddess of Evil, to whom the hippopotamus was sacred, and who was herself figured as a hippopotamus erect. This would be merely equivalent to relating that he succumbed to death. Manetho gave him a reign of sixty-two years.

The question is asked by the modern critics, who will take nothing on trust, " Have we in Menes a real Egyptian, a being of flesh and blood, one who truly lived, breathed, fought, built, ruled, and at last died? Or are we still dealing with a phantom, as much as when we spoke of Seb, and Thoth, and Osiris, and Set, and Horus?" The answer seems to be, that we cannot tell. The Egyptians believed in Menes as a man; they placed him at the head of their dynastic lists; but they had no contemporary monument to show inscribed with his name. A name like that of Menes is found at the beginning of things in so many nations, that on that account alone the word would be suspicious; in Greece it is Minos, in Phrygia Manis, in Lydia Manes, in India Menu, in Germany Mannus. And again, the name of the founder is so like that of the city which he founded, that another suspicion arises—Have we not here one of the many instances of a personal name made out of a local one, as Nin or Ninus from Nineveh (Ninua), Romulus from Roma, and the like ? Probably we shall do best to acquiesce in the judgment of Dr. Birch: "Menes must be placed among those founders of monarchies whose personal existence a severe and enlightened criticism doubts or denies."

The city was, however, a reality, the embankment was a reality, the temple of Phthah was a reality, and the founding of a kingdom in Egypt, which included both the Upper and the Lower country some considerable time before the date of Abraham, was a reality, which the sternest criticism need not—nay, cannot—doubt. All antiquity attests that the valley of the Nile was one of the first seats of civilization. Abraham found a settled government established there when he visited the country, and a consecutive series of monuments carries the date of the first civilization at least as far back as B.C. 2700—probably further.

If the great Menes, then, notwithstanding all that we are told of his doings, be a mere shadowy personage, little more than *magni nominis umbra*, what shall we say of his twenty or thirty successors of the first, second, and third dynasties? What but that they are shadows of shadows? The native monuments of the early Ramesside period (about B.C. 1400–1300) assign to this time some twenty-five names of kings; but they do not agree in their order, nor do they altogether agree in the names. The kings, if they were kings, have left no history—we can only by conjecture attach to them any particular buildings, we can give no account of their actions, we can assign no chronology to their reigns. They are of no more importance in the "story of Egypt" than the Alban kings in the "story of Rome." "Non ragionam di loro, ma guarda e passi."

The first living, breathing, acting, flesh-and-blood personage, whom so-called histories of Egypt present to us, is a certain Sneferu, or Seneferu, whom the Egyptians seem to have regarded as the first monarch of their fourth dynasty. Sneferu—called by Manetho, we know not why, Soris—has left us a representation of himself, and an inscription. On the rocks of Wady Magharah, in the Sinaitic peninsula, may be seen to this day an incised tablet representing the monarch in the act of smiting an enemy, whom he holds by the hair of his head, with a mace. The action is apparently emblematic, for at the side we see the words *Ta satu*, "Smiter of the nations;" and it is a fair explanation of the tablet, that its intention was to signify that the Pharaoh in question had reduced to subjection the tribes which in his time inhabited the Sinaitic regions. The motive of the attack was not mere lust of conquest, but rather the desire of gain. The Wady Magharah contained mines of copper and of turquoise, which the Egyptians desired to work ; and for this purpose it was necessary to hold the country by a set of military posts, in order that the miners might pursue their labours without molestation. Some ruins of the fortifications are still to be seen ; and the mines themselves, now exhausted, pierce the sides of the rocks, and bear in

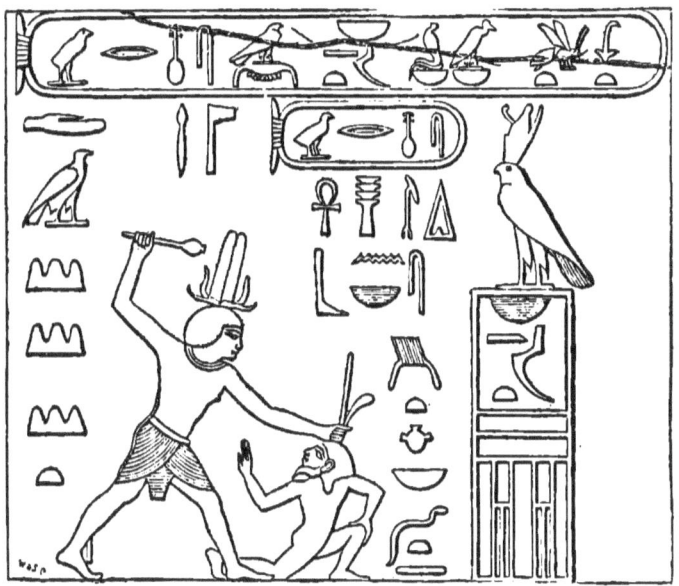

TABLET AT SNEFERU AT WADY-MAGHARAH.

many places traces of hieroglyphical inscriptions. The remains of temples show that the expatriated colonists were not left without the consolations of religion, while a deep well indicates the care that was taken to supply their temporal needs. Thousands of stone arrow-heads give evidence of the presence of a strong garrison, and make us acquainted with the weapon which they found most effectual against their enemies.

Sneferu calls himself *Neter aa*, "the Great God," and *Neb mat*, "the Lord of Justice." He is also "the Golden Horus," or "the Conqueror." *Neb mat* is not a usual title with Egyptian monarchs; and its assumption by Sneferu would seem to mark, at any rate, his appreciation of the excellence of justice, and his desire to have the reputation of a just ruler. Later ages give him the title of "the beneficent king," so that he would seem to have been a really unselfish and kindly sovereign. His form, however, only just emerges from the mists of the period to be again concealed from our view, and we vainly ask ourselves what exactly were the benefits that he conferred on Egypt, so as to attain his high reputation.

Still, the monuments of his time are sufficient to tell us something of the Egypt of his day, and of the amount and character of the civilization so early attained by the Egyptian people. Besides his own tablet in the Wady Magharah, there are in the neighbourhood of the pyramids of Ghizeh a number of tombs which belong to the officials of his court and the members of his family. These tombs contain both sculptures and inscriptions, and throw considerable light on the condition of the country.

In the first place, it is apparent that the style of writing has been invented which is called hieroglyphical, and which has the appearance of a picture writing, though it is almost as absolutely phonetic as any other. Setting apart a certain small number of "determinatives," each sign stands for a sound—the

CIVILIZATION OF SNEFERU'S TIME. 57

greater part for those elementary sounds which we express by letters. An eagle is *a*, a leg and foot *b*, a horned serpent *f*, a hand *t*, an owl *m*, a chicken *u*, and the like. It is true that there are signs which express a compound sound, a whole word, even a word of two syllables. A bowl or basin represents the sound of *neb*, a hatchet that of *neter*, a guitar that of *nefer*, a crescent that of *aah*, and so on. Secondly, it is clear that artistic power is considerable. The animal forms used in the hieroglyphics—the bee, the vulture, the uræus, the hawk, the chicken, the eagle—are well drawn. In the human forms there is less merit, but still they are fairly well proportioned and have spirit. No rudeness or want of finish attaches either to the writing or to the drawing of Sneferu's time; the artists do not attempt much, but what they attempt they accomplish.

Next, we may notice the character of the tombs. Already the tomb was more important than the house; and while every habitation constructed for the living men of the time has utterly perished, scores of the dwellings assigned to the departed still exist, many in an excellent condition. They are stone buildings resembling small houses, each with its door of entrance, but with no windows, and forming internally a small chamber generally decorated with sculptures. The walls slope at an angle of seventy-five or eighty degrees externally, but in the interior are perpendicular. The roof is composed of large flat stones. Strictly speaking, the chambers are not actual tombs, but mortuary chapels. The embalmed body of the deceased, encased in its wooden coffin

(Gen. 1. 26), was not deposited in the chamber, but in an excavation under one of the walls, which was carefully closed up after the coffin had been placed inside it. The chamber was used by the relations for sacred rites, sacrificial feasts, and the like, held in honour of the deceased, especially on the anniversary of his death and entrance into Amenti. The early Egyptians indulged, like the Chinese, in a worship of ancestors. The members of a family met from time to time in the sepulchral chamber of their father, or their grandfather, and went through various ceremonies, sang hymns, poured libations, and made offerings, which were regarded as pleasing to the departed, and which secured their protection and help to such of their descendants as took part in the pious practices.

Sometimes a tomb was more pretentious than those above described. There is an edifice at Meydoum, improperly termed a pyramid, which is thought to be older than Sneferu, and was probably erected by one of the "shadowy kings" who preceded him on the throne. Situated on a natural rocky knoll of some considerable height, it rises in three stages at an angle of $74° 10'$ to an elevation of a hundred and twenty-five feet. It is built of a compact limestone, which must have been brought from some distance. The first stage has a height a little short of seventy feet; the next exceeds thirty-two feet; the third is a little over twenty-two feet. It is possible that originally there were more stages, and probable that the present highest stage has in part crumbled away; so that we may fairly reckon the original height to have been between a hundred and forty and a hundred and fifty feet. The monument is generally regarded as a tomb, from its situation in the Memphian necropolis and its remote resemblance to the pyramids ; but as yet it has not been penetrated, and consequently has not been proved to have been sepulchral.

A construction, which has even a greater appearance of antiquity than the Meydoum tower, exists at

PYRAMID OF MEYDOUM.

Saccarah. Here the architect carried up a monument to the height of two hundred feet, by constructing it in six or seven sloping stages, having an angle of 73° 30'. The core of his building was composed of rubble, but this was protected on every side by a thick casing of limestone roughly hewn, and apparently quarried on the spot. The sepulchral intention of the construction is unquestionable. It covered a spacious chamber excavated in the rock, whereon the monument was built, which, when first discovered, contained a sarcophagus and was lined with slabs of granite. Carefully concealed passages connected the chamber with the outer world, and allowed of its being entered by those in possession of the "secrets of the prison-house." In this structure we have, no doubt, the tomb of a king more ancient than Sneferu—though for our own part we should hesitate to assign the monument to one king rather than another.

If we pass from the architecture of the period to its social condition, we remark that grades of society already existed, and were as pronounced as in later times. The kings were already deities, and treated with superstitious regard. The state-officials were a highly privileged class, generally more or less connected with the royal family. The land was partly owned by the king (Gen. xlvii. 6), who employed his own labourers and herdsmen upon it; partly, mainly perhaps, it was in the hands of great landed proprietors—nobles, who lived in country houses upon their estates, maintaining large households, and giving employment to scores of peasants, herdsmen, artizans, huntsmen, and fishermen. The "lower orders" were of very little account. They were at the beck and call of the landed aristocracy in the country districts, of the state-officials in the towns. Above all, the monarch had the right of impressing them into his service whenever he pleased, and employing them in the "great works" by which he strove to perpetuate his name.

There prevailed, however, a great simplicity of manners. The dress of the upper classes was wonderfully

THE GREAT PYRAMID OF SACCARAH. 61

plain and unpretending, presenting little variety and scarcely any ornament. The grandee wore, indeed, an elaborate wig, it being imperative on all men to shave

GREAT PYRAMID OF SACCARAH (*Present appearance*).

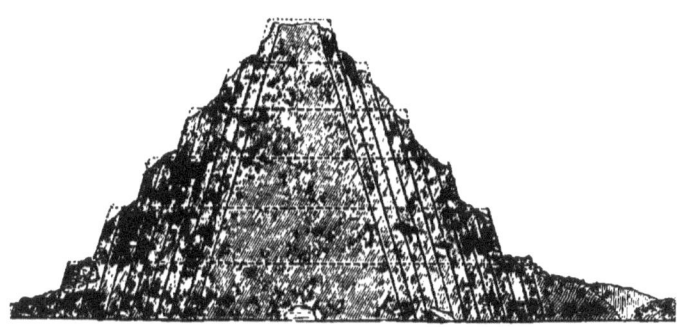

SECTION OF THE SAME, SHOWING ORIGINAL CONSTRUCTION.

the head for the sake of cleanliness. But otherwise his costume was of the simplest and the scantiest. Ordinarily, when he was employed in the common duties of life, a short tunic, probably of white linen, reaching from the waist to a little above the knee, was his sole garment. His arms, chest, legs, even his feet, were naked ; for sandals, not to speak of stockings or shoes, were unknown. The only decoration which he wore was a chain or riband round the neck, to which was suspended an ornament like a locket— probably an amulet. In his right hand he carried a long staff or wand, either for the purpose of belabouring his inferiors, or else to use it as a walking-stick. On special occasions he made, however, a more elaborate toilet. Doffing his linen tunic, he clothed himself in a single, somewhat scanty, robe, which reached from the neck to the ankles ; and having exchanged his chain and locket for a broad collar, and adorned his wrists with bracelets, he was ready to pay visits or to receive company. He had no carriage, so far as appears, not even a palanquin ; no horse to ride, nor even a mule or a donkey. The great men of the East rode, in later times, on " white asses " (Judges v. 10) ; the Egyptian of Sneferu's age had to trudge to court, or to make calls upon his friends, by the sole aid of those means of locomotion which nature had given him.

Women, who in most civilized countries claim to themselves far more elaboration in dress and variety of ornament than men, were content, in the Egypt of which we are here speaking, with a costume, and a personal decoration, scarcely less simple than that of their husbands. The Egyptian *materfamilias* of the time wore her hair long, and gathered into three masses, one behind the head, and the other two in front of either shoulder. Like her spouse, she had but a single garment—a short gown or petticoat reaching from just below the breasts to half way down the calf of the leg, and supported by two broad straps passed over the two shoulders. She exposed her

GROUP OF STATUARY, CONSISTING OF A HUSBAND AND WIFE.

arms and bosom to sight, and her feet were bare, like her husband's. Her only ornaments were bracelets.

There was no seclusion of women at any time among the ancient Egyptians. The figure of the wife on the early monuments constantly accompanies that of her husband. She is his associate in all his occupations. Her subordination is indicated by her representation being on an unduly smaller scale, and by her ordinary position, which is behind the figure of her "lord and master." In statuary, however, she appears seated with him on the same seat or chair. There is no appearance of her having been either a drudge or a plaything. She was regarded as man's true "helpmate," shared his thoughts, ruled his family, and during their early years had the charge of his children. Polygamy was unknown in Egypt during the primitive period; even the kings had then but one wife. Sneferu's wife was a certain Mertitefs, who bore him a son, Nefer-mat, and after his death became the wife of his successor. Women were entombed with as much care, and almost with as much pomp, as men. Their right to ascend the throne is said to have been asserted by one of the kings who preceded Sneferu; and from time to time women actually exercised in Egypt the royal authority.

IV.

THE PYRAMID BUILDERS.

It is difficult for a European, or an American, who has not visited Egypt, to realize the conception of a Great Pyramid. The pyramidal form has gone entirely out of use as an architectural type of monumental perfection ; nay, even as an architectural embellishment. It maintained an honourable position in architecture from its first discovery to the time of the Maccabee kings (1 Mac. xiii. 28) ; but, never having been adopted by either the Greeks or the Romans, it passed into desuetude in the Old World with the conquest of the East by the West. In the New World it was found existent by the early discoverers, and then held a high place in the regards of the native race which had reached the furthest towards civilization ; but Spanish bigotry looked with horror on everything that stood connected with an idolatrous religion, and the pyramids of Mexico were first wantonly injured, and then allowed to fall into such a state of decay, that their original form is by some questioned. A visit to the plains of Teotihuacan will not convey to the mind which is a blank on the subject the true conception of a great pyramid. It requires a pilgrimage to Ghizeh or Saccarah, or a lively and *well-instructed* imagination, to enable a man to call up before his mind's eye the true form and appearance and impressiveness of such a structure.

Lord Houghton endeavoured to give expression to the feelings of one who sees for the first time these wondrous, these incomprehensible creations in the following lines :

> After the fantasies of many a night,
>   After the deep desires of many a day,
> Rejoicing as an ancient Eremite
>   Upon the desert's edge at last I lay :
> Before me rose, in wonderful array,
>   Those works where man has rivalled Nature most,
> Those Pyramids, that fear no more decay
>   Than waves inflict upon the rockiest coast,
> Or winds on mountain-steeps, and like endurance boast.
>
> Fragments the deluge of old Time has left
>   Behind in its subsidence—long long walls
> Of cities of their very names bereft,—
>   Lone columns, remnants of majestic halls,
> Rich traceried chambers, where the night-dew falls,—
>   All have I seen with feelings due, I trow,
> Yet not with such as these memorials
>   Of the great unremembered, that can show
> The mass and shape they wore four thousand years ago.

The Egyptian idea of a pyramid was that of a structure on a square base, with four inclining sides, each one of which should be an equilateral triangle, all meeting in a point at the top. The structure might be solid, and in that case might be either of hewn stone throughout, or consist of a mass of rubble merely held together by an external casing of stone; or it might contain chambers and passages, in which case the employment of rubble was scarcely possible.

THE THREE PYRAMIDS OF GHIZEH. 67

It has been demonstrated by actual excavation, that all the *great* pyramids of Egypt were of the latter character—that they were built for the express purpose of containing chambers and passages, and of preserving those chambers and passages intact. They required, therefore, to be, and in most cases are, of a good construction throughout.

There are from sixty to seventy pyramids in Egypt, chiefly in the neighbourhood of Memphis Some of them are nearly perfect, some more or less in ruins, but most of them still preserving their ancient shape, when seen from afar. Two of them greatly exceed all the others in their dimensions, and are appropriately designated as "the Great Pyramid" and "the Second Pyramid." A third in their immediate vicinity is of very inferior size, and scarcely deserves the pre-eminence which has been conceded to it by the designation of "the Third Pyramid."

Still, the three seem all of them, to deserve description, and to challenge a place in "the story of Egypt," which has never yet been told without some account of the marvels of each of them. The smallest of the three was a square of three hundred and fifty-four feet each way, and had a height of two hundred and eighteen feet. It covered an area of two acres, three roods, and twenty-one poles, or about that of an ordinary London square. The cubic contents amounted to above nine million feet of solid masonry, and are calculated to have weighed 702,460 tons. The height was not very impressive. Two hundred and twenty feet is an altitude attained by the towers of many churches, and the "Pyramid of the Sun" at Teotihuacan did not fall much short of it; but the mass was immense, the masonry was excellent, and the ingenuity shown in the construction was great. Sunk in the rock from which the pyramid rose, was a series of sepulchral chambers. One, the largest, almost directly under the apex of the pyramid, was empty. In another, which had an arched roof, constructed in the most careful and elaborate way, was found the sarcophagus of the king, Men-kau-ra, to whom tradition assigned the building, formed of a single mass of blue-black basalt, exquisitely polished and beautifully carved, externally eight feet long, three feet high, and three feet broad, internally six feet by two. In the sarcophagus was the wooden coffin of the monarch, and on the lid of the coffin was his name. The chambers were connected by two long passages with the open air; and another passage had, apparently, been used for the same purpose before the pyramid attained its ultimate size. The tomb-chamber, though carved in the rock, had been paved and lined with slabs of solid stone, which were fastened to the native rock by iron cramps. The weight of the sarcophagus which it contained, now unhappily lost, was three tons.

The "Second Pyramid," which stands to the north-east of the Third, at the distance of about two hundred and seventy yards, was a square of seven hundred and seven feet each way, and thus covered an area of almost eleven acres and a half, or nearly double that of the greatest building which Rome ever produced—the Coliseum. The sides rose at an angle of 52° 10′; and the perpendicular height was four hundred and fifty-four feet, or fifty feet more than that of the spire

VIEW OF THE GREAT AND SECOND PYRAMIDS.

of Salisbury Cathedral. The cubic contents are estimated at 71,670,000 feet; and their weight is calculated at 5,309,000 tons. Numbers of this vast amount convey but little idea of the reality to an ordinary reader, and require to be made intelligible by comparisons. Suppose, then, a solidly built stone house, with walls a foot thick, twenty feet of frontage, and thirty feet of depth from front to back; let the walls be twenty-four feet high and have a foundation of six feet; throw in party-walls to one-third the extent of the main walls—and the result will be a building containing four thousand cubic feet of masonry. Let there be a town of eighteen thousand such houses, suited to be the abode of a hundred thousand inhabitants—then pull these houses to pieces, and pile them up into a heap to a height exceeding that of the spire of the Cathedral of Vienna, and you will have a rough representation of the "Second Pyramid of Ghizeh." Or lay down the contents of the structure in a line a foot in breadth and depth—the line would be above 13,500 miles long, and would reach more than half-way round the earth at the equator. Again, suppose that a single man can quarry a ton of stone in a week, then it would have required above twenty thousand to be employed constantly for five years in order to obtain the material for the pyramid; and if the blocks were required to be large, the number employed and the time occupied would have had to be greater.

The internal construction of the "Second Pyramid" is less elaborate than that of the Third, but not very different. Two passages lead from the outer air to a sepulchral chamber almost exactly under the apex of the pyramid, and exactly at its base, one of them commencing about fifty feet from the base midway in the north side, and the other commencing a little outside the base, in the pavement at the foot of the pyramid. The first passage was carried through the substance of the pyramid for a distance of a hundred and ten feet at a descending angle of 25° 55', after which it became horizontal, and was tunnelled through the native rock on which the pyramid was built. The second passage was wholly in the rock. It began with a descent at an angle of 21° 40', which continued for a hundred feet; it was then horizontal for fifty feet; after which it ascended gently for ninety-six feet, and joined the first passage about midway between the sepulchral chamber and the outer air. The sepulchral chamber was carved mainly out of the solid rock below the pyramid, but was roofed in by some of the basement stones, which were sloped at an angle. The chamber measured forty-six feet in length and sixteen feet in breadth; its height in the centre was twenty-two feet. It contained a plain granite sarcophagus, without inscription of any kind, eight feet and a half in length, three feet and a half in breadth, and in depth three feet. There was no coffin in the sarcophagus at the time of its discovery, and no inscription on any part of the pyramid or of its contents. The tradition, however, which ascribed it to the immediate predecessor of Men-kau-ra, may be accepted as sufficient evidence of its author.

Come we now to the "Great Pyramid," "which is still," says Lenormant, "at least in respect of its mass,

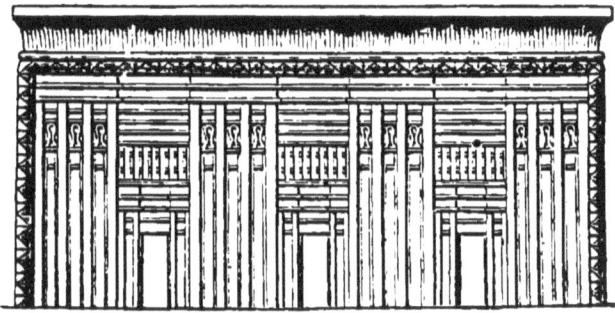

SARCOPHAGUS OF MYCERINUS.

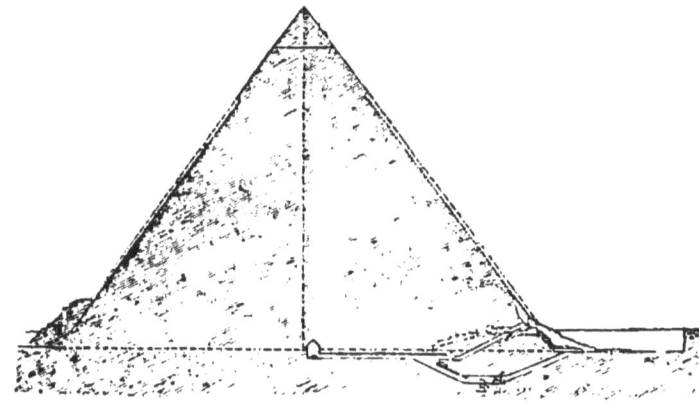

SECTION OF THE SECOND PYRAMID.

THE GREAT PYRAMID. 75

the most prodigious of all human constructions." The "Great Pyramid," or "First Pyramid of Ghizeh," as it is indifferently termed, is situated almost due northeast of the "Second Pyramid," at the distance of about two hundred yards. The length of each side at the base was originally seven hundred and sixty-four feet, or fifty-seven feet more than that of the sides of the "Second Pyramid." Its original perpendicular height was something over four hundred and eighty feet, its cubic contents exceeded eighty-nine million feet, and the weight of its mass 6,840,000 tons. In height it thus exceeded Strasburg Cathedral by above six feet, St. Peter's at Rome by above thirty feet, St. Stephen's at Vienna by fifty feet, St. Paul's, London, by a hundred and twenty feet, and the Capitol at Washington by nearly two hundred feet. Its area was thirteen acres, one rood, and twenty-two poles, or nearly two acres more than the area of the "Second Pyramid," which was fourfold that of the "Third Pyramid," which, as we have seen, was that of an ordinary London square. Its cubic contents would build a city of twenty-two thousand such houses as were above described, and laid in a line of cubic squares would reach a distance of nearly seventeen thousand miles, or girdle two-thirds of the earth's circumference at the equator. Herodotus says that its construction required the continuous labour of a hundred thousand men for the space of twenty years, and moderns do not regard the estimate as exaggerated.

The "Great Pyramid" presents, moreover, many other marvels besides its size. First, there is the massiveness of the blocks of which it is composed.

The basement stones are in many cases thirty feet long by five feet high, and four or five wide: they must contain from six hundred to seven hundred and fifty cubic feet each, and weigh from forty-six to fifty-seven tons. The granite blocks which roof over the upper sepulchral chamber are nearly nineteen feet long, by two broad and from three to four deep. The relieving stones above the same chamber, and those

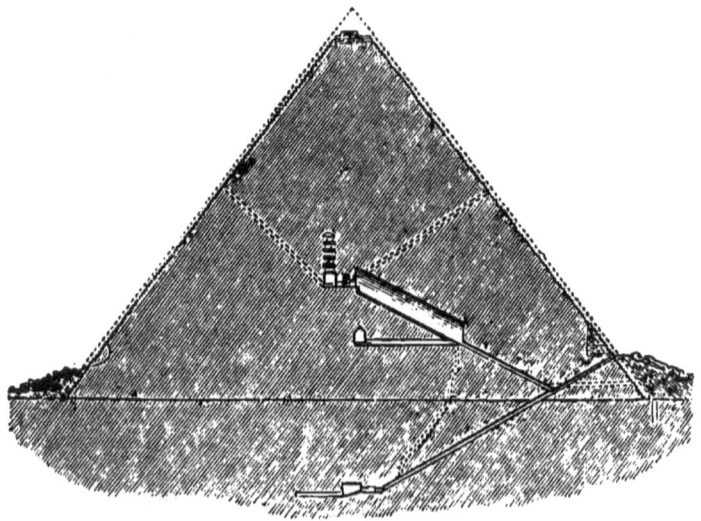

SECTION OF THE GREAT PYRAMID.

of the entrance passage, are almost equally massive. Generally the external blocks are of a size with which modern builders scarcely ever venture to deal, though the massiveness diminishes as the pyramid is ascended. The bulk of the interior is, however, of comparatively small stones; but even these are carefully hewn and squared, so as to fit together compactly.

Further, there are the passages, the long gallery,

the ventilation shafts, and the sepulchral chambers all of them remarkable, and some of them simply astonishing. The "Great Pyramid" guards three chambers. One lies deep in the rock, about a hundred and twenty feet beneath the natural surface of the ground, and is placed almost directly below the apex

KING'S CHAMBER AND CHAMBERS OF CONSTRUCTION, GREAT PYRAMID.

of the structure. It measures forty-six feet by twenty-seven, and is eleven feet high. The access to it is by a long and narrow passage which commences in the north side of the pyramid, about seventy feet above the original base, and descends for forty yards through the masonry, and then for seventy more in the same line through the solid rock, when it changes its direction, becoming horizontal for nine yards, and so entering the chamber itself. The two other chambers are reached by an ascending passage, which branches off from the descending one at the distance of about thirty yards from the entrance, and mounts up through the heart of the pyramid for rather more than forty yards, when it divides into two. A low horizontal gallery, a hundred and ten feet long, leads to a chamber which has been called "the Queen's"—a room about nineteen feet long by seventeen broad, roofed in with sloping blocks, and having a height of twenty feet in the centre. Another longer and much loftier gallery continues on for a hundred and fifty feet in the line of the ascending passage, and is then connected by a short horizontal passage with the uppermost or "King's Chamber." Here was found a sarcophagus believed to be that of King Khufu, since the name of Khufu was scrawled in more than one place on the chamber walls.

The construction of this chamber—the very kernel of the whole building — is exceedingly remarkable. It is a room of thirty-four feet in length, with a width of seventeen feet, and a height of nineteen, composed wholly of granite blocks of great size, beautifully polished, and fitted together with great care. The construction of the roof is particularly admirable. First, the chamber is covered in with nine huge blocks, each nearly nineteen feet long and four feet wide, which are laid side by side upon the walls so as to form a complete ceiling. Then above these blocks is a low chamber similarly covered in, and this is

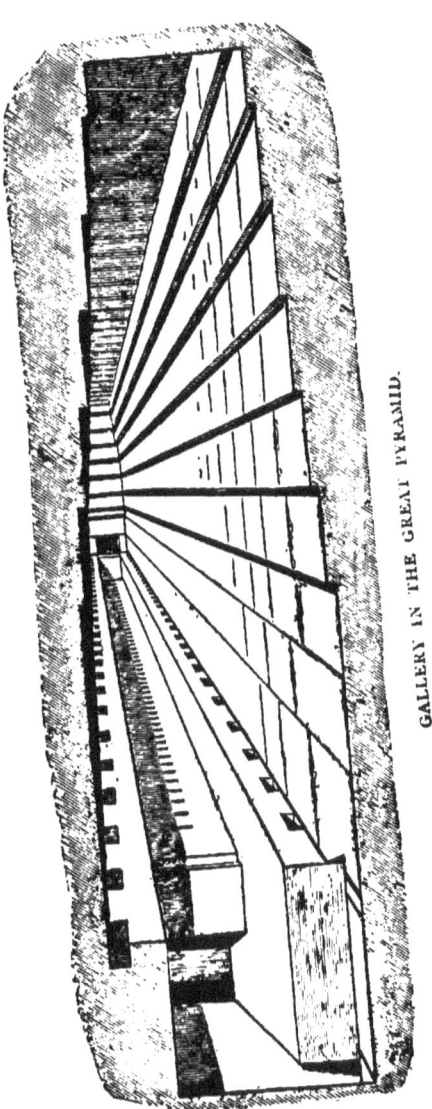

GALLERY IN THE GREAT PYRAMID.

GALLERY IN THE GREAT PYRAMID.

repeated four times; after which there is a fifth opening, triangular, and roofed in by a set of huge sloping blocks, which meet at the apex and support each other. The object is to relieve the chamber from any superincumbent weight, and prevent it from being crushed in by the mass of material above it ; and this object has been so completely attained that still, at the expiration of above forty centuries, the entire chamber, with its elaborate roof, remains intact, without crack or settlement of any kind.

Further, from the great chamber are carried two ventilation-shafts, or air-passages, northwards and southwards, which open on the outer surface of the pyramid, and are respectively two hundred and thirty-three and one hundred and ninety-four feet long. These passages are square, or nearly so, and have a diameter varying between six and nine inches. They give a continual supply of pure air to the chamber, and keep it dry at all seasons.

The Great Gallery is also of curious construction. Extending for a distance of one hundred and fifty feet, and rising at an angle of 26° 18', it has a width of five feet at the base and a height of above thirty feet. The side walls are formed of seven layers of stone, each projecting a few inches over that below it. The gallery thus gradually contracts towards the top, which has a width of four feet only, and is covered in with stones that reach across it, and rest on the walls at either side. The exact object of so lofty a gallery has not been ascertained ; but it must have helped to keep the air of the interior pure and sweet, by increasing the space through which it had to circulate.

The "Pyramid Builders," or kings who constructed the three monuments that have now been described, were, according to a unanimous tradition, three consecutive monarchs, whose native names are read as Khufu, Shafra, and Menkaura. These kings belonged to Manetho's fourth dynasty; and Khufu, the first of the three, seems to have been the immediate successor of Sneferu. Theorists have delighted to indulge in speculations as to the objects which the builders had in view when they raised such magnificent constructions. One holds that the Great Pyramid, at any rate, was built to embody cosmic discoveries, as the exact length of the earth's diameter and circumference, the length of an arc of the meridian, and the true unit of measure. Another believes the great work of Khufu to have been an observatory, and the ventilating passages to have been designed for "telescopes," through which observations were to be made upon the sun and stars; but it has not yet been shown that there is any valid foundation for these fancies, which have been spun with much art out of the delicate fabric of their propounders' brains. The one hard fact which rests upon abundant evidence is this—the pyramids were built for tombs, to contain the mummies of deceased Egyptians. The chambers in their interiors, at the time of their discovery, held within them sarcophagi, and in one instance the sarcophagus had within it a coffin. The coffin had an inscription upon it, which showed that it had once contained the body of a king. If anything more is necessary, we may add that every pyramid in Egypt—and there are, as we have said, more than sixty of them—was built for the same purpose, and that they all occupy sites in the great necropolis, or burial-ground opposite Memphis, where the inhabitants are known to have laid their dead.

The marvel is, how Khufu came suddenly to have so magnificent a thought as that of constructing an edifice double the height of any previously existing, covering five times the area, and containing ten times the mass. Architecture does not generally proceed by "leaps and bounds;" but here was a case of a sudden extraordinary advance, such as we shall find it difficult to parallel elsewhere. An attempt has been made to solve the mystery by the supposition that all pyramids were gradual accretions, and that their size marks simply the length of a king's reign, each monarch making his sepulchral chamber, with a small pyramid above it, in his first year, and as his reign went on, adding each year an outer coating; so that the number of these coatings tells the length of his reign, as the age of a tree is known from the number of its annual rings. In this case there would have been nothing ideally great in the conception of Khufu—he would simply have happened to erect the biggest pyramid because he happened to have the longest reign; but, except in the case of the "Third Pyramid," there is a unity of design in the structures which implies that the architect had conceived the whole structure in his mind from the first. The lengths of the several parts are proportioned one to another. In the "Great Pyramid," the main chamber would not have needed the five relieving chambers above it unless it was known that it would have to be pressed down by a superincumbent mass, such as actually lies upon it. Moreover, how is it possible to conceive that in the later years of a decrepid monarch, the whole of an enormous pyramid could be coated over with huge blocks—and the blocks are largest at the external surface—the work requiring to be pushed each year with more vigour, as becoming each year greater and more difficult? Again, what shall we say of the external finish? Each pyramid was finally smoothed down to a uniform sloping surface. This alone must have been a work of years. Did a pyramid builder leave it to his successor to finish his pyramid? It is at least doubtful whether any pyramid at all would ever have been finished had he done so.

We must hold, therefore, that Khufu did suddenly conceive a design without a parallel—did require his architect to construct him a tomb, which should put to shame all previous monuments, and should with difficulty be surpassed, or even equalled. He must have possessed much elevation of thought, and an intense ambition, together with inordinate selfishness, an overweening pride, and entire callousness to the sufferings of others, before he could have approved the plan which his master-builder set before him. That plan, including the employment of huge blocks of stone, their conveyance to the top of a hill a hundred feet high, and their emplacement, in some cases, at a further elevation of above 450 feet, involved, under the circumstances of the time, such an amount of human suffering, that no king who had any regard for the happiness of his subjects could have consented to it. Khufu must have forced his subjects to labour for a long term of years—twenty, according to Herodotus—at a servile work which was wholly unproductive, and was carried on amid their sighs and groans for no object but his own glorification, and the supposed safe custody of his remains. Shafra must have done nearly the same. Hence an evil repute attached to the pyramid builders, whose names were handed down to posterity as those of evil-minded and impious kings, who neglected the service of the gods to gratify their own vanity, and, so long as they could exalt themselves, did not care how much they oppressed their people. There was not even the poor apology for their conduct that their oppression fell on slaves, or foreigners, or prisoners of war. Egypt was not yet a conquering power; prisoners of war were few, slaves not very common. The labourers whom the pyramid builders employed were their own free subjects whom they impressed into the heavy service.

It is by a just Nemesis that the kings have in a great measure failed to secure the ends at which they aimed, and in hope of which they steeled their hearts against their subjects' cries. They have indeed handed down their names to a remote age : but it is as tyrants and oppressors. They are world-famous, or rather world-infamous. But that preservation of their corporeal frame which they especially sought, is exactly what they have missed attaining.

> Let not a monument give you or me hopes,
> Since not a pinch of dust remains of Cheóps,

says the doggerel of the satiric Byron ; and it is the

absolute fact that while thousands of mummies buried in common graves remain untouched even to the present day, the very grandeur of the pyramid builders' tombs attracted attention to them, caused the monuments to be opened, the sarcophagi to be rifled, and the remains inclosed in them to be dispersed to the four winds of heaven.

Still, whatever gloomy associations attach to the pyramids in respect of the sufferings caused by their erection, as monuments they must always challenge a certain amount of admiration. A great authority declares: "No one can possibly examine the interior of the Great Pyramid without being struck with astonishment at the wonderful mechanical skill displayed in its construction. The immense blocks of granite brought from Syene, a distance of five hundred miles, polished like glass, and so fitted that the joints can scarcely be detected! Nothing can be more wonderful than the extraordinary amount of knowledge displayed in the construction of the discharging chambers over the roof of the principal apartment, in the alignment of the sloping galleries, in the provision of the ventilating shafts, and in all the wonderful contrivances of the structure. All these, too, are carried out with such precision that, notwithstanding the immense superincumbent weight, no settlement in any part can be detected to an appreciable fraction of an inch. Nothing more perfect mechanically has ever been erected since that time." [1]

The architectural effect of the two greatest of the pyramids is certainly magnificent. They do not

[1] Fergusson, "History of Architecture," vol. i. pp. 91, 92.

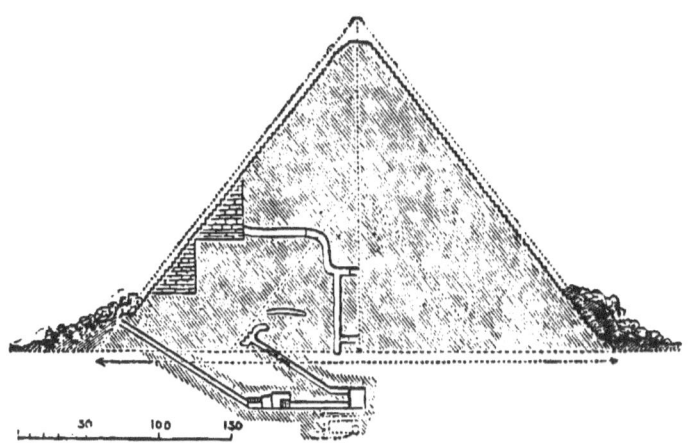

SECTION OF THE THIRD PYRAMID, SHOWING PASSAGES.

TOMB-CHAMBER OF THE THIRD PYRAMID.

greatly impress the beholder at first sight, for a pyramid, by the very law of its formation, never looks as large as it is—it slopes away from the eye in every direction, and eludes rather than courts observation. But as the spectator gazes, as he prolongs his examination and inspection, the pyramids gain upon him, their impressiveness increases. By the vastness of their mass, by the impression of solidity and durability which they produce, partly also, perhaps, by the symmetry and harmony of their lines and their perfect simplicity and freedom from ornament, they convey to the beholder a sense of grandeur and majesty, they produce within him a feeling of astonishment and awe, such as is scarcely caused by any other of the erections of man. In all ages travellers have felt and expressed the warmest admiration for them. They impressed Herodotus as no works that he had seen elsewhere, except, perhaps, the Babylonian. They astonished Germanicus, familiar as he was with the great constructions of Rome. They furnished Napoleon with the telling phrase, " Soldiers, forty centuries look down upon you from the top of the pyramids." Greece and Rome reckoned them among the Seven Wonders of the world. Moderns have doubted whether they could really be the work of human hands. If they possess only one of the elements of architectural excellence, they possess that element to so great an extent that in respect of it they are unsurpassed, and probably unsurpassable.

These remarks apply especially to the first and second pyramids. The "Third" is not a work of any very extraordinary grandeur. The bulk is not greater than that of the chief pyramid of Saccarah, which has never attracted much attention; and the height did not greatly exceed that of the chief Mexican temple-mound. Moreover, the stones of which the pyramid was composed are not excessively massive. The monument aimed at being beautiful rather than grand. It was coated for half its height with blocks of pink granite from Syene, bevelled at the edges, which remain still in place on two sides of the structure. The entrance to it, on the north side, was conspicuous, and seems to have had a metal ornamentation let into the stone. The sepulchral chamber was beautifully lined and roofed, and the sarcophagus was exquisitively carved. Menkaura, the constructor, was not regarded as a tyrant, or an oppressor, but as a mild and religious monarch, whom the gods ill-used by giving him too short a reign. His religious temper is indicated by the inscription on the coffin which contained his remains: " O Osiris," it reads, " King of Upper and Lower Egypt, Menkaura, living eternally, engendered by the Heaven, born of Nut, substance of Seb, thy mother Nut stretches herself over thee in her name of the abyss of heaven. She renders thee divine by destroying all thy enemies, O King Menkaura, living eternally."

The fashion of burying in pyramids continued to the close of Manetho's sixth dynasty, but no later monarchs rivalled the great works of Khufu and Shafra. The tombs of their successors were monuments of a moderate size, involving no oppression of the people, but perhaps rather improving their condition by causing a rise in the rate of wages.

Certainly, the native remains of the period give a cheerful representation of the condition of all classes. The nation for the most part enjoys peace, and applies itself to production. The wealth of the nobles increases, and the position of their dependents is improved. Slaves were few, and there was ample employment for the labouring classes. We do not see the stick at work upon the backs of the labourers in the sculptures of the time ; they seem to accomplish their various tasks with alacrity and gaiety of heart. They plough, and hoe, and reap; drive cattle or asses ; winnow and store corn ; gather grapes and tread them, singing in chorus as they tread ; cluster round the winepress or the threshingfloor, on which the animals tramp out the grain ; gather lotuses ; save cattle from the inundation ; engage in fowling or fishing ; and do all with an apparent readiness and cheerfulness which seems indicative of real content. There may have been a darker side to the picture, and undoubtedly was while Khufu and Shafra held the throne; but kings of a morose and cruel temper seem to have been the exception, rather than the rule, in Egypt ; and the moral code, which required kindness to be shown to dependents, seems, at this period at any rate, to have had a hold upon the consciences, and to have influenced the conduct, of the mass of the people. "Happy the nation that has no history!" Egypt during this golden age was neither assailed by any aggressive power beyond her borders, nor had herself conceived the idea of distant conquest. An occasional raid upon the negroes of the South, or chastisement of the nomades of the East, secured her interests in those quarters, and prevented her warlike virtues from dying out through lack of use. But otherwise tranquillity was undisturbed, and the energies of the nation were directed to increasing its material prosperity, and to progress in the arts.

Among the marvels of Egypt perhaps the Sphinx is second to none. The mysterious being with the head of a man and the body of a lion is not at all uncommon in Egyptian architectural adornment, but the one placed before the Second Pyramid (the Pyramid of Shafra), and supposed to be contemporary with it, astonishes the observer by its gigantic proportions. It is known to the Arabs as Abul-hôl, the father of terror. It measures more than one hundred feet in length, and was partially carved from the rocks of the Lybian hills. Between its outstretched feet there stands a chapel, uncovered in 1816, three walls of which are formed by tablets bearing inscriptions indicative of its use and origin.

A small temple behind the great Sphinx, probably also built by Shafra, is formed of great blocks of the hardest red granite, brought from the neighbourhood of Syene and fitted to each other with a nicety astonishing to modern architects, who are unable to imagine what tools could have proved equal to the difficult achievement. Mysterious passages pierce the great Sphinx and connect it with the Second Pyramid, three hundred feet west of it. In the face of this mystery all questions are vain, and yet every visitor adds new queries to those that others have asked before him.

THE GREAT SPHINX.

Since what unnumbered year
  Hast thou kept watch and ward,
And o'er the buried land of fear
  So grimly held thy guard?
No faithless slumber snatching,
  Still couched in silence brave,
Like some fierce hound, long watching
  Above her master's grave. . . .

  Dost thou in anguish thus
  Still brood o'er Œdipus?
And weave enigmas to mislead anew,
  And stultify the blind
  Dull heads of human-kind,
    And inly make thy moan,
That, mid the hated crew,
  Whom thou so long couldst vex,
  Bewilder and perplex,
Thou yet couldst find a subtler than thine own?

  Even now, methinks that those
  Dark, heavy lips which close
  In such a stern repose,
Seem burdened with some thought unsaid,
And hoard within their portals dread
  Some fearful secret there,
  Which to the listening earth
  She may not whisper forth,
    Not even to the air!

  Of awful wonders hid
  In yonder dread Pyramid,
    The home of magic fears;
  Of chambers vast and lonely,
  Watched by the Genii only,
Who tend their masters' long-forgotten biers,
  And treasures that have shone
  On cavern walls alone,
    For thousand, thousand years.

  Would she but tell. She knows
  Of the old Pharaohs;

Could count the Ptolemies' long line ;
Each mighty myth's original hath seen,
Apis, Anubis,—ghosts that haunt between
   The bestial and divine,—
(Such he that sleeps in Philæ,—he that stands
   In gloom unworshipped, 'neath his rock-hewn fane,—
And they who, sitting on Memnonian sands,
   Cast their long shadows o'er the desert plain :)
     Hath marked Nitocris pass,
     And Oxymandyas
Deep-versed in many a dark Egyptian wile,—
   The Hebrew boy hath eyed
   Cold to the master's bride ;
And that Medusan stare hath frozen the smile
Of all her love and guile,
   For whom the Cæsar sighed,
   And the world-loser died,—
The darling of the Nile.

V.

THE RISE OF THEBES TO POWER, AND THE EARLY THEBAN KINGS.

HITHERTO Egypt had been ruled from a site at the junction of the narrow Nile valley with the broad plain of the Delta—a site sufficiently represented by the modern Cairo. But now there was a shift of the seat of power. There is reason to believe that something like a disruption of Egypt into separate kingdoms took place, and that for a while several distinct dynasties bore sway in different parts of the country. Disruption was naturally accompanied by weakness and decline. The old order ceased, and opportunity was offered for some new order—some new power—to assert itself. The site on which it arose was one three hundred and fifty miles distant from the ancient capital, or four hundred and more by the river. Here, about lat. 26°, the usually narrow valley of the Nile opens into a sort of plain or basin. The mountains on either side of the river recede, as though by common consent, and leave between themselves and the river's bank a broad amphitheatre, which in each case is a rich green plain—an alluvium of the most productive character—dotted with *dom* and date palms, sometimes growing single, sometimes collected into clumps or groves. On the western side the Libyan range gathers itself up into a single considerable peak, which has an elevation of twelve hundred feet. On the east the desert-wall maintains its usual level character, but is pierced by valleys conducting to the coast of the Red Sea. The situation was one favourable for commerce. On the one side was the nearest route through the sandy desert to the Lesser Oasis, which commanded the trade of the African interior; on the other the way led through the valley of Hammamât, rich with *breccia verde* and other valuable and rare stones, to a district abounding in mines of gold, silver, and lead, and thence to the Red Sea coast, from which, even in very early times, there was communication with the opposite coast of Arabia, the region of gums and spices.

In this position there had existed, probably from the very beginnings of Egypt, a provincial city of some repute, called by its inhabitants Apé or Apiu, and, with the feminine article prefixed, Tapé, or Tapiu, which some interpret "The city of thrones." To the Greeks the name "Tapé" seemed to resemble their own well-known "Thebai," whence they transferred the familiar appellation from the Bœotian to the Mid-Egyptian town, which has thus come to be known to Englishmen and Anglo-Americans as "Thebes." Thebes had been from the first the capital of a "nome." It lay so far from the court that it acquired a character of its own—a special cast of religion, manners, speech, nomenclature, mode of writing, and the like—which helped to detach it from Lower or Northern Egypt more even than its isolation. Still, it was not until the northern kingdom sank into decay from internal weakness and exhaustion, and disintegration supervened in the Delta and elsewhere, that Thebes resolved to assert herself and claim independent sovereignty. Apparently, she achieved her purpose without having recourse to arms. The kingdoms of the north were content to let her go. They recognized their own weakness, and allowed the nascent power to develop itself unchecked and unhindered.

The first known Theban monarch is a certain Antef or Enantef, whose coffin was discovered in the year 1827 by some Arabs near Qurnah, to the west of Thebes. The mummy bore the royal diadem, and the epigraph on the lid of the coffin declared the body which it contained to be that of "Antef, king of *the two Egypts.*" The phrase implied a claim to dominion over the whole country, but a claim as purely nominal as that of the kings of England from Edward IV. to George III. to be monarchs of France and Navarre. Antef's rule may possibly have reached to Elephantine on the one hand, but is not likely to have extended much beyond Coptos on the other. He was a local chieftain posing as a great sovereign, but probably with no intention to deceive either his own contemporaries or posterity. His name appears in some of the later Egyptian dynastic lists; but no monument of his time has come down to us except the one that has been mentioned.

Antef I. is thought to have been succeeded by Mentu-hotep I., a monarch even more shadowy, known to us only from the " Table of Karnak." This prince, however, is followed by one who possesses a greater amount of substance—Antef-aa, or " Antef the Great," grandson, as it would seem, of the first Antef—a sort of Egyptian Nimrod, who delighted above all things in the chase. Antefaa's sepulchral monument shows him to us standing in the midst of his dogs, who wear collars, and have their names engraved over them. The dogs are four in number, and are of distinct types. The first, which is called *Mahut*, or " Antelope," has drooping ears, and long but somewhat heavy legs; it resembles a foxhound, and was no doubt both swift and strong, though it can scarcely have been so swift as its namesake. The second was called *Abakaru*, a name of unknown meaning; it has pricked up, pointed ears, a pointed nose, and a curly tail. Some have compared it with the German *spitz* dog, but it seems rather to be the original dog of nature, a near congener of the jackal, and the type to which all dogs revert when allowed to run wild and breed indiscriminately. The third, named *Pahats* or *Kamu, i.e.* " Blacky," is a heavy animal, not unlike a mastiff; it has a small, rounded, drooping ear, a square, blunt nose, a deep chest, and thick limbs. The late Dr. Birch supposed that it might have been employed by Antefaa in " the chase of the lion ;" but we should rather regard it as a watch-dog, the terror of thieves, and we suspect that the artist gave it the sitting attitude to indicate that its business was not to hunt, but to keep watch and ward at its master's gate. The fourth dog, who bears the name of *Tekal*, and walks between his master's legs, has ears that seem

ANTEF II. AND HIS DOGS. 99

to have been cropped. He has been said to resemble "the Dalmatian hound"; but this is questionable. His peculiarities are not marked; but, on the whole, it seems most probable that he is "a pet house-dog"[1] of the terrier class, the special favourite of his master. Antefaa's dogs had their appointed keeper, the master of his kennel, who is figured on the sepulchral tablet behind the monarch, and bears the name of Tekenru.

The hunter king was buried in a tomb marked only by a pyramid of unbaked brick, very humble in its character, but containing a mortuary chapel in which the monument above described was set up. An inscription on the tablet declared that it was erected to the memory of Antef the Great, Son of the Sun, King of Upper and Lower Egypt, in the fiftieth year of his reign.

Other Mentu-hoteps and other Antefs continued on the line of Theban kings, reigning quietly and ingloriously, and leaving no mark upon the scroll of time, yet probably advancing the material prosperity of their country, and preparing the way for that rise to greatness which gives Thebes, on the whole, the foremost place in Egyptian history. Useful projects occupied the attention of these monarchs. One of them sank wells in the valley of Hammamât, to provide water for the caravans which plied between Coptos and the Red Sea. Another established military posts in the valley to protect the traffic and the Egyptian quarrymen. Later on, a king called Sankh-ka-ra launched a fleet upon the Red Sea waters,

[1] So Mr. A. D. Bartlett, F.Z.S., in the "Transactions of the Society of Biblical Archæology," vol. iv. p. 195.

and opened direct communications with the sacred land of Punt, the region of odoriferous gums and of strange animals, as giraffes, panthers, hunting leopards, cynocephalous apes, and long-tailed monkeys. There is some doubt whether " Punt " was Arabia Felix, or the Somauli country. In any case, it lay far down the Gulf, and could only be reached after a voyage of many days.

The dynasty of the Antefs and Mentu-hoteps, which terminated with Sankh-ka-ra, was followed by one in which the prevailing names were Usurtasen and Amenemhat. This dynasty is Manetho's twelfth, and the time of its rule has been characterized as " the happiest age of Egyptian history?"[1] The second phase of Egyptian civilization now set in—a phase which is regarded by many as outshining the glories of the first. The first civilization had subordinated the people to the monarch, and had aimed especially at eternizing the memory and setting forth the power and greatness of king after king. The second had the benefit and advantage of the people for its primary object; it was utilitarian, beneficent, appealing less to the eye than to the mind, far-sighted in its aims, and most successful in the results which it effected. The wise rulers of the time devoted their energies and their resources, not, as the earlier kings, to piling up undying memorials of themselves in the shape of monuments that "reached to heaven," but to useful works, to the excavation of wells and reservoirs, the making of roads, the encouragement of commerce, and the development of the vast agricultural wealth

[1] R. Stuart Poole, "Cities of Egypt," p. 52.

of the country. They also diligently guarded the frontiers, chastised aggressive tribes, and checked invasion by the establishment of strong fortresses in positions of importance. They patronized art, employing themselves in building temples rather than tombs, and adorned their temples not only with reliefs and statues, but also with the novel architectural embellishment of the obelisk, a delicate form, and one especially suited to the country.

The founder of the "twelfth dynasty," Amenemhat I., deserves a few words of description. He found Thebes in a state of anarchy; civil war raged on every side; all the traditions of the past were forgotten; noble fought against noble; the poor were oppressed; life and property were alike insecure; "there was stability of fortune neither for the ignorant nor for the learned man." One night, after he had lain down to sleep, he found himself attacked in his bedchamber; the clang of arms sounded near at hand. Starting from his couch, he seized his own weapons and struck out; when lo! his assailants fled; detected in their attempt to assassinate him, they dared not offer any resistance, thus showing themselves alike treacherous and cowardly. Amenemhat, having once taken arms, did not lay them down till he had defeated every rival, and so fought his way to the crown. Once acknowledged as king, he ruled with moderation and equity; he "gave to the humble, and made the weak to live;" he "caused the afflicted to cease from their afflictions, and their cries to be heard no more;" he brought it to pass that none hungered or thirsted in the land; he gave such orders to his servants as continually increased the love of his people towards him. At the same time, he was an energetic warrior. He "stood on the boundaries of the land, to keep watch on its borders," personally leading his soldiers to battle, armed with the *khopesh* or falchion. He carried on wars with the Petti, or bowmen of the Libyan interior, with the Sakti or Asiatics, with the Maxyes or Mazyes of the northwest, and with the Ua-uat and other negro tribes of the south; not, however, as it would seem, with any desire of making conquests, but simply for the protection of his own frontier. With the same object he constructed on his north-eastern frontier a wall or fortress "to keep out the Sakti," who continually harassed the people of the Eastern Delta by their incursions.

The wars of Amenemhat I. make it evident that by his time Thebes had advanced from the position of a petty kingdom situated in a remote part of Egypt, and held in check by two or more rival kingdoms in the lower Nile valley and the Delta, to that of a power which bore sway over the whole land from Elephantine to the Mediterranean. "I sent my messengers up to Abu (Elephantine) and my couriers down to Athu" (the coast lakes), says the monarch in his "Instructions" to his son—the earliest literary production from a royal pen that has come down to our days; and there is no reason to doubt the truth of his statement. In the Delta alone could he come into contact with either the Mazyes or the Sakti, and a king of Thebes could not hold the Delta without being master also of the lower Nile valley from

Coptos to Memphis. We must regard Egypt, then, under the "twelfth dynasty," as once more consolidated into a single state—a state ruled, however, not from Memphis, but from Thebes, a decidedly inferior position.

Amenemhat I. is the only Egyptian king who makes a boast of his hunting prowess. "I hunted the lion," he says, "and brought back the crocodile a prisoner." Lions do not at the present time frequent Egypt, and, indeed, are not found lower down the Nile valley than the point where the Great Stream

SPEARING THE CROCODILE.

receives its last tributary, the Atbara. But anciently they seem to have haunted the entire desert tracts on either side of the river. The Roman Emperor Hadrian is said to have hunted one near Alexandria, and the monuments represent lions as tamed and used in the chase by the ancient inhabitants. Sometimes they even accompanied their masters to the battlefield. We know nothing of Amenemhat's mode of hunting the king of beasts, but may assume that it was not very different from that which prevailed at a later date in Assyria. There, dogs and beaters were employed to rouse the animals from their lairs, while the king and his fellow-sportsmen either plied them with flights of arrows, or withstood their onset with swords and spears. The crocodile was certainly sometimes attacked while he was in the water, the hunters using a boat, and endeavouring to spear him at the point where the head joins the spine; but this could not have been the mode adopted by Amenemhat, since it would have resulted in instant death, whereas he tells us that he "brought the crocodile home a prisoner." Possibly, therefore, he employed the method which Herodotus says was in common use in his day. This was to bait a hook with a joint of pork and throw it into the water at a point where the current would carry it out into mid-stream; then to take a live pig to the river-side, and belabour him well with a stick till he set up the squeal familiar to most ears. Any crocodile within hearing was sure to come to the sound, and falling in with the pork on the way, would instantly swallow it down. Upon this the hunters hauled at the rope to which the hook was attached, and, notwithstanding his struggles, drew "leviathan" to shore. Amenemhat, having thus "made the crocodile a prisoner," may have carried his captive in triumph to his capital, and exhibited him before the eyes of the people.

Amenemhat, having reigned as sole king for twenty years, was induced to raise his eldest son, Usurtasen, to the royal dignity, and associate him with himself in the government of the empire. Usurtasen was a prince of much promise. He "brought prosperity to the affairs of his father. He was, as a god, without fears; before him was never one like to him. Most skilful in affairs, beneficent in his mandates, both in his going out and in his coming in he made Egypt flourish." His courage and his warlike capacity were great. Already, in the lifetime of his father, he had distinguished himself in combats with the Petti and the Sakti. When he was settled upon the throne, he made war upon the Cushite tribes who bordered Egypt upon the south, employing the services of a general named Ameni, but also taking a part personally in the campaign. The Cushites or Ethiopians, who in later times became such dangerous neighbours to Egypt, were at this early period weak and insignificant. After the king had made his expedition, Ameni was able with a mere handful of four hundred troops to penetrate into their country, to "conduct the golden treasures" which it contained to the presence of his master, and to capture and carry off a herd of three thousand cattle.

It was through his sculptures and his architectural works that the first Usurtasen made himself chiefly conspicuous. Thebes, Abydos, Heliopolis or On, the Fayoum and the Delta, were equally the scenes of his constructive activity, and still show traces of his presence. At Thebes, he carried to its completion the cell, or *naos*, of the great temple of Ammon, in later times the innermost sanctuary of the building, and reckoned so sacred, that when Thothmes III. rebuilt and enlarged the entire edifice he reproduced the structure of Usurtasen, unchanged in form, and merely turned from limestone into granite. At Abydos and other cities of Middle Egypt, he constructed temples adorned with sculptures, inscriptions, and colossal statues. At Tanis, he set up his own statue, exhibiting himself as seated upon his throne. In the Fayoum he erected an obelisk forty-one feet high to the honour of Ammon, Phthah, and Mentu, which now lies prone upon the ground near the Arab village of Begig. Indications of his ubiquitous activity are found also at the Wady Magharah, in the Sinaitic peninsula, and at Wady Halfa in Nubia, a little above the Second Cataract; but his grandest and most elaborate work was his construction of the great temple of the Sun at Heliopolis, and his best memorial is that tall finger pointing to the sky which greets the traveller approaching Egypt from the east as the first sample of its strange and mystic wonders. This temple the king began in his third year. After a consultation with his lords and counsellors, he issued the solemn decree : " It is determined to execute the work ; his majesty chooses to have it made. Let the superintendent carry it on in the way that is desired ; let all those employed upon it be vigilant ; let them see that it is made without weariness ; let every due ceremony be performed ; let the beloved place arise." Then the king rose up, wearing a diadem, and holding the double pen ; and all present followed him. The scribe read the holy book, and extended the measuring cord, and laid the foundations on the spot which the temple was to occupy. A grand building arose ; but it has been wholly demolished by the ruthless hand of time and the barbarity of conquerors. Of all its

OBELISK OF USERTASEN I, ON THE SITE OF HELIOPOLIS.

glories nothing now remains but the one taper obelisk of pink granite, which rises into the soft sleepy air above the green cornfields of Matariych, no longer tipped with gold, but still catching on its summit the earliest and latest sun-rays, while wild-bees nestle in the crannies of the weird characters cut into the stone.

Usurtasen, after reigning ten years in conjunction with his father and thirty-two years alone, associated his son, Amenemhat II., who became sole king about three years later. His reign, though long, was undistinguished, and need not occupy our attention. He followed the example of his predecessors in associating a son in the government; and this son succeeded him, and is known as Usurtasen II. One event of interest alone belongs to this time. It is the reception by one of his great officials of a large family or tribe of Semitic immigrants from Asia, who beg permission to settle permanently in the fertile Egypt under the protection of its powerful king. Thirty-seven Amu, men, women, and children, present themselves at the court which the great noble holds near the eastern border, and offer him their homage, while they solicit a favourable hearing. The men are represented draped in long garments of various colours, and wearing sandals unlike the Egyptian—more resembling, in fact, open shoes with many straps. Their arms are bows, arrows, spears, and clubs. One plays on a seven-stringed lyre by means of a plectrum. Four women, wearing fillets round their heads, with garments reaching below the knee, and wearing anklets but no sandals, accompany them. A boy, armed with a spear, walks at the side of the women; and two children, seated in a kind of pannier placed on the back of an ass, ride on in front. Another ass, carrying a spear, a shield, and a pannier, precedes the man who plays on the lyre. The great official, who is named Khnum-hotep, receives the foreigners, accompanied by an attendant who carries his sandals and a staff, and who is followed by three dogs. A scribe, named Nefer-hotep, unrolls before his master a strip of papyrus, on which are inscribed the words, "The sixth year of the reign of King Usurtasen Sha-khepr-ra: account rendered of the Amu who in the lifetime of the chief, Khnum-hotep, brought to him the mineral, *mastemut*, from the country of Pit-shu—they are in all thirty-seven persons." The mineral *mastemut* is thought to be a species of stibium or antimony, used for dying the skin around the eyes, and so increasing their beauty. Besides this offering, the head of the tribe, who is entitled *khak*, or "prince," and named Abusha, presents to Khnum-hotep a magnificent wild-goat, of the kind which at the present day frequents the rocky mountain tract of Sinai. He wears a richer dress than his companions, one which is ornamented with a fringe, and has a wavy border round the neck. The scene has been generally recognized as strikingly illustrating the coming of Jacob's family into Egypt (Gen. xlvi. 28–34), and was at one time thought by some to represent that occurrence; but the date of Abusha's coming is long anterior to the arrival in Egypt of Jacob's family, the number is little more than half that of the Hebrew immigrants, the names do not accord; and it is now agreed on all hands, that the interest of the representation is confined to its illustrative force.

Usurtasen II. reigned for nineteen years. He does not seem to have associated a son, but was succeeded by another Usurtasen, most probably a nephew. The third Usurtasen was a conquering monarch, and advanced the power and glory of Egypt far more than any other ruler belonging to the Old Empire. He began his military operations in his eighth year, and starting from Elephantine in the month Epiphi, or May, moved southward, like another Lord Wolseley, with a fixed intention, which he expressed in writing upon the rocks of the Elephantine island, of permanently reducing to subjection " the miserable land of Cush." His expedition was so far successful that in the same year he established two forts, one on either side of the Nile, and set up two pillars with inscriptions warning the black races that they were not to proceed further northward, except with the object of importing into Egypt cattle, oxen, goats, or asses. The forts are still visible on either bank of the river a little above the Second Cataract, and bear the names of Koommeh and Semneh. They are massive constructions, built of numerous squared blocks of granite and sandstone, and perched upon two steep rocks which rise up perpendicularly from the river. Usurtasen, having made this beginning proceeded, from his eighth to his sixteenth year, to carry on the war with perseverance and ferocity in the district between the Nile and the Red Sea—to kill the men, fire the crops, and carry off the women and children, much as recently did the Arab traders whom Baker and Gordon strove to crush. The memory of his razzias was perpetuated upon stone columns set up to record his successes. Later on, in his nineteenth year he made a last expedition, to complete the conquest of "the miserable Kashi," and recorded his victory at Abydos.

The effect of these inroads was to advance the Egyptian frontier one hundred and fifty miles to the south, to carry it, in fact, from the First to above the Second Cataract. Usurtasen drew the line between Egypt and Ethiopia at this period, very much where the British Government drew it between Egypt and the Soudan in 1885. The boundary is a somewhat artificial one, as any boundary must be on the course of a great river; but it is probably as convenient a point as can be found between Assouan (Syene) and Khartoum. The conquest was regarded as redounding greatly to Usurtasen's glory, and made him the hero of the Old Empire. Myths gathered about his name, which, softened into Sesostris, became a favourite one in the mouths of Egyptian minstrels and minnesingers. Usurtasen grew to be a giant more than seven feet high, who conquered, not only all Ethiopia, but also Europe and Asia; his columns were said to be found in Palestine, Asia Minor, Scythia, and Thrace; he left a colony at Colchis, the city of the golden fleece; he dug all the canals by which Egypt was intersected; he invented geometry; he set up colossi above fifty feet high; he was the greatest monarch that had ruled Egypt since the days of Osiris!

No doubt these tales were, in the main, imaginary; but they marked the fact that in Usurtasen III. the military glories of the Old Empire culminated.

VI.

THE GOOD AMENEMHAT AND HIS WORKS.

THE great river to which Egypt owes her being, is at once the source of all her blessings and her chiefest danger. Swelling with a uniformity, well calculated to call forth man's gratitude and admiration, almost from a fixed day in each year, and continuing to rise steadily for months, it gradually spreads over the lands, covering the entire soil with a fresh coating of the richest possible alluvium, and thus securing to the country a perpetual and inexhaustible fertility. Nature's mechanism is so perfect, that the rise year after year scarcely varies a foot, and is almost exactly the same now as it was when the first Pharaoh poured his libation to the river-god from the embankment which he had made at Memphis; but though this uniformity is great, and remarkable, and astonishing, it is not absolute. There are occasions, once in two or three centuries, when the rainfall in Abyssinia is excessive. The Blue Nile and the Atbara pour into the deep and steady stream of the White Nile torrents of turbid water for months together. The windows of heaven seem to have been opened, and the rain pours down as if it would never cease. Then the river of the Egyptians assumes a threatening character; faster and faster it rises, and higher and higher ; and further and further it spreads, until it begins to creep up the sides of the two ranges of hills. Calamitous results ensue. The mounds erected to protect the cities, the villages, and the pasture lands, are surmounted, or undermined, or washed away ; the houses, built often of mud, and seldom of any better material than crude brick, collapse ; cattle are drowned by hundreds ; human life is itself imperilled ; the population has to betake itself to boats, and to fly to the desert regions which enclose the Nile valley to the east and west, regions of frightful sterility, which with difficulty support the few wandering tribes that are their normal inhabitants. If the excessive rise continues long, thousands or millions starve ; if it passes off rapidly, then the inhabitants return to find their homes desolated, their cattle drowned, their household goods washed away, and themselves dependent on the few rich men who may have stored their corn in stone granaries which the waters have not been able to penetrate. Disasters of this kind are, however, exceedingly rare, though, when they occur, their results are terrible to contemplate.

The more usual form of calamity is of the opposite kind. Once or twice in a century the Abyssinian rainfall is deficient. The rise of the Nile is deferred beyond the proper date. Anxious eyes gaze daily on the sluggish stream, or consult the " Nilometers " which kings and princes have constructed along its course to measure the increase of the waters. Hopes and fears alternate as good or bad news reaches the inhabitants of the lower valley from those who dwell higher up the stream. Each little rise is expected to herald a greater one, and the agony of suspense is prolonged until the "hundred days," traditionally assigned to the increase, have gone by, and there is no longer a doubt that the river has begun to fall. Then hope is swallowed up in despair. Only the lands lying nearest to the river have been inundated ; those at a greater distance from it lie parched and arid during the entire summer-time, and fail to produce a single blade of grass or spike of corn. Famine stares the poorer classes in the face, and unless large supplies of grain have been laid up in store previously, or can be readily imported from abroad, the actual starvation of large numbers is the inevitable consequence. We have heartrending accounts of such famines. In the year 457 of the Hegira (A.D. 1064) a famine began, which lasted seven years, and was so severe that dogs and cats, and even human flesh, were eaten ; all the horses of the Caliph but three perished, and his family had to fly into Syria. Another famine in A.D. 1199 is recorded by Abd-el-Latif, an eye-witness, in very similar terms.

There is reason to believe that, under the twelfth dynasty, some derangement of meteoric or atmospheric conditions passed over Abyssinia and Upper Egypt, either in both the directions above noticed, or, at any rate, in the latter and more ordinary one. An official belonging to the later part of this period, in enumerating his merits upon his tomb, tells us, " There was no poverty in my days, no starvation in my time, even when there were years of famine. I ploughed all the fields of Mah to its southern and northern boundaries; I gave life to its inhabitants, making its food; no one was starved in it. I gave to the widow as to the married woman." As the late Dr. Birch observes, " Egypt was occasionally subject to famines; and these, at the time of the twelfth dynasty, were so important, that they attracted great attention, and were considered worthy of record by the princes or hereditary lords who were buried at Beni-Hassan. Under the twelfth dynasty, also, the tombs of Abydos show the creation of superintendents, or storekeepers of the public granaries, a class of functionaries apparently created to meet the contingency."[1]

The distress of his subjects under these circumstances seems to have drawn the thoughts of "the good Amenemhat" to the devising of some system which should effectually remedy these evils, by preventing their occurrence. In all countries where the supply of water is liable to be deficient, it is of the utmost importance to utilize to the full that amount of the life-giving fluid, be it more or be it less, which the bounty of nature furnishes. Rarely, indeed, is nature absolutely a niggard. Mostly she gives far more than is needed, but the improvidence or the apathy of man allows her gifts to run to waste. Careful and provident husbanding of her store will generally make it suffice for all man's needs and requirements. Sometimes this has been effected in a thirsty land by conducting all the rills and brooks that flow from the highlands or hills into subterranean conduits, where they are shielded from the sun's rays, and prolonging these ducts for miles upon miles, till

[1] " Records of the Past," vol. xii. p. 60.

every drop of the precious fluid has been utilized for irrigation. Such is the *karees* or *kanat* system of Persia. In other places vast efforts have been made to detain the abundant supply of rain which nature commonly provides in the spring of the year, to store it, and prevent it from flowing off down the river-courses to the sea, where it is absolutely lost. For this purpose, either huge reservoirs must be constructed by the hand of man, or else advantage must be taken of some facility which nature offers for storing the water in convenient situations. Valleys may be blocked by massive dams, and millions of gallons thus imprisoned for future use, as is done in many parts of the North of England, but for manufacturing and not for irrigation purposes. Or naturally land-locked basins may be found, and the overflow of streams at their flood-time turned into them and arrested, to be made use of later in the year.

In Egypt the one and only valley was that of the Nile, and the one and only stream that which had formed it, and flowed along it, at a lower or higher level, ceaselessly. It might perhaps have been possible for Egyptian engineering skill to have blocked the valley at Silsilis, or at the Gebelein, and to have thus turned Upper Egypt into a huge reservoir always full, and always capable of supplying Lower Egypt with enough water to eke out a deficient inundation. But this could only have been done by an enormous work, very difficult to construct, and at the sacrifice of several hundred square miles of fertile territory, thickly inhabited, which would have been covered permanently by the artificial lake. Moreover, the

Egyptians would have known that such an embankment can under no circumstances be absolutely secure, and may have foreseen that its rupture would spread destruction over the whole of the lower country. Amenemhat, at any rate, did not venture to adopt so bold a design. He sought for a natural depression, and found one in the Libyan range of hills to the west of the Nile valley, about a degree south of the latitude of Memphis—a depression of great depth and of ample expanse, fifty miles or more in length by thirty in breadth, and containing an area of six or seven hundred square miles. It was separated from the Nile valley by a narrow ridge of hills about two hundred feet high, through which ran from south-east to north-west a narrow rocky gorge, giving access to the depression. It is possible that in very high floods some of the water of the inundation passed naturally into the basin through this gorge; but whether this were so or no, it was plain that by the employment of no very large amount of labour a canal or cutting might be carried along the gorge, and the Nile water given free access into the depression, not only in very high floods, but annually when the inundation reached a certain moderate height. This is, accordingly, what Amenemhat did. He dug a canal from the western branch of the Nile—the modern Bahr Yousuf—leaving it at El-Lahoun, carried his canal through the gorge, in places cutting deep into its rocky bottom, and by a system of sluices and flood-gates retained such an absolute control over the water that he could either admit or exclude the inundation at his will, as it rose; and when it fell, could either allow the water that had flowed in to return, or imprison it and keep it back. Within the gorge he had thus at all times a copious store of the invaluable fluid, banked up to the height of high Nile, and capable of being applied to purposes of cultivation both within and without the depression by the opening and shutting of the sluices.

So much appears to be certain. The exact size and position of Amenemhat's reservoir within the depression, which a French *savant* was supposed to have discovered, are now called in question, and must be admitted to be still *sub judice*. M. Linant de Bellefonds regarded the reservoir as occupying the south-eastern or upper portion of the depression only, as extending from north to south a distance of fourteen miles only, and from east to west a distance varying from six to eleven miles. He regarded it as artificially confined towards the west and north by two long lines of embankment, which he considered that he had traced, and gave the area of the lake as four hundred and five millions of square mètres, or about four hundred and eighty millions of square yards. Mr. Cope Whitehouse believes that the water was freely admitted into the whole of the depression, which it filled, with the exception of certain parts, which stood up out of the water as islands, from one hundred and fifty to two hundred feet high. He believes that it was in places three hundred feet deep, and that the circuit of its shores was from three hundred to five hundred miles. It is to be hoped that a scientific expedition will ere long set this dispute at rest, and enable the modern student distinctly to grasp and understand the great work of Amenemhat. Whatever may be the truth regarding "Lake Mœris," as this great reservoir was called, it is certain that it furnished the ancients one of the least explicable of all the many problems that the remarkable land of the Nile presented to them. Herodotus added to the other marvels of the place a story about two sitting statues based upon pyramids, which stood three hundred feet above the level of the lake, and a famous labyrinth, of which we shall soon speak.

Whether the reservoir of Amenemhat had the larger or the smaller dimensions ascribed to it, there can be no doubt that it was a grand construction, undertaken mainly for the benefit of his people, and greatly conducing to their advantage. Even if the reservoir had only the dimensions assigned to it by M. de Bellefonds, it would, according to his calculations, have contained water sufficient, not only for irrigating the northern and western portions of the Fayoum throughout the year, but also for the supply of the whole western bank of the Nile from Beni-Souef to the embouchure at Canopus for six months. This alone would in dry seasons have been a sensible relief to a large portion of the population. If the dimensions exceeded those of De Bellefonds, the relief would have been proportionately greater.

The good king was not, however, content merely to benefit his people by increasing the productiveness of Egypt and warding off the calamities that occasionally befell the land ; he further gave employment to large numbers, which was not of a severe or oppressive kind, but promoted their comfort and welfare. In

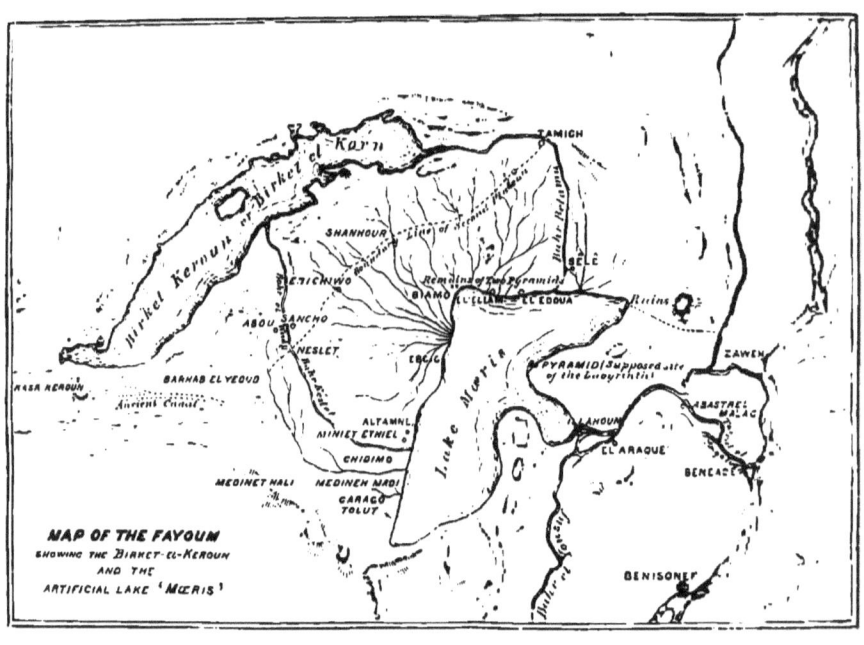

connection with his hydraulic works in the Fayoum he constructed a novel species of building, which after ages admired even above the constructions of the pyramid-builders, and regarded as the most wonderful edifice in all the world. "I visited the place," says Herodotus,[1] "and found it to surpass description; for if all the walls and other great works of the Greeks could be put together in one, they would not equal, either for labour or expense, this Labyrinth; and yet the temple of Ephesus is a building worthy of note, and so is the temple of Samos. The pyramids likewise surpass description, and are severally equal to a number of the greatest works of the Greeks; but the Labyrinth surpasses the pyramids. It has twelve courts, all of them roofed, with gates exactly opposite one another, six looking to the north, and six to the south. A single wall surrounds the whole building. It contains two different sorts of chambers, half of them underground, and half above-ground, the latter built upon the former; the whole number is three thousand, of each kind fifteen hundred. The upper chambers I myself passed through and saw, and what I say of them is from my own observation; of the underground chambers I can only speak from report, for the keepers of the building could not be induced to show them, since they contained (they said) the sepulchres of the kings who built the Labyrinth, and also those of the sacred crocodiles. Thus it is from hearsay only that I can speak of them; but the upper chambers I saw with my own eyes, and found them to excel all other human pro-

[1] Euterpe, ch. 148.

ductions; for the passages through the houses, and the varied windings of the paths across the courts, excited in me infinite admiration, as I passed from the courts into chambers, and from the chambers into colonnades, and from the colonnades into fresh houses, and again from these into courts unseen before. The roof was, throughout, of stone, like the walls; and the walls were carved all over with figures; every court was surrounded with a colonnade, which was built of white stones, exquisitely fitted together. At the corner of the Labyrinth stands a pyramid, forty fathoms high, with large figures engraved upon it, which is entered by a subterranean passage."

The pyramid intended is probably that examined by Perring and Lepsius, which had a base of three hundred feet, and an elevation, probably, of about one hundred and eighty-five feet. It was built of crude brick mixed with a good deal of straw, and cased with a white silicious limestone. The same material was employed for the greater part of the so-called "Labyrinth," but many of the columns were of red granite, and some perhaps of porphyry. Most likely the edifice was intended as a mausoleum for the sacred crocodiles, and was gradually enlarged for their accommodation—Amenemhat, whose præ-nomen was found on the pyramid, being merely the first founder. The number of the pillared courts, and their similarity, made the edifice confusing to foreigners, and got it the name of "The Labyrinth"; but it is not likely the designers of the building had any intention to mislead or to confuse.

Amenemhat's præ-nomen, or throne-name, assumed

(according to ordinary custom) on his accession, was Ra-n-mat, "Sun of Justice" or "Sun of Righteousness." The assumption of the title indicates his desire to leave behind him a character for justice and equity. It is perhaps noticeable that the name by which the Greeks knew him was Mœris, which may mean "the beloved." With him closes the first period of Theban greatness. A cloud was impending, and darker days about to follow; but as yet Egypt enjoyed a time of progressive, and in the main peaceful, development. Commerce, art, religion, agriculture, occupied her. She did not covet other men's lands, nor did other men covet hers. The world beyond her borders knew little of her, except that she was a fertile and well-ordered land, whereto, in time of dearth, the needy of other countries might resort with confidence.

it with walls of great thickness, which he guarded with a body of two hundred and forty thousand men. Each summer he visited the place, to see their supplies of corn measured out for his soldiers and their pay delivered to them, as well as to superintend their military exercises, in order that foreigners might hold them in respect."

The king, Timæus, does not appear either in the lists of Manetho or upon the monuments, nor is it possible to determine the time of the invasion more precisely than this—that it fell into the interval between Manetho's twelfth and his eighteenth dynasties. The invaders are characterized by the Egyptians as Menti or Sati; but these terms are used so vaguely that nothing definite can be concluded from them. On the whole, it is perhaps most probable that the invading army, like that of Attila, consisted of a vast variety of races—"a collection of all the nomadic hordes of Syria and Arabia"—who made common cause against a foe known to be wealthy, and who all equally desired settlements in a land reputed the most productive in the East. An overwhelming flood of men—a quarter of a million, if we may believe Manetho—poured into the land, impetuous, irresistible. All at once, a danger had come beyond all possible previous calculation—a danger from which there was no escape. It was as when the northern barbarians swooped down in their countless thousands on the outlying provinces of the Roman Empire, or as when the hordes of Jingis Khan overran Kashgar and Kharesm—the contest was too unequal for anything that can be called a struggle to

VII.

ABRAHAM IN EGYPT.

"Now there was a famine in the land of Canaan; and Abram went down into Egypt to sojourn there" (Gen. xii. 10). Few events in the history of mankind are more interesting than the visit which the author of the Pentateuch thus places before us in less than a dozen words. The "father of the faithful," the great apostle of Monotheism, the wanderer from the distant "Ur of the Chaldees," familiar with Babylonian greatness, and Babylonian dissoluteness, and Babylonian despotism, having quitted his city home and adopted the simple habits of a Syrian nomadic sheikh, finds himself forced to make acquaintance with a second form of civilization, a second great organized monarchy, and to become for a time a sojourner among the people who had held for centuries the valley of the Nile. He had obeyed the call which took him from Ur to Haran, from Haran to Damascus, from Damascus to the hills of Canaan; he had divorced himself from city life and city usages; he had embraced the delights of that free, wandering existence which has at all times so singular a charm for many, and had dwelt for we know not how many years in different parts of Palestine, the chief of a tribe rich in flocks and herds, moving with them from place to place as the fancy took him. It was assuredly with much reluctance that he quitted the open downs and fresh breezes and oak groves of Canaan—the land promised to him and to his seed after him, and took his way through the "desert of the south" to the great kingdom with which he and his race could never hope to be on terms of solid friendship. But the necessity which constrained him was imperative. When, from the want of the ordinary spring rains, drought and famine set in on the Palestinian uplands, there was in ancient times but one resource. Egypt was known as a land of plenty. Whether it were Hebrew nomads, or Hittite warriors, or Phœnician traders that suffered, Egypt was the sole refuge, the sole hope. There the river gave the plenteous sustenance which would be elsewhere sought in vain. There were granaries and storehouses, and an old established system whereby corn was laid up as a reserve in case of need, both by private individuals of the wealthier classes and by the kings. There among the highest officers of state was the "steward of the public granary," whose business it was, when famine pressed, to provide, so far as was possible, both for natives and foreigners, alleviating the distress of all, while safeguarding, of course, the king's interests (Gen. xlvii. 13-26).

Abraham, therefore, when he found that "the famine was grievous in the land" of Canaan, did the only thing that it was possible for him to do—left Palestine, and wended his way through the desert to the Egyptian frontier. What company he took with him is uncertain. A few years later we find him at the head of a body of three hundred and eighteen men capable of bearing arms—"trained servants born in his house"—which implies the headship over a tribe of at least twelve hundred persons. He can scarcely have entered Egypt with a much smaller number. It was before his separation from his nephew, Lot, whose followers were not much fewer than his own. And to leave any of his dependents behind would have been to leave them to starvation. We must suppose a numerous caravan organized, with asses and camels to carry provisions and household stuff, and with the women and the little ones conveyed as we see them in the sculpture representing the arrival of Abusha from the same quarter, albeit with a smaller *entourage*. The desert journey would be trying, and probably entail much loss, especially of the cattle and beasts; but at length, on the seventh or eighth day, as the water was getting low in the skins and the camels were beginning to faint and groan with the scant fare and the long travel, a dark low line would appear upon the edge of the horizon in front, and soon the line would deepen into a delicate fringe, sparkling here and there as though it were sown with diamonds.[1] Then it would be recognized that there lay before the travellers the fields and gardens and palaces and obelisks of Egypt, the broad flood and rich plain of the Nile, and their hearts would leap with joy, and lift themselves up in thanksgiving to the Most High, who had brought them through the great and terrible wilderness to a land of plenty.

But now a fresh anxiety fell upon the spirit of the

[1] Adapted from Kinglake's "Eothen," p. 201.

chief. Tradition tells us that already in Babylonia he had had experience of the violence and tyranny of earthly potentates, and had with difficulty escaped from an attempt which the king of Babylon made upon his life. Either memory recalled this and similar dangers, or reason suggested what the unbridled licence of irresponsible power might conceive and execute under the circumstances. The Pharaohs had, it is plain, already departed from the simple manners of the earlier times, when each prince was contented with a single wife, and had substituted for the primitive law of monogamy that corrupt system of hareem life which has kept its ground in the East from an ancient date to the present day. Abraham was aware of this, and "as he was come near to enter into Egypt," but was not yet entered, he was seized with a great fear. " Behold," he said to Sarai his wife, " Behold now, I know that thou art a fair woman to look upon ; therefore it shall come to pass, when the Egyptians shall see thee, that they shall say, This is his wife: and they will kill me, but they will save thee alive." Under these circumstances Abraham, with a craft not unnatural in an Oriental, but certainly far from commendable, resolved to dissemble his relationship towards Sarah, and to represent her as not his wife, but his sister. She was, in point of fact, his half-sister, as he afterwards pleaded to Abimelech (Gen. xx. 12), being the daughter of Terah by a secondary wife, and married to her half-brother. " Say, I pray thee," he said, " thou art my sister, that it may be well with me for thy sake ; and my soul shall live because of thee." Sarah acquiesced ; and no doubt the whole tribe was made acquainted with the resolution come to, so that they might all be in one story.

The frontier was then approached. We learn from the history of Abusha, as well as from other scattered notices in the papyri, how carefully the eastern border was always guarded, and what precautions were taken to apprise the Court when any considerable body of immigrants arrived. The chief official upon the frontier, either Khnumhotep or some one occupying a similar position, would receive the incomers, subject them to interrogation, and cause his secretary to draw up a report, which would be forwarded by courier to the capital. The royal orders would be awaited, and meantime perhaps fresh reports would be sent by other officials of the neighbourhood. In the present instance, we are told that several "princes of Pharaoh," having been struck with the beauty of Sarah, commended her to their royal master, who sent for her and had her brought into his own house. Abraham himself was well received and treated with much distinction "for her sake." According to Eupolemus, he and his were settled in the sacred city of On or Heliopolis; and there, in that seat of learning and religion, the Patriarch, as the same authority declares, lived peacefully for many years and taught the Egyptians the sciences of astronomy and arithmetic. The author of Genesis says nothing of the place of his abode, but simply informs us of his well-being. "Pharaoh entreated Abram well for Sarai's sake; and he had sheep, and oxen, and he-asses, and men-servants, and maid-servants, and she-asses, and camels." The collocation of the clauses implies that all these were presents from the king. The pleased monarch lavished on his brother-in-law such gifts of honour as were usual at the time and suitable to his circumstances. Abraham became "very rich in cattle, in silver, and in gold " (Gen. xiii. 2). He flourished greatly, whether for months or for years the scripture does not say. He was separated from his wife, and she was an inmate of Pharaoh's hareem ; but he kept his secret, and no one betrayed him. Apparently, he was content.

Ere long, however, a discovery was made. Calamity came upon the royal house in some marked way, probably either in the form of sickness or of death. The king became convinced that he was the object of a Divine chastisement, and cast about for a cause to which his sufferings might reasonably be attributed. How had he provoked God's anger ? Either, as Josephus thinks, the priests had by this time found out the truth, and made the suggestion to him, that he was being punished for having taken another man's wife into his seraglio ; or possibly, as others have surmised, Sarah herself divined the source of the calamities, and made confession of the truth. At any rate, by some means or other, the facts of the case became known ; and the Pharaoh thereupon hastened to set matters right. Sarah, though an inmate of the hareem, was probably still in the probationary condition, undergoing the purification necessary before the final completion of her nuptials (Esth. ii. 12), and could thus be restored intact. The Pharaoh sent for Abraham, reproached him with his deceit, pointed out the ill consequences which had followed, and, doubtless in some displeasure, required him to take his wife and depart. The famine was at an end, and there was no reason why he should linger. Beyond reproach, however, Pharaoh inflicted no punishment. He "commanded his men concerning Abraham; and they sent him away, and his wife, and *all that he had.*"

Such is the account which has come down to us of Abraham's sojourn in Egypt. If it be asked, Why is it inserted into the "story of Egypt" at this point? the reply must be, because, on a dispassionate consideration of all the circumstances, chronological and other, which attach to the narrative, it has been generally agreed that the event belongs to *about* this time. There is no special reign to which it can be definitely assigned; but the best critics acquiesce in the judgment of Canon Cook upon the point, who says: "For my own part, I regard it as all but certain that Abraham visited Egypt in some reign between the middle of the eleventh and the thirteenth dynasty, and most probably under one of the earliest Pharaohs of the twelfth."[1]

This is not the only entrance of Hebrews or people of Semitic race into Egypt. Emigrants from less favoured countries had frequently looked with interest to the fertile Delta of the Nile, hoping that there they might find homes free from the vicissitudes of their own. Previous to this, one Amu had entered Egypt, perhaps from Midian, with his family, counting thirty-seven, the little ones riding upon asses, and had sought the protection of the reigning sovereign. It was again

[1] See "Speaker's Commentary," vol. i. p. 447, col. i.

the experience of Egypt to receive emigrants from the north-east, from Syria or Northern Arabia, at a little later period, when the nomads in those regions looked over to the south and, by contrast with their over-peopled country, thought they saw a sort of "fairy-land of wealth, culture, and wisdom," which they hoped to enjoy by force ; and they were not the last to seek asylum there. We shall soon have to remark on the familiar case of the immigration of the sons of Jacob with their households. In process of time the Semitic wanderers increased so materially that the population in the eastern half of the Delta became half Asiatic, prepared to submit readily to Asiatic rule and to worship Semitic deities ; they had already imposed a number of their words upon the language of Egypt.

VIII.

THE GREAT INVASION—THE HYKSÔS OR SHEPHERD KINGS—JOSEPH AND APEPI.

THE prowess of the Egyptians had not yet been put to any severe proof. They had themselves shown little of an aggressive spirit. Attracted by the mineral wealth of the Sinaitic peninsula, they had indeed made settlements in that region, which had involved them in occasional wars with the natives, whom they spoke of as "Mena" or "Menti"; and they had had a contest of more importance with the tribes of the south, negro and Ethiopic, in which they had shown a decided superiority over those rude barbarians; but, as yet, they had attempted no important conquest, and had been subjected to no serious attack. The countries upon their borders were but sparsely peopled, and from neither the Berber tribes of the northern African coast, nor from the Sinaitic nomads, nor even from the negroes of the south, with their allies—the "miserable Cushites"—was any dangerous invasion to be apprehended. Egypt had been able to devote herself almost wholly to the cultivation of the arts of peace, and had not been subjected to the severe ordeal, which most nations pass through in their infancy, of a struggle for existence with warlike and powerful enemies.

The time was now come for a great change. Movements had begun among the populations of Asia which threatened a general disturbance of the peace of the world. Asshur had had to "go forth" out of the land of Shinar, and to make himself a habitation further to the northward, which must have pressed painfully upon other races. In Elam an aggressive spirit had sprung up, and military expeditions had been conducted by Elamitic kings, which started from the shores of the Persian Gulf and terminated in Southern Syria and Palestine. The migration of the tribes which moved with Terah and Abraham from Ur to Haran, and from Haran to Hebron, is but one of many indications of the restlessness of the period. The Hittites were growing in power, and required an enlarged territory for their free expansion. It was now probably that they descended from the hills of Cappadocia upon the region below Taurus and Amanus, where we find them dominant in later ages. Such a movement on their part would displace a large population in Upper Syria, and force it to migrate southwards. There are signs of a pressure upon the north-eastern frontier of Egypt on the part of Asiatics needing a home as early as the commencement of the twelfth dynasty; and it is probable that, while the dynasty lasted, the pressure was continually becoming greater. Asiatics were from time to time received within the barrier of Amenemhat I., some to sojourn and some to dwell. The eastern Delta was more or less Asiaticized; and a large portion of its inhabitants was inclined to welcome a further influx from Asia.

We have one account only of the circumstances of the great invasion by which Egypt fell under a foreign yoke. It purports to come from the native historian, Manetho ; but it is delivered to us directly by Josephus, who, in his reports of what other writers had narrated, is not always to be implicitly trusted. Manetho, according to him, declared as follows : " There was once a king of Egypt named Timæus, in whose reign the gods being offended, for I know not what cause, with our nation, certain men of ignoble race, coming from the eastern regions, had the courage to invade the country, and falling upon it unawares, conquered it easily without a battle. After the submission of the princes, they conducted themselves in a most barbarous fashion towards the whole of the inhabitants, slaying some, and reducing to slavery the wives and the children of the others. Moreover they savagely set the cities on fire, and demolished the temples of the gods. At last, they took one of their number called Salatis, and made him king over them. Salatis resided at Memphis, where he received tribute both from Upper and Lower Egypt, while at the same time he placed garrisons in all the most suitable situations. He strongly fortified the frontier, especially on the side of the east, since he foresaw that the Assyrians, who were then exceedingly powerful, might desire to make themselves masters of his kingdom. Having found, moreover, in the Sethroïte nome, to the east of the Bubastite branch of the Nile, a city very favourably situated, and called, on account of an ancient theological tradition, Avaris, he rebuilt it and strengthened be made. Egypt collapsed before the invader. Manetho says that there was no battle; and we can readily understand that in the divided condition of the country, with two or three subordinate dynasties ruling in different parts of the Delta, and another dynasty at Thebes, no army could be levied which could dare to meet the enemy in the field. The inhabitants fled to their cities, and endeavoured to defend themselves behind walls; but it was in vain. The walls of the Egyptian cities were rather banks to keep out the inundation than ramparts to repel an enemy. In a short time the strongholds that resisted were taken, the male population put to the sword, the women and children enslaved, the houses burnt, the temples ruthlessly demolished. An iconoclastic spirit possessed the conquerors. The gods and worship of Egypt were hateful to them. Wherever the flood passed, it swept away the existing civilization, deeply impregnated as it was with religion; it covered the ground with the *débris* of temples and shrines, with the fragments of statues and sphinxes; it crushed existing religious usages, and for a time, as it would seem, substituted nothing in their place. "A study of the monuments," says M. François Lenormant, "attests the reality of the frightful devastations which took place at the first moment of the invasion. With a solitary exception, all the temples anterior to the event have disappeared, and no traces can be found of them except scattered ruins which bear the marks of a destructive violence. To say what during these centuries Egypt had to endure in the way of upsetting of her past is impossible. The only fact which can be stated as certain is, that not a single monument of this desolate epoch has come down to our days to show us what became of the ancient splendour of Egypt under the Hyksôs. We witness under the fifteenth and sixteenth dynasties a fresh shipwreck of Egyptian civilization. Vigorous as it had been, the impulse given to it by the Usurtasens suddenly stops ; the series of monuments is interrupted, and Egypt informs us by her very silence of the calamities with which she was smitten."[1]

It was, fortunately, not the entire country that was overrun. So far as appears, the actual occupation of Egypt by the Hyksôs was confined to the Delta, to the Lower Nile valley, and to the district of the Fayoum. Elephantine, Thebes, Abydos, escaped the destroyers, and though forced to certain formal acts of submission, to an acknowledgment of the Hyksôs suzerainty, and to the payment of an annual tribute, retained a qualified independence. The Theban monuments of the eleventh and twelfth dynasties were undisturbed. Even in Lower Egypt there were structures that suffered little or nothing at the conqueror's hands, being too humble to attract his attention or too massive to yield to the means of destruction known to him. Thus the pyramids scarcely suffered, though it is possible that at this time their sanctity was first violated and their contents rifled. The great obelisk of Usurtasen I., which still stands at Heliopolis, was not overthrown. The humbler tombs at Ghizeh, so precious to the antiquary,

[1] "Manuel d'Histoire Ancienne de l'Orient, ' vol i. p. 360.

were for the most part untouched. Amenemhat's buildings in the Fayoum may have been damaged, but they were not demolished. Though Egyptian civilization received a rude shock from the invasion, it was not altogether swallowed up or destroyed; and when the deluge had passed it emerged once more, and soon reached, and even surpassed, its ancient glories.

The Hyksôs king who led the invasion, or who, at any rate, was brought to the front in its course, bore, we are told, either the name of Salatis, or that of Saites. Of these two forms the second is undoubtedly to be preferred, since the first has in its favour only the single authority of Josephus, while the second is supported by Africanus, Eusebius, George the Syncellus, and to a certain extent by the monuments. The "tablet of four hundred years" contains the name of Sut-Aapehti as that of a king of Egypt who must have belonged to the Middle Empire, and this name may fairly be regarded as represented in an abbreviated form by the Greek "Saïtes." Saïtes, having made himself absolute master of the Lower Country, and forced the king of the Upper Country to become his tributary, fixed his residence at Memphis, at the same time strongly fortifying and garrisoning various other towns in important positions. Of these the most considerable was the city, called Auaris, or Avaris, in the Sethroïte nome, which lay east of the Pelusiac branch of the Nile, and was probably not far from Pelusium itself, if indeed it was not identical with that city. Another strong fort, by means of which the Delta was held and overawed, seems to have been

Zan or Tanis, now San, situated on what was called the Tanitic branch of the Nile, the next most easterly branch to the Pelusiac. A third was in the Fayoum, on the site now called Mit-Fares. A large body of troops must also have been maintained at Memphis, if the king, as we are told, ordinarily held his court there.

How long the Egyptians groaned under the tyranny of the "Shepherds," it is difficult to say. The epitomists of Manetho are hopelessly at variance on the subject, and the monuments are silent, or nearly so. Moderns vary in the time, which they assign to the period between two centuries and five. On the whole, criticism seems to incline towards the shorter term, though why Manetho, or his epitomists, should have enlarged it, remains an insoluble problem. There is but one dynasty of " Shepherd Kings " that has any distinct historical substance, or to which we can assign any names. This is a dynasty of six kings only, whose united reigns are not likely to have exceeded two centuries. Nor does it seem possible that, if the duration of the foreign oppression had been much longer, Egypt could have returned, so nearly as she did, to the same manners and customs, the same religious usages, the same rules of art, the same system of government, even the very same proper names, at the end of the period, as had been in use at its beginning. One cannot but think that the *bouleversement* which Egypt underwent has been somewhat exaggerated by the native historian for the sake of rhetorical effect, to enhance by contrast the splendour of the New Empire.

In another respect, too, if he has not misrepresented the rule of the "Shepherd Kings," he has failed to do it justice. He has painted in lurid colours the advent of the foreign race, the war of extermination in which they engaged, the cruel usage to which they subjected the conquered people ; he has represented the invaders as rude, savage, barbarous, bent on destruction, careless of art, the enemies of progress and civilization. He has neglected to point out, that, as time went on, there was a sensible change. The period of constant bitter hostilities came to an end. Peace succeeded to war. In Lower Egypt the "Shepherds" reigned over quiet and unresisting subjects ; in Upper Egypt they bore rule over submissive tributaries. Under these circumstances a perceptible softening of their manners and general character took place. As the Mongols and the Mandchus in China suffered themselves by degrees to be conquered by the superior civilization of the people whom they had overrun and subdued, so the Hyksôs yielded little by little to the influences which surrounded them, and insensibly assimilated themselves to their Egyptian subjects. They adopted the Egyptian dress, titles, official language, art, mode of writing, architecture. In Tanis, especially, temples were built and sculptures set up under the later "Shepherd Kings," differing little in their general character from those of purely Egyptian periods. The foreign monarchs erected their effigies at this site, which were sculptured by native artists according to the customary rules of Egyptian glyptic art, and only differ from those of the earlier native Pharaohs in the head-dress, the expression of the

BUST OF A SHEPHERD KING.

countenance, and a peculiar arrangement of the beard. A friendly intercourse took place during this period between the kings of the North, established at Tanis and Memphis, and those of the South, resident at Thebes; frequent embassies were interchanged; and blocks of granite and syenite were continually floated down the Nile, past Thebes, to be employed by the "Shepherds" in their erections at the southern capitals.

The "Shepherds" brought with them into Egypt the worship of a deity, whom they called Sut or Sutekh, and apparently identified with the sun. He was described as "the great ruler of heaven," and identified with Baal in later times. The kings regarded themselves as especially under his protection. At the time of the invasion, they do not seem to have considered this deity as having any special connection with any of the Egyptian gods, and they consequently made war indiscriminately against the entire Egyptian Pantheon, plundering and demolishing all the temples alike. But when the first burst of savage hostility was gone by, when more settled times followed, and the manners and temper of the conquerors grew softened by pacific intercourse with their subjects, a likeness came to be seen between Sutekh, their own ancestral god, and the "Set" of the Egyptians. Set in the old Egyptian mythology was recognized as "the patron of foreigners, the power which swept the children of the desert like a sand-storm over the fertile land." He was a representative of physical, but not of moral, evil; a strong and powerful deity, worthy of reverence and worship, but less an object of love than of fear. The "Shepherds" acknowledged in this god their Sutekh; and as they acquired settled habits, and assimilated themselves to their subjects, they began to build temples to him, after the Egyptian model, in their principal towns. After the dynasty had borne rule for five reigns, covering the space perhaps of one hundred and fifty years, a king came to the throne named Apepi, who has left several monuments, and is the only one of the "Shepherds" that stands out for us in definite historical consistency as a living and breathing person. Apepi built a great temple to Sutekh at Zoan, or Tanis, his principal capital, composed of blocks of red granite, and adorned it with obelisks and sphinxes. The obelisks are said to have been fourteen in number, and must have been dispersed about the courts, and not, as usual, placed only at the entrance. The sphinxes, which differed from the ordinary Egyptian sphinx in having a mane like a lion and also wings, seem to have formed an avenue or vista leading up to the temple from the town. They are in diorite, and have the name of Apepi engraved upon them.

The pacific rule of Apepi and his predecessors allowed Thebes to increase in power, and her monuments now recommence. Three kings who bore the family name of Taa, and the throne name of Ra-Sekenen, bore rule in succession at the southern capital. The third of these, Taa-ken, or "Taa the Victorious," was contemporary with Apepi, and paid his tribute punctually, year by year, to his lawful suzerain. He does not seem to have had any desire to provoke war; but Apepi probably thought that he

APEPI AND JOSEPH.

was becoming too powerful, and would, if unmolested, shortly make an effort to throw off the Hyksôs yoke. He therefore determined to pick a quarrel with him, and proceeded to send to Thebes a succession of embassies with continually increasing demands. First of all he required Taa-ken to relinquish the worship of all the Egyptian gods except Amen-Ra, the chief god of Thebes, whom he probably identified with his own Sutekh. It is not quite clear whether Taa-ken consented to this demand, or politely evaded it. At any rate, a second embassy soon followed the first, with a fresh requirement; and a third followed the second. The policy was successful, and at last Taa-ken took up arms. It would seem that he was successful, or was at any rate able to hold his own; for he maintained the war till his death, and left it to his successor, Aahmes.

There was an ancient tradition, that the king who made Joseph his prime minister, and committed into his hands the entire administration of Egypt, was Apepi. George the Syncellus says that the synchronism was accepted by all. It is clear that Joseph's arrival did not fall, like Abraham's, into the period of the Old Empire, since under Joseph horses and chariots are in use, as well as wagons or carts, all of which were unknown till after the Hyksôs invasion. It is also more natural that Joseph, a foreigner, should have been advanced by a foreign king than by a native one, and the favour shown to his brethren, who were shepherds (Gen. xlvi. 32), is consonant at any rate with the tradition that it was a "Shepherd King" who held the throne at the time of their arrival. A priest of Heliopolis, moreover, would scarcely have given Joseph his daughter in marriage unless at a time when the priesthood was in a state of depression. Add to this that the Pharaoh of Joseph is evidently resident in Lower Egypt, not at Thebes, which was the seat of government for many hundred years both before and after the Hyksôs rule.

If, however, we are to place Joseph under one of the " Shepherd Kings," there can be no reason why we should not accept the tradition which connects him with Apepi. Apepi was dominant over the whole of Egypt, as Joseph's Pharaoh seems to have been. He acknowledged a single god, as did that monarch (Gen. xli. 38, 39). He was a thoroughly Egyptianized king. He had a council of learned scribes, a magnificent court, and a peaceful reign until towards its close. His residence was in the Delta, either at Tanis or Auaris. He was a prince of a strong will, firm and determined; one who did not shrink from initiating great changes, and who carried out his resolves in a somewhat arbitrary way. The arguments in favour of his identity with Joseph's master are, perhaps, not wholly conclusive; but they raise a presumption, which may well incline us, with most modern historians of Egypt, to assign the touching story of Joseph to the reign of the last of the Shepherds.

IX.

HOW THE HYKSÔS WERE EXPELLED FROM EGYPT.

AT first sight it seems strange that the terrible warriors who, under Set or Saïtes, so easily reduced Egypt to subjection, and then still further weakened the population by massacre and oppression, should have been got rid of, after two centuries or two centuries and a half, with such comparative ease. But the rapid deterioration of conquering races under certain circumstances is a fact familiar to the historian. Elamites, Babylonians, Assyrians, Medes, Persians, Greeks, rapidly succeeded each other as the dominant power in Western Asia, each race growing weaker and becoming exhausted, after a longer or a shorter interval, through nearly the same causes. Nor are the reasons for the deterioration far to seek. Each race when it sets out upon its career of conquest is active, energetic, inured to warlike habits, simple in its manners, or at any rate simpler than those which it conquers, and, comparatively speaking, poor. It is urged on by the desire of bettering its condition. If it meets with a considerable resistance, if the conquest occupies a long space, and the conquered are with difficulty held under, rebelling from time to time, and making frantic efforts to throw off the yoke which galls and frets them, then the warlike habits of the conquerors are kept up, and their dominion may continue for several centuries. Or, if the nation is very energetic and unresting, not content with its earlier conquests, or willing to rest upon its oars, but continually seeking out fresh enemies upon its borders, and regarding war as the normal state of its existence, then the centuries may be prolonged into millennia, and it may be long indeed before any tendency to decline shows itself; but, ordinarily, there is no very prolonged resistance on the one side, and no very constant and unresting energy on the other. A poor and hardy people, having swooped down upon one that is softer and more civilized, easily carries all before it, acquires the wealth and luxury which it desires, and being content with them, seeks for nothing further, but assimilates itself by degrees to the character and condition of the people whom it has conquered. A standing army, disposed in camps and garrisons, may be kept up; but if there is a cessation of actual war even for a generation, the severity of military discipline will become relaxed, the use of arms will grow unfamiliar, the physical type will decline, the belligerent spirit will die away, and the conquerors of a century ago will have lost all the qualities which secured them success when they made their attack, and have sunk to the level of their subjects. When this point is reached, thoughts of rebellion are apt to arise in the hearts of these latter; the old terror which made the conqueror appear irresistible is gone, and is perhaps succeeded by contempt —the subjects feel that they have at least the advantage of numbers on their side; they have also probably been leading harder and more bracing lives; they see that, man for man, they are physically stronger than their conquerors; and at last they rebel, and are successful.

In Egypt there was, further, this peculiarity—the conquered people occupied two entirely distinct positions. In the Delta, the Fayoum, and the northern Nile valley, they were completely reduced, and lived intermixed with their conquerors, a despised class, suffering more or less of oppression. In Upper Egypt the case was different. There the people had submitted in a certain sense, acknowledged the Hyksôs monarchs as their suzerains, and indicated their subjection by the payment of an annual tribute; but they retained their own native princes, their own administration and government, their own religion, their own laws; they did not live intermixed with the new comers; they were not subject to daily insult or ill-treatment; the fact that they paid a tribute did not hinder their preserving their self-respect, and consequently they suffered neither moral nor physical deterioration. Further, it would seem to have been possible for them to engage in wars on their own account with the races living further up the Nile, or with the wild tribes of the desert, and thus to maintain warlike habits among themselves, while the Hyksôs were becoming unaccustomed to them. The Ra-Sekenens of Thebes, who called themselves " great " and " very great," had probably built up a considerable power in Upper Egypt during the reigns of the later " Shepherd Kings;" had improved their military system by the adoption of the horse and the chariot, which the Hyksôs had introduced; had practised their people in arms, and acquired a reputation as warriors.

More particularly must this have been the case with Ra-Sekenen III., the contemporary of Apepi. Ra-Sekenen the Third called himself "the great victorious Taa." He surrounded himself with a council of "mighty chiefs, captains, and expert leaders." He acquired so much repute, that he provoked Apepi's jealousy before he had in any way transgressed the duties which he owed him as a feudatory. In the long negotiation between the two, of which the "First Sallier Papyrus" gives an account, it is evident that, while Ra-Sekenen has committed no act whereof Apepi has any right to complain, he has awoke in him feelings of such hostility, that Apepi will be content with nothing less than either unqualified submission to every demand that he chooses to make, or war *à outrance*. Never was a subject monarch more goaded and driven into rebellion against his inclination by over-bearing conduct on the part of his suzerain than was Ra-Sekenen by the last "Shepherd King." The disinclination of himself and his court to fight is almost ludicrous: they "are silent and in great dismay; they know not how to answer the messenger sent to them, good or ill." Ra-Sekenen, powerful as he had become, "victorious" as he may have been against Libyans and negroes, and even Cushites, dreaded exceedingly to engage in a struggle with the redoubted people which, two centuries previously, had shown itself so irresistible.

WAR FORCED UPON RA-SEKENEN. 151

It would seem, however, that he was forced to take up arms at last. We have, unfortunately, no description of the war which followed, so far as it was conducted by this monarch. But it is evident that Apepi was completely disappointed in his hope of crushing the rising native power before it had grown too strong. He had in fact delayed too late. Ra-Sekenen, compelled to defend himself against his aggressive suzerain, raised the standard of national independence, invited aid from all parts of Egypt, and succeeded in bringing a large army into the field. At the first he simply held his own against Apepi, but by degrees he was able to do more. The Hyksôs, who marched against Thebes, found enemies rise up against them in their rear, as first one and then another native chief declared against them in this or that city; their difficulties continually increased; they had to re-descend the Nile valley and to concentrate their forces nearer home. But each year they lost ground. First the Fayoum was yielded, then Memphis, then Tanis. At last nothing remained to the invaders but their great fortified camp, Uar or Auaris, which they had established at the time of their arrival upon the eastern frontier, and had ever since kept up. In this district, which was strongly fortified by walls and moats, and watered by canals derived from the Pelusiac branch of the Nile, they had concentrated themselves, we are told, to the number of 240,000 men, determined to make there a final stand against the Egyptians.

It was when affairs were in this position that Ra-Sekenen died, and was succeeded by a king of a different family, the first monarch of the "Eighteenth Dynasty," Aahmes. Aahmes was a prince of great force of character, brave, active, energetic, liberal, beloved by his subjects. He addressed himself at once to the task of completing the liberation of his country by dislodging the Hyksôs from Auaris, and driving them beyond his borders. With this object he collected a force, which is said to have amounted to nearly half a million of men, and at the same time placed a flotilla of ships upon the Nile, which was of the greatest service in his later operations. Auaris was not only defended by broad moats connected with the waters of the Nile, but also bordered upon a lake, or perhaps rather a lagoon, of considerable dimensions. Hence it was necessary that it should be attacked not only by land, but also by water. Aahmes seems to have commanded the land forces in person, riding in a war-chariot, the first of which we have distinct mention. A favourite officer, who bore the same name as his master, accompanied him, sometimes marching at his side as he rode in his chariot, sometimes taking his place in one of the war-vessels, and directing the movements of the fleet. After a time formal siege was laid to Auaris; the fleet was ordered to attack the walls on the side of the lagoon, while the land force was engaged in battering the defences elsewhere. Assaults were made day after day with only partial success; but at last the defenders were wearied out—a panic seized them, and, hastily evacuating the place, they retired towards Syria, the quarter from which they had originally come. Aahmes may have been willing that they should escape; since, if they had been completely blocked in and driven to bay, they might have made a desperate resistance, and caused the Egyptians an enormous loss. He followed, however, upon their footsteps, to make sure that they did not settle anywhere in his neighbourhood, and was not content till they had crossed the desert and entered the hill country of Palestine. Even then he still hung upon their rear, harassing them and cutting off their stragglers; finally, when they made a stand at Sharuhen in Southern Palestine, he laid siege to the town, took it, and made a great slaughter of the hapless defenders.

The war did not terminate until the fifth year of Aahmes' reign. Its result was the complete defeat of the invading hordes which had held Lower and Middle Egypt for so long, and their expulsion from Egypt with such ignominy and loss that they made no effort to retaliate or to recover themselves. Vast numbers must have been slain in the battles, or have perished amid the hardships of the retreat; and many thousands were, no doubt, made prisoners and carried back into Egypt as slaves. It is thought that these captives were so numerous as to become an important element in the population of the eastern Delta, and even to modify the character of the Egyptian race in that quarter. The lively imagination of M. François Lenormant sees their descendants in the "strange people, with robust limbs, an elongated face, and a severe expression, which to this day inhabits the tract bordering on Lake Menzaleh."[1]

[1] "Manuel d'Histoire Ancienne de l'Orient," vol. i. p. 368.

It is probable that Aahmes had for allies in his war with the "Shepherds" the great nation which adjoined Egypt on the south, and which was continually growing in power—the Kashi, Cushites, or Ethiopians. His wife appears by her features and complexion to have been a Cushite princess, and the marriage is likely to have been less one of inclination than of policy. The Egyptians admired fair women rather than dark ones, as is plain from the unduly light complexions which the artists, in their desire to flatter, ordinarily assign to women, as well as from the attractiveness of Sarah, even in advanced age. When a Theban king contracted marriage with an Ethiopian of ebon blackness, we are entitled to assume a political motive; and the most probable political motive under the circumstances of the time was the desire for military assistance. Though in the early wars between the Kashi and the Egyptians the prowess of the former is not represented as great, and the designation of "miserable Cushites" is evidently used in depreciation of their warlike qualities, yet the very use of the epithet implies a feeling of hostility which could scarcely have been provoked by a weak people. And the Cushites certainly advanced in prowess and in military vigour as time went on. They formed the most important portion of the Egyptian troops for some centuries; at a later period they conquered Egypt, and were the dominant power for a hundred years; still further on, they defied the might of Persia when Egypt succumbed to it. Aahmes, in contracting his marriage with the Ethiopian princess, to whom he gave the name of Nefertari-Aahmes—or

HEAD OF NEFERTARI-AAHMES.

"the good companion of Aahmes"—was, we may be tolerably sure, bent on obtaining a contingent of those stalwart troops whose modern representatives are either the Blacks of the Soudan or the Gallas of the highlands of Abyssinia. The "Shepherds" thus yielded to a combination of the North with the South, of the Egyptians with the Ethiopians, such as in later times, on more than one occasion, drove the Assyrians out of the country.

X.

THOTHMES I., THE FIRST GREAT EGYPTIAN CONQUEROR.

THOTHMES I. was the grandson of the Aahmes who drove out the Hyksôs. He had thus hereditary claims to valour and military distinction. The Ethiopian blood which flowed in his veins through his grandmother, Nefertari-Aahmes, may have given him an additional touch of audacity, and certainly showed itself in his countenance, where the short depressed nose and the unduly thick lips are of the Cushite rather than of the Egyptian type. His father, Amen-hotep I., was a somewhat undistinguished prince; so that here, as so often, where superior talent runs in a family, it seems to have skipped a generation, and to have leapt from the grandsire to the grandson. Thothmes began his military career by an invasion of the countries upon the Upper Nile, which were still in an unsettled state, notwithstanding the campaigns which had been carried on, and the victories which had been gained in them, during the two preceding reigns, by King Aahmes, and by the generals of Amen-hotep. He placed a flotilla of ships upon the Nile above the Second Cataract, and supporting it with his land forces on either side of the river, advanced from Semneh, the boundary established by Usurtasen III., which is in lat. 21° 50' to Tombos, in lat. 19°, conquering the tribes, Nubian and Cushite, as he proceeded, and from time to time distinguishing himself in ·personal combats with his enemies. On one occasion, we are told, "his majesty became more furious than a panther," and placing an arrow on his bowstring,

BUST OF THOTHMES I.

directed it against the Nubian chief so surely that it struck him, and remained fixed in his knee, whereupon the chief "fell fainting down before the royal diadem." He was at once seized and made a prisoner; his followers were defeated and dispersed; and he himself, together with others, was carried off on board the royal ship, hanging with his head downwards, to the royal palace at the capital. This victory was the precursor of others; everywhere "the Petti of Nubia were hewed in pieces, and scattered all over their lands," till "their stench filled the valleys." At last a general submission was made, and a large tract of territory was ceded. The Egyptian terminus was pushed on from the twenty-second parallel to the nineteenth, and at Tombos, beyond Dongola, an inscription was set up, at once to mark the new frontier, and to hand down to posterity the glory of the conquering monarch. The inscription still remains, and is couched in inflated terms, which show a departure from the old official style. Thothmes declares that "he has taken tribute from the nations of the North, and from the nations of the South, as well as from *those of the whole earth;* he has laid hold of the barbarians; he has not let a single one of them escape his gripe upon their hair; the Petti of Nubia have fallen beneath his blows; he has made their waters to flow backwards; he has overflowed their valleys like a deluge, like waters which mount and mount. He has resembled Horus, when he took possession of his eternal kingdom; all the countries included within the circumference of the entire earth are prostrate under his feet." Having effected his conquest, Thothmes sought to secure it by the appointment of a new officer, who was to govern the newly-annexed country under the title of "Prince of Cush," and was to have his ordinary residence at Semneh.

Flushed with his victories in this quarter, and intoxicated with the delight of conquest, Thothmes, on his return to Thebes, raised his thoughts to a still grander and more adventurous enterprize. Egypt had a great wrong to avenge, a huge disgrace to wipe out. She had been invaded, conquered, plundered, by an enemy whom she had not provoked by any aggression ; she had seen her cities laid in ashes, her temples torn down and demolished, the images of her gods broken to pieces, her soil dyed with her children's blood ; she had been trampled under the iron heel of the conqueror for centuries ; she had been exhausted by the payment of taxes and tribute ; she had had to bow the knee, and lick the dust under the conqueror's feet—was not retribution needed for all this? True, she had at last risen up and expelled her enemy, she had driven him beyond her borders, and he seemed content to acquiesce in his defeat, and to trouble her no more ; but was this enough ? Did not the law of eternal justice require something more ?

"Nec lex justior ulla est,
Quàm necis artifices arte perire sua."

Was it not proper, fitting, requisite for the honour of Egypt, that there should be retaliation, that the aggressor should suffer what he had inflicted, should be attacked in his own country, should be made to feel the grief, the despair, the rage, the shame, that he had forced Egypt to feel for so many years; should expiate his guilt by a penalty, not only proportioned to the offence, but its exact counterpart ? Such thoughts, we may be sure, burned in the mind of the young warrior, when, having secured Egypt on the south, he turned his attention to the north, and asked himself the question how he should next employ the power that he had inherited, and the talents with which nature had endowed him.

It is uncertain what amount of knowledge the Egyptians of the time possessed concerning the internal condition, population, and resources, of the continent which adjoined them on the north-east. We cannot say whether Thothmes and his counsellors could, or could not, bring before their mind's eye a fairly correct view of the general position of Asiatic affairs, and form a reasonable estimate of the probabilities of success or discomfiture, if a great expedition were led into the heart of Asia. Whatever may have been their knowledge or ignorance, it will be necessary for the historical student of the present day to have some general ideas on the subject, if he is to form an adequate conception either of the dangers which Thothmes affronted, or of the amount of credit due to him for his victories. We propose, therefore, in the present place, to glance our eye over the previous history of Western Asia, and to describe, so far as is possible, its condition at the time when Thothmes began to contemplate the invasion which it is his great glory to have accomplished.

Western Asia is generally allowed to have been the cradle of the human race. Its more fertile portions were thickly peopled at a very early date. Monarchy, it is probable, first grew up in Babylonia, towards the mouths of the Tigris and Euphrates. But it was not long ere a sister kingdom established itself in Susiana, or Elam, the fertile tract between the Lower Tigris and the Zagros mountains. The ambition of conquest first showed itself in this latter country, whence

Kudur-Nakhunta, about B.C. 2300, made an attack on Erech, and Chedor-laomer (about B.C. 2000) established an empire which extended from the Zagros mountains on the one hand to the shores of the Mediterranean on the other (Gen. xiv. 1-4) Shortly after this, a third power, that of the Hittites, grew up towards the north, chiefly perhaps in Asia Minor, but with a tendency to project itself southward into the Mesopotamian region. Upper Mesopotamia, Syria, and Palestine, were at this time inhabited by weak tribes, each under its own chief, with no coherence, and no great military spirit. The chief of these tribes, at the time when Thothmes I. ascended the Egyptian throne, were the Rutennu in Syria, and the Nahari or Naïri in Upper Mesopotamia. The two monarchies of the south, Elam and Babylon were not in a flourishing condition, and exercised no suzerainty beyond their own natural limits. They were, in fact, a check upon each other, constantly engaged in feuds and quarrels, which prevented either from maintaining an extended sway for more than a few years. Assyria had not yet acquired any great distinction, though it was probably independent, and ruled by monarchs who dwelt at Asshur (Kileh-Sherghat). The Hittites, about B.C. 1900, had received a severe check from the Babylonian monarch, Sargon, and had withdrawn themselves into their northern fortresses. Thus the circumstances of the time were, on the whole, favourable to the enterprize of Thothmes. No great organized monarchy was likely to take the field against him, or to regard itself as concerned to interfere with the execution of his projects, unless they assumed extraordinary dimensions. So long as he did not proceed further north than Taurus, or further east than the western Khabour, the great affluent of the Euphrates, he would come into contact with none of the "great powers" of the time; he would have, at the worst, to contend with loose confederacies of tribes, distrustful of each other, unaccustomed to act together, and, though brave, possessing no discipline or settled military organization. At the same time, his adversaries must not be regarded as altogether contemptible. The Philistines and Canaanites in Palestine, the Arabs of the Sinaitic and Syrian deserts, the Rutennu of the Lebanon and of Upper Syria, the Naïri of the western Mesopotamian region, were individually brave men, were inured to warfare, had a strong love of independence, and were likely to resist with energy any attempt to bring them under subjection. They were also, most of them, well acquainted with the value of the horse for military service, and could bring into the field a number of war-chariots, with riders well accustomed to their management. Egypt had only recently added the horse to the list of its domesticated animals, and followed the example of the Asiatics by organizing a chariot force. It was open to doubt whether this new and almost untried corps would be able to cope with the experienced chariot-troops of Asia.

The country also in which military operations were to be carried on was a difficult one. It consisted mainly of alternate mountain and desert. First, the sandy waste called El Tij—the "Wilderness of the

Wanderings "—had to be passed, a tract almost wholly without water, where an army must carry its own supply. Next, the high upland of the Negeb would present itself, a region wherein water may be procured from wells, and which in some periods of the world's history has been highly cultivated, but which in the time of Thothmes was probably almost as unproductive as the desert itself. Then would come the green rounded hills, the lofty ridges, and the deep gorges of Palestine, untraversed by any road, in places thickly wooded, and offering continually greater obstacles to the advance of an army, as it stretched further and further towards the north. From Palestine the Lebanon region would have to be entered on, where, though the Cœle-Syrian valley presents a comparatively easy line of march to the latitude of Antioch, the country on either side of the valley is almost untraversable, while the valley itself contains many points where it can be easily blocked by a small force. The Orontes, moreover, and the Litany, are difficult to cross, and in the time of Thothmes I. would be unbridged, and form no contemptible obstacles. From the lower valley of the Orontes, first mountains and then a chalky desert had to be crossed in order to reach the Euphrates, which could only be passed in boats, or else by swimming. Beyond the Euphrates was another dreary and infertile region, the tract about Haran, where Crassus lost his army and his life.

How far Thothmes and his counsellors were aware of these topographical difficulties, or of the general condition of Western Asia, it is, as already observed, impossible to determine. But, on the whole, there are reasons for believing that intercourse between nation and nation was, even in very early times, kept up, and that each important country had its "intelligence department," which was not badly served. Merchants, refugees, spies, adventurers desirous of bettering their condition, were continually moving, singly or in bodies, from one land to another, and through them a considerable acquaintance with mundane affairs generally was spread abroad. The knowledge was, of course, very inexact. No surveys were made, no plans of cities or fortresses, no maps; the military force that could be brought into the field by the several nations was very roughly estimated; but still, ancient conquerors did not start off on their expeditions wholly in the dark as to the forces which they might have to encounter, or the difficulties which were likely to beset their march.

Thothmes probably set out on his expedition into Asia in about his sixth or seventh year. He was accompanied by two officers, who had served his father and his grandfather, known respectively as "Aahmes, son of Abana," and "Aahmes Pennishem." Both of them had been engaged in the war which he had conducted against the Petti of Nubia and their Ethiopian allies, and both had greatly distinguished themselves. Aahmes, the son of Abana, boasts that he seven times received the prize of valour—a collar of gold—for his conduct in the field; and Aahmes Pennishem gives a list of twenty-nine presents given to him as military rewards by three kings. It does not appear that any resistance was offered to the invading force as it passed through Palestine; but in Syria Thothmes engaged the Rutennu, and "exacted satisfaction" from them, probably on account of the part which they had taken in the Hyksôs struggle; after which he crossed the Euphrates and fell upon the far more powerful nation of the Naïri. The Naïri, when first attacked by the Assyrians, had twenty-three cities, and as many kings; they were rich in horses and mules, and had so large a chariot force that we hear of a hundred and twenty chariots being taken from them in a single battle. At this time the number of the chariots was probably much smaller, for each of the two officers named Ahmes takes great credit to himself on account of the capture of one such vehicle. It is uncertain whether more than a single battle was fought. All that we are told is, that "His Majesty, having arrived in Naharina" (*i.e.* the Naïri country), "encountered the enemy, and organized an attack. His Majesty made a great slaughter of them; an immense number of live captives was carried off by His Majesty." These words would apply equally to a single battle and to a series of battles. All that can be said is, that Thothmes returned victorious from his Asiatic expedition, having defeated the Rutennu and the Naïri, and brought with him into Egypt a goodly booty, and a vast number of Asiatic prisoners.

The warlike ambition of Thothmes I. was satisfied by his Nubian and Asiatic victories. On his return to Egypt at the close of his Mesopotamian campaign, he engaged in the peaceful work of adorning and beautifying his capital cities. At Thebes he greatly enlarged the temple of Ammon, begun by Amenemhat I., and continued under his son, the first Usurtasen. by adding to it the cloistered court in front of the central cell—a court two hundred and forty feet long by sixty-two broad, surrounded by a colonnade, of which the supports were Osirid pillars, or square piers with a statue of Osiris in front. This is the first known example of the cloistered court, which became afterwards so common; though it is possible that constructions of a similar character may have been made by the "Shepherd Kings" at Tanis. Thothmes also adorned this temple with obelisks. In front of the main entrance to his court he erected two vast monoliths of granite, each of them seventy-five feet in height, and bearing dedicatory inscriptions, which indicated his piety and his devotion to all the chief deities of Egypt.

Further, at Memphis he built a new royal palace, which he called "The Abode of Aa-khepr-ka-ra," a grand building, afterwards converted into a magazine for the storage of grain.

The greatness of Thothmes I. has scarcely been sufficiently recognized by historians. It may be true that he did not effect much; but he broke ground in a new direction; he set an example which led on to grand results. To him it was due that Egypt ceased to be the isolated, unaggressive power that she had remained for perhaps ten centuries, that she came boldly to the front and aspired to bring Asia into subjection. Henceforth she exercised a potent influence beyond her borders—an influence which affected, more or less, all the western Asiatic powers. She had forced her way into the comity of the great nations. Henceforth, whether it was for good or for evil, she had to take her place among them, to reckon with them, as they reckoned with her, to be a factor in the problem which the ages had to work out—What should be the general march of events, and what states and nations should most affect the destiny of the world.

XI.

QUEEN HATASU AND HER MERCHANT FLEET.

HASHEPS, or Hatasu, was the daughter of the great warrior king, Thothmes the First, and, according to some, was, during his later years, associated with him in the government. An inscription is quoted in which he assigns to her her throne-name of Ra-ma-ka, and calls her " Queen of the South and of the North." But it was not till after the death of her father that she came prominently forward, and assumed a position not previously held by any female in Egypt, unless it were Net-akret (Nitocris). Women in Egypt had been, it is true, from very early times held in high estimation, were their husbands' companions, not their playthings or their slaves, appeared freely in public, and enjoyed much liberty of action. One of the ancient mythical monarchs, of the time before Sneferu, is said to have passed a law permitting them to exercise the sovereign authority. Nitocris of the sixth dynasty of Manetho ruled, apparently, as sole queen ; and Sabaknefru-ra of the twelfth, the wife of Amenemhat IV., reigned for some years conjointly with her husband. Hatasu's position was intermediate between these. Her father had left behind him two sons, as well as a daughter ; and the elder of these, according to Egyp-

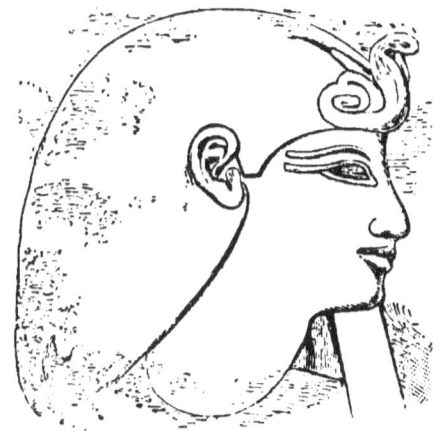

HEAD OF THOTHMES II.

HEAD OF HATASU.

tian law, succeeded him. He reigned as Thothmes-nefer-shau, and is known to moderns as Thothmes the Second. He was, however, a mere youth, of a weak and amiable temper ; while Hatasu, his senior by some years, was a woman of great energy and of a masculine mind, clever, enterprizing, vindictive, and unscrupulous. The contrast of their portrait busts is remarkable, and gives a fair indication of the character of each of them. Thothmes has the appearance of a soft and yielding boy: he has a languishing eye, a short upper lip, a sensuous mouth and chin. Hatasu looks the Amazon : she holds her head erect, has a bold aquiline nose, a firmly-set mouth, and a chin that projects considerably, giving her an indescribable air of vigour and resolution. The effect is increased, no doubt, by her having attached to it the male appendage of an artificial beard ; but even apart from this, her face would be a strong one, expressive of firmness, pride, and decision. It is thought that she contracted a marriage with her brother, such unions being admissible by the Egyptian marriage law, and not infrequent among the Pharaohs, whether of the earlier or the later dynasties. In any case, it is certain that she took the direction of affairs under his reign, reducing him to a cipher, and making her influence paramount in every department of the government.

At this period of her life the ambition of Queen Hatasu was to hand her name down to posterity as a constructor of buildings. She made many additions to the old temple of Ammon at Karnak ; and she also built at Medinet Abou, in the vicinity of Thebes, a temple of a more elaborate character than any that had preceded it, the remains of which are still standing, and have attracted much attention from architects. Egyptian temple-architecture is here seen tentatively making almost its first advances from the simple cell of Usurtasen I. towards that richness of complication and multiplicity of parts which it ultimately reached. Pylons, courts, corridors supported by columns, pillared apartments, meet us here in their earliest germ; while there are also indications of constructive weakness, which show that the builders were aspiring to go beyond previous models. The temple is cruciform in shape, but the two arms of the cross are unequal. In front, two pylons of moderate dimensions, not exceeding twenty-four feet in height, and built with the usual sloping sides and strongly projecting cornice, guarded a doorway which gave entrance into a court, sixty feet long by thirty broad. At the further end of the court stood a porch, thirty feet long and nine deep, supported by four square stone piers, emplaced at equal distances. The porch led into the cell, a long, narrow chamber of extreme plainness, about twenty-five feet long by nine wide, with a doorway at either end. At either side of the cell were corridors, supported, like the porch, by square piers, and roofed in by blocks of stone from nine to ten feet long. These blocks have in some instances shown signs of giving way; and, to counteract the tendency, octagonal pillars have been introduced at the weak points, without regard to exact regularity or correspondence. Behind the cell are chambers for the officiating priests, which are six in number, and on either side of the porch are also

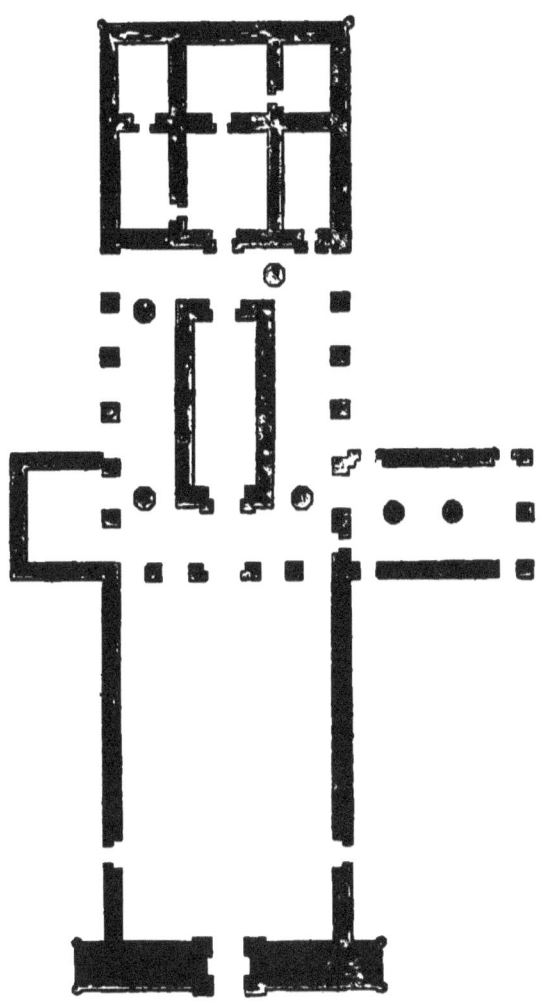

GROUND-PLAN OF TEMPLE AT MEDINET-ABOU.

chambers, forming the arms of the cross, but of unequal dimensions. That on the left is nearly square, about fifteen feet by twelve ; that on the right is oblong, twenty-seven feet by fifteen, and has needed the support of two pillars internally, which seem, however, to have been part of the original design. This chamber is open towards the north-east, terminating in a porch of three square piers.

The joint reign of Hatasu and Thothmes II. did not continue for more than a few years. It is suspected that she engaged in a conspiracy against him in order to rid herself of the small restraint which his participation in the sovereignty exercised upon her, and was privy to his murder. But there is no sufficient evidence to substantiate these charges, which have been somewhat recklessly made. All that distinctly appears is, that Thothmes II. died while he was still extremely young, and when he had reigned only a short time, and that after his death Hatasu showed her hostility to his memory by erasing his name wherever it occurred on the monuments, and substituting for it either her own name or that of her father. She appears also at the same time to have taken full possession of the throne, and to have been accepted as actual sovereign of the Egyptian people. She calls herself "The living Horus, abounding in divine gifts, the mistress of diadems, rich in years, the golden Horus, goddess of diadems, Queen of Upper and Lower Egypt, daughter of the Sun, consort of Ammon, living for ever, and daughter of Ammon, dwelling in his heart." Nor was she content with attributes which made acknowledgment of her sex. She wished to be regarded as a man, assumed male apparel and an artificial beard, and gave herself on many of her monuments the style and title of a king. Her name of Hatasu she changed into Hatasu-Khnum-Ammon, thus identifying herself with two of the chief Egyptian gods. She often represented herself as crowned with the tall plumes of Ammon. She took the titles of "*son* of the sun," "the good *god*," "*lord* of the two lands," "beloved of Ammon, the protector of *kings*." A curious anomaly appears in some of her inscriptions, where masculine and feminine forms are inextricably mixed up; though spoken of consistently as "the king," and not "the queen," yet the personal and possessive pronouns which refer to her are feminine for the most part, while sometimes such perplexing expressions occur as "le roi qui est bien *aimée* par Ammon," or "His Majesty herself."

The legal position which Hatasu occupied during the sixteen years that followed the death of Thothmes II. was probably that of regent for Thothmes III., his (and her) younger brother; but practically she was full sovereign of Egypt. It was now that she formed her grand schemes of foreign commerce, and had them carried out by her officers. First of all, she caused to be built, in some harbour on the western coast of the Red Sea, a fleet of ships, certainly not fewer than five, each constructed so as to be propelled both by oars and sails, and each capable of accommodating some sixty or seventy passengers. Of these thirty were the rowers, whose long sweeps were to plough the waves, and bring the vessels into port, whether the wind were favourable or no; some ten or

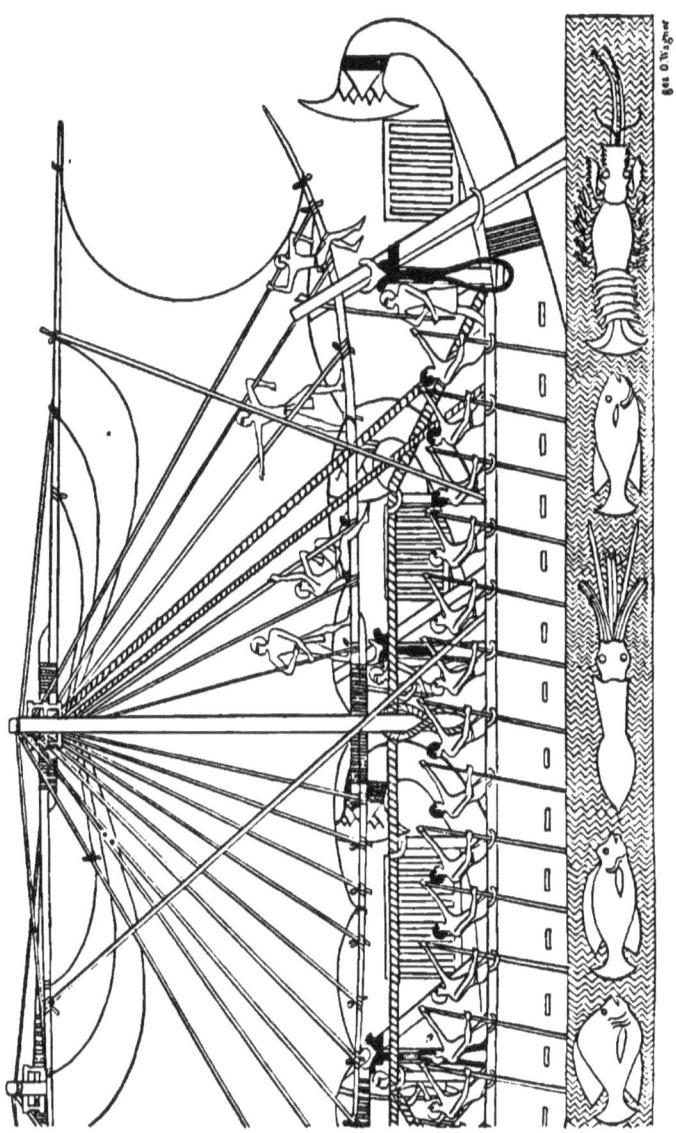

EGYPTIAN SHIP IN THE TIME OF HATASU.

twelve formed the crew ; and the remainder consisted of men-at-arms, whose services, it was felt, might be required, if the native tribes were not sufficiently impressed with the advantages of commercial dealings. An expedition then started from Thebes under the conduct of a royal ambassador, who was well furnished with gifts for distribution among the barbarian chiefs, and instructed to proceed with his fleet down the Red Sea to its mouth, or perhaps even further, and open communications with the land of " Punt," which was in this quarter. " Punt " has been generally identified with Southern Arabia, and it is certainly in favour of this view that the chief object of the expedition was to procure incense and spices, which Arabia is known to have produced anciently in profusion. But among the other products of the land mentioned in the inscriptions of Hatasu, there are several which Arabia could not possibly have furnished ; and the conjecture has therefore been made that Punt, or at any rate the Punt of this expedition, was not the Arabian peninsula, or any part of it, but the African tract outside the Gulf, known to moderns as "the Somauli country." However this may have been, it is certain that the fleet weighed anchor, and sailed down the Red Sea, borne by favourable winds, which were ascribed to the gracious majesty of Ammon, and reached their destination, the Ta-neter, or " Holy Land "—the " abode of Athor," and perhaps the original home of Ammon himself—without accident or serious difficulty. The natives gave them a good reception. They were simple folk, living in rounded huts or cabins, which were perched on floors supported by piles, probably on account of the marshiness of the ground, and which had to be entered by means of ladders. Cocoa-nut palms overshadowed the huts, interspersed with incense trees, while near them flowed a copious stream, in which were a great variety of fishes. The principal chief of the country was a certain Parihu, who was married to a wife of an extraordinary appearance. A dwarf, hunchbacked, with a drawn face and short, deformed legs, she can scarcely,

HOME BUILT ON PILES IN THE LAND OF PUNT

one would think, have been a countrywoman or the Queen of Sheba. She belonged, more probably, to one of the dwarfish tribes of which Africa has so many, as Dokos, Bosjesmen, and others. The royal couple were delighted with their visitors, and with the presents which they received from them; they made a sort of acknowledgment of the suzerainty of the Pharaohs, but at the same time stipulated that the peace and liberty of the land of Punt should be re-

FREE TRADE IN THE LAND OF PUNT. 183

spected by the Egyptians. Perfect freedom of trade was established. The Egyptians had permission to enter the incense forests, and either to cut down the trees for the sake of the resin which they exuded, or to dig them up and convey them to the ships. We see the trees, or rather bushes, dug up with as much earth as possible about their roots, then slung on poles and carried to the sea-shore, and finally placed

THE QUEEN OF PUNT, AS SHE APPEARED AT THE COURT OF HATASU.

upright upon the ships' decks, and screened from the heat of the sun's rays by an awning. Thirty-one trees were thus embarked, with the object of transplanting them to Egypt, where it was hoped that they might grow and flourish. A large quantity of the resin was also collected and packed in sacks, which were tied at the mouth and piled up upon the decks. Various other products and commodities were likewise brought to the beach by the natives, and exchanged for those which the Egyptians had taken care to bring with them in their ships' holds. The most prized were gold, silver, ivory, ebony and other woods, cassia, kohl or stibium, apes, baboons, dogs, slaves, and leopard skins. The utmost friendliness prevailed during the whole period of the Egyptians' stay in the country; and at their departure, a number of the natives, of their own free-will, accompanied them to Egypt. Among these would seem to have been the deformed queen and several chiefs.

The return journey to Thebes was effected partly by way of the Nile. No doubt the sea-going ships sailed back to the harbour from which they had started; while the incense trees and other commodities were disembarked, and conveyed across the desert tract which borders the Nile valley towards the east; but instead of being brought to Thebes by land they were re-shipped on board a number of large Nile boats, and conveyed down the river to the capital. The day of their arrival was made a grand gala-day. All the city went out to meet the returning travellers. There was a grand parade of the household troops, and also of those which had accompanied the expedition; the incense trees, the strange animals, the many products of the distant country, were exhibited; a tame leopard, with his negro keeper, followed the soldiers; a band of natives, called Tamahu, engaged in a sort of sham-fight or war-dance. The misshapen queen and the chiefs of the land of Punt, together with a number of Nubian hunters from the region of Chent-hen-nefer, which lay far up the course of the Nile, were conducted to the presence of Hatasu, offered their homage to her as she sat upon her throne, and presented her with valuable gifts. " Homage to thy countenance," they said, " O Queen of Egypt, Sun beaming like the sun-disk, Aten, Arabia's mistress." An offering was then made by Hatasu to the god Ammon ; a bull was sacrificed, and two vases of the precious frankincense presented to him by the queen herself. Sacrifice was likewise made and prayers offered to Athor, " Queen of Punt " and " Mistress of Heaven." The incense trees were finally planted in ground prepared for them, and the day concluded with general festivity and rejoicing.

The complete success of so important and difficult an enterprize might well please even a great queen. Hatasu, delighted with the result, did her best to prevent it fading away from human remembrance by building a new temple to Ammon, and representing the entire expedition upon its walls. At Tel-el-Bahiri, in the valley of El-Assasif, near Thebes, she found a convenient site for her new structure, which she imposed upon four steps, and covered internally with a series of bas-reliefs, highly coloured, depicting the chief scenes of the expedition. Here are to be seen, even at the present day, the ships—the most ancient representations of sea-going ships that the world contains—the crews, the incense-trees, the chiefs and queen of Punt, the native dwellings, the trees and fish of the land, the arrival of the expedition at Thebes in twelve large boats, the prostration of the native chiefs before Hatasu, the festival held on the occasion, and the offerings made to the gods. It is seldom that any single event of ancient history is so profusely illustrated as this expedition of Queen Hatasu, which is placed before our eyes in all its various phases, from the gathering of the fleet on the Red Sea coast to the return of those engaged in it, in gladness and triumph, to Thebes.

After exercising all the functions of sovereignty for fifteen years, during which she kept her royal brother in a subjection that probably became very galling to him, Hatasu found herself under the necessity of admitting him to a share in the royal authority, and allowed his name to appear on her monuments in a secondary and subordinate position. About this time she was especially engaged in the ornamentation of the old temple of Ammon at Thebes, begun by Usurtasen I., and much augmented by her father, Thothmes I. The chief of all her works in this quarter were two obelisks of red granite, or syenite, drawn from the quarries of Elephantine, and set up before the entrance, which her father had made in front of Usurtasen's construction. These great works are unexcelled, in form, colour, and beauty of engraving, by any similar productions of Egyptian art, either earlier or later. They measure nearly a hundred feet in height, and are covered with the most delicately finished hieroglyphics. On them Hatasu declares that she "has made two great obelisks for her father, Ammon, from a heart that is full of love for him." They are "of hard granite of the South, each of a single stone, without any joining or division." The summit of each, or cap of the pyramidion, is "of pure gold, taken from the chiefs of nations," so that they "are seen from a distance of many leagues—Upper and Lower Egypt are bathed in their splendour" (!).

Hatasu reigned conjointly with Thothmes III. for the space of seven years. Their common monuments have been found at Thebes, in the Wady Magharah, and elsewhere. It is not probable that the relations of the brother and sister during this period were very cordial. Hatasu still claimed the chief authority, and placed her name before that of her brother on all public documents. She was, as she has been called, "a bold, ambitious woman," and evidently admitted with reluctance any partner of her greatness. Thothmes III., a man of great ambition and no less ability, is not likely to have acquiesced very willingly in the secondary position assigned to him. Whether he openly rebelled against it, broke with Hatasu, and deprived her of the throne, or even put her to death, is wholly uncertain. The monuments hitherto discovered are absolutely silent as to what became of this great queen. She may have died a natural death, opportunely for her brother, who must have wished to find himself unshackled ; or she may have been the victim of a conspiracy within the palace walls. All that we know is that she disappears from history in about her fortieth year, and that her brother and successor, the third Thothmes, actuated by a strong and settled animosity, caused her name to be erased, as far as possible, from all her monuments. There is scarcely one on which it remains intact. The greatest of Egyptian queens—one of the greatest of Egyptian sovereigns—is indebted for the continuance of her memory among mankind to the accident that the stonemasons employed by Thothmes to carry out his plan of vengeance were too careless or too idle to effect the actual obliteration of the name, which they everywhere marred with their chisels. Hatred, for once, though united with absolute power, missed its aim; and Hatasu's great constructions, together with her "Merchant Fleet," are among the indisputable facts of history which can never be forgotten.

XII.

THOTHMES THE THIRD AND AMENHOTEP THE SECOND.

No sooner had Thothmes III. burst the leading-strings in which his sister had held him for above twenty years, then he showed the metal of which he was made by at once placing himself at the head of his troops, and marching into Asia. Persuaded that the great god, Ammon, had promised him a long career of victory, he lost no time in setting to work to accomplish his glorious destiny. Starting from an Egyptian post on the Eastern frontier, called Garu or Zalu, in the month of February, he took his march along the ordinary coast route, and in a short time reached Gaza, the strong Philistine city, which was already a fortress of repute, and regarded as "the key of Syria." The day of his arrival was the anniversary of his coronation, and according to his reckoning the first day of his twenty-third year. Gaza made no resistance: its chief was friendly to the Egyptians, and gladly opened his gates to the invading army. Having rested at Gaza no more than a single night, Thothmes resumed his march, and continuing to skirt the coast, arrived on the eleventh day at a fortified town called Jaham, probably Jamnia. Here he was met by his scouts, who brought the intelligence that the enemy was collected at Megiddo, on the edge of the great plain of Esdraelon, the ordinary battle-field of the Palestinian nations. They consisted of "all the people dwelling between the river of Egypt on the one hand and the land of Naharaïn (Mesopotamia) on the other." At their head was the king of Kadesh, a great city on the upper Orontes, which afterwards became one of the chief seats of the Hittite power, but was at this time in the possession of the Rutennu (Syrians). They were strongly posted at the mouth of a narrow pass, behind the ridge of hills which connects Carmel with the Samaritan upland, and Thothmes was advised by his captains to avoid a direct attack, and march against them by a circuitous route, which was undefended. But the intrepid warrior scorned this prudent counsel. "His generals," he said, "might take the roundabout road, if they liked; *he* would follow the straight one." The event justified his determination. Megiddo was reached in a week without loss or difficulty, and a great battle was fought in the fertile plain to the north-west of the fortress, in which the Egyptian king was completely victorious, and his enemies were scattered like chaff before him. The Syrians must have fled precipitately at the first attack; for they lost in killed no more than eighty-three, and in prisoners no more than two hundred and forty, or according to another account three hundred and forty, while the chariots taken were nine hundred and twenty-four, and the captured horses 2,132. Megiddo was near at hand, and the bulk of the fugitives would reach easily the shelter of its walls. Others may have dispersed themselves among the mountains. The Syrian camp was, however, taken, together with vast treasures in silver and gold, lapis lazuli, turquoise, and alabaster; and the son of the king of Kadesh fell into Thothmes' hands. Megiddo itself, soon afterwards, surrendered, as did the towns of Inunam, Anaugas, and Hurankal or Herinokol. An immense booty in corn and cattle was also carried off. Thothmes returned to Egypt in triumph, and held a prolonged festival to Ammon-Ra in Thebes, accompanied by numerous sacrifices and offerings. Among the last we find included three of the cities taken from the Rutennu, which were assigned to the god in order that they might "supply a yearly contribution to his sacred food."

It is a familiar saying, that "increase of appetite doth grow by what it feeds on." Thothmes certainly found his appetite for conquest whetted, not satiated, by his Syrian campaign. If we may trust M. Lenormant, he took the field in the very year that followed his victory of Megiddo, and after traversing the whole of Syria, and ravaging the country about Aleppo, proceeded to Carchemish, the great Hittite town on the Upper Euphrates, and there crossed the river into Naharaïn, or Mesopotamia, whence he carried off a number of prisoners. Two other campaigns, which cannot be traced in detail, belong to the period between his twenty-fourth and his twenty-ninth year. Thenceforward to his fortieth year his military expeditions scarcely knew any cessation. At one time he would embark his troops on board a fleet, and make descents upon the coast of Syria, coming as unexpectedly and ravaging as ruthlessly as the Normans of the Middle Ages. He would cut down the fruit trees, carry off the crops, empty the magazines of grain, lay hands upon all valuables that were readily removable, and carry them on board his ships, returning to Egypt with a goodly store of gold and silver, of lapis lazuli and other precious stones, of vases in silver and in bronze, of corn, wine, incense, balsam, honey, iron, lead, emery, and male and female slaves. At another, he would march by land, besiege and take the inland towns, demand and obtain the sons of the chiefs as hostages, exact heavy war contributions, and bring back with him horses and chariots, flocks and herds, strange animals, trees, and plants.

Of all his expeditions, that undertaken in his thirty-third year was perhaps the most remarkable. Starting from the country of the Rutennu, he on this occasion directed the main force of his attack upon the Mesopotamian region, which he ravaged far and wide, conquering the towns, and "reducing to a level plain the strong places of the miserable land of Naharaïn," capturing thirty kings or chiefs, and erecting two tablets in the region, to indicate its subjection. It is possible that he even crossed the Tigris into Adiabene or the Zab country, since he relates that on his return he passed through the town of Ni or Nini, which many of the best historians of Egypt identify with Nineveh. Nineveh was not now (about B.C. 1500) the capital of Assyria, which was lower down the Tigris, at Asshur or Kileh Sherghat, but was only a provincial town of some magnitude. Still, it was within the dominions of the Assyrian monarch of the time, and any attack upon it would have been an insult and a challenge to the great power of Upper Mesopotamia, which ruled from the alluvium to the mountains. It is certain that the king of Assyria did not accept the challenge, but preferred to avoid an encounter with the Egyptian troops. Both at this time and subsequently he sent envoys with rich presents to court the favour of Thothmes, who accepted the gifts as " tribute," and counted " the chief of Assuru" among his tributaries. Submission was also made to him at the same time by the " prince of Senkara," a name which still exists in the lower Babylonian marsh region. Among the gifts which this prince sent was "lapis lazuli of Babylon." It is an exaggeration to represent the expedition as having resulted in the conquest of the great empires of Assyria and Babylon; but it is quite true to say that it startled and shook those empires, that it filled them with a great fear of what might be coming, and brought Egypt into the position of the principal military power of the time. Assyrian influence especially was checked and curtailed. There is reason to believe, from the Egyptian remains found at Arban on the Khabour,[1] that Thothmes added to the Egyptian empire the entire region between the Euphrates and its great eastern affluent—a broad tract of valuable territory—and occupied it with permanent garrisons. The Assyrian monarch bought off the further hostility of his dangerous neighbour by an

[1] Layard, "Nineveh and Babylon," pp. 280-282.

annual embassy which conveyed rich gifts to the court of the Pharaohs, gifts that were not reciprocated. Among these we find enumerated gold and silver ornaments, lapis lazuli, vases of Assyrian stone (alabaster?), slaves, chariots adorned with gold and silver, silver dishes and silver beaten out into sheets, incense, wine, honey, ivory, cedar and sycomore wood, mulberry trees, vines, and fig trees, buffaloes, bulls, and a gold habergeon with a border of lapis lazuli.

A curious episode of the expedition is related by Amenemheb, an officer who accompanied it, and was in personal attendance upon the Egyptian monarch. It appears that in the time of Thothmes III. the elephant haunted the woods and jungles of the Mesopotamian region, as he now does those of the peninsula of Hindustan. The huge unwieldy beasts were especially abundant in the neighbourhood of Ni or Nini, the country between the middle Tigris and the Zagros range. As Amenemhat I. had delighted in the chase of the lion and the crocodile, so Thothmes III. no sooner found a number of elephants within his reach than he proceeded to hunt and kill them, mainly no doubt for the sport, but partly in order to obtain their tusks. No fewer than a hundred and twenty are said to have been killed or taken. On one occasion, however, the monarch ran a great risk. He was engaged in the pursuit of a herd, when the "rogue," or leading elephant, turned and made a rush at the royal sportsman, who would probably have fallen a victim, gored by a tusk or trampled to death under the huge beast's feet, had not Amenemheb hastened to the rescue, and by wounding the creature's trunk drawn its rage upon himself. The brute was then, after a short struggle, overpowered and captured.

Further expeditions were led by Thothmes into Asia in his thirty-fourth, thirty-fifth, thirty-eighth, thirty-ninth, fortieth, and forty-second years; but in none of them does he seem to have outdone the exploits of the great campaign of the year 33. The brunt of his attacks at this time fell upon the Zahi, or Tahai, of northern Phœnicia, and upon the Naïri of the Mesopotamian region, who continually rebelled, and had to be reconquered. The Rutennu seem for the most part to have paid their tribute without resistance and without much difficulty. This may have been partly owing to the judicious system which Thothmes had established among them, whereby each chief was forced to give a son or brother as hostage for his good behaviour, and if the hostage died to send another in his place. It was certainly not because the tribute was light, since it consisted of a number of slaves, silver vases of the weight of 762 pounds, nineteen chariots, 276 head of cattle, 1,622 goats, several hundredweight of iron and lead, a number of suits of armour, and "all kinds of good plants." The Rutennu had also to supply the stations along the military road, whereby Thothmes kept up the communications between Egypt and Mesopotamia, with bread, wine, dates, incense, honey, and figs.

While thus engaged in enlarging the limits of his empire towards the north and the north-east, the careful monarch did not allow the regions brought under

Egyptian influence by former rulers to escape him. He took a tribute of gold, spices, male and female slaves, cattle, ivory, ebony, and panther skins from the land of Punt, of cattle and slaves from Cush, and of the same products from the Uauat. Altogether he is said to have carried off from the subject countries above 11,000 captives, 1,670 chariots, 3,639 horses, 4,491 of the larger cattle, more than 35,000 goats, silver to the amount of 3,940 pounds, and gold to the amount of 9,054 pounds. He also conveyed to Egypt from the conquered lands enormous quantities of corn and wine, together with incense, balsam, honey, ivory, ebony and other rare woods, lapis lazuli, furniture, statues, vases, dishes, basins, tent-poles, bows, habergeons, fruit trees, live birds, and monkeys! With a curiosity which was insatiable, he noted all that was strange or unusual in the lands which he visited, and sought to introduce the various novelties into his own proper country. Two unknown kinds of birds, and a variety of the goose, which he found in Mesopotamia, and transported from the valley of the Khabour to that of the Nile, are said to have been "dearer to the king than anything else." His artists had instructions to make careful studies of the different objects, and to represent them faithfully on his monuments. We see on these "water-lilies as high as trees, plants of a growth like cactuses, all sorts of trees and shrubs, leaves, flowers, and fruits, including melons and pomegranates; oxen and calves also figure, and among them a wonderful animal with three horns. There are likewise herons, sparrow-hawks, geese, and doves. All these objects appear gaily intermixed in the pictures, as suited the simple childlike conception of the artist."[1] An inscription tells the intention of the monarch. "Here," it runs, "are all sorts of plants and all sorts of flowers of the Holy Land, which the king discovered when he went to the land of Ruten to conquer it. Thus says the king—I swear by the sun, and I call to witness my father Ammon, that all is plain truth; there is no trace of deception in that which I relate. What the splendid soil brings forth in the way of productions, I have had portrayed in these pictures, with the intention of offering them to my father Ammon, as a memorial for all times."

Besides his army, Thothmes also maintained a naval force, and used it largely in his expeditions. According to one writer, he placed a fleet on the Euphrates, and in an action which took place with the Assyrians, defeated and chased the enemy for a distance of between seven and eight miles. He certainly upon some occasions made his attacks on Syria and Phœnicia from the sea; nor is it improbable that his maritime forces reduced Cyprus (which was conquered and held in a much less flourishing period by Amasis) and plundered the coast of Cilicia; but a judicious criticism will scarcely extend the voyages of his fleet, as has been done by another writer, to Crete, and the islands of the Ægean, the sea-boards of Greece and Asia Minor, the southern coast of Italy, Algeria, and the waters of the Euxine! There is no evidence in the historical inscriptions of Thothmes of any such far-reaching expeditions. The supposed

[1] Brugsch, "History of Egypt," vol. i. pp. 367, 368.

evidence for them is in a song of victory, put into the mouth of the god, Ammon, and inscribed on one of the walls of the great temple of Karnak. The song is interesting, but it scarcely bears out the deductions that have been drawn from it, as will appear from the subjoined translation.

(AMMON *loquitur.*)

I came, and thou smotest the princes of Zahi;
I scattered them under thy feet over all their lands;
I made them regard thy Holiness as the blazing sun;
Thou shinest in sight of them in my form.

I came, and thou smotest them that dwell in Asia;
Thou tookest captive the goat-herds of Ruten;
I made them behold thy Holiness in thy royal adornments,
As thou graspest thy weapons in the war-chariot.

I came, and thou smotest the land of the East;
Thou marchedst against the dwellers in the Holy Land;
I made them behold thy Holiness as the star Canopus,
Which sends forth its heat and disperses the dew.

I came, and thou smotest the land of the West;
Kefa and Asebi (*i.e.* Phœnicia and Cyprus) held thee in fear;
I made them look upon thy Holiness as a young bull,
Courageous, with sharp horns, which none can approach.

I came, and thou smotest the subjects of their lords;
The land of Mathen trembled for fear of thee;
I made them look upon thy Holiness as upon a crocodile,
Terrible in the waters, not to be encountered.

I came, and thou smotest them that dwelt in the Great Sea;
The inhabitants of the isles were afraid of thy war-cry;
I made them behold thy Holiness as the Avenger,
Who shews himself at the back of his victim.

I came, and thou smotest the land of the Tahennu;
The people of Uten submitted themselves to thy power;
I made them see thy Holiness as a lion, fierce of eye,
Who leaves his den and stalks through the valleys.

I came, and thou smotest the hinder (*i.e.* northern) lands;
The circuit of the Great Sea is bound in thy grasp ;
I made them behold thy Holiness as the hovering hawk,
Which seizes with his glance whatever pleases him.

I came, and thou smotest the lands in front ;
Those that sat upon the sand thou carriedst away captive ;
I made them behold thy Holiness like the jackal of the South,
Which passes through the lands as a hidden wanderer.

I came, and thou smotest the nomad tribes of Nubia,
Even to the land of Shut, which thou holdest in thy grasp ;
I made them behold thy Holiness like thy pair of brothers,
Whose hands I have united to give thee power.[1]

It is impossible to conclude this sketch of Thothmes III. without some notice of his buildings. He was the greatest of Egyptian conquerors, but he was also one of the greatest of Egyptian builders and patrons of art. The grand temple of Ammon at Thebes was the especial object of his fostering care ; and he began his career of builder and restorer by repairs and restorations, which much improved and beautified that edifice. Before the southern propylæa he re-erected, in the first year of his independent reign, colossal statues of his father, Thothmes I., and his grandfather, Amenhotep, which had been thrown down in the troublous time succeeding Thothmes the First's death. He then proceeded to rebuild the central sanctuary, the work of Usurtasen I., which had probably begun to decay, and, recognizing its importance as the very *penetrale* of the temple, he resolved to reconstruct it in granite, instead of common stone, that he might render it, practically,

[1] Brugsch, " History of Egypt " (first ed., 1879), vol. i. pp. 371, 372.

imperishable. With a reverence and a self-restraint that it might be wished restorers possessed more commonly, he preserved all the lines and dimensions of the ancient building, merely reproducing in a better material the work of his great predecessor. Having accomplished this pious task, he gave a vent to his constructive ambition by a grand addition to the temple on its eastern side. Behind the cell, at the distance of about a hundred and fifty feet, he erected a magnificent hall, or pillared chamber, of dimensions previously unknown in Egypt, or elsewhere in the world at the time—an oblong square, one hundred and forty-three feet long by fifty-three feet wide, or nearly half as large again as the nave of Canterbury Cathedral. The whole of the apartment was roofed in with slabs of solid stone; it was divided in its longest direction into five avenues or vistas by means of rows of pillars and piers, the former being towards the centre, and attaining a height of thirty feet, with bell capitals, and the latter towards the sides, with a height of twenty feet. This arrangement enabled the building to be lighted by means of a clerestory, in the manner shown by the accompanying woodcut. In connection with this noble hall, on three sides of it, northwards, eastwards, and southwards, Thothmes further erected chambers and corridors, partly open, partly supported by pillars, which might form convenient store-chambers for the vestments of the priests and the offerings of the people.

Thothmes also added propylæa to the temple on the south, and erected in front of the grand entrance —which was (as usual) between the pylons of the propylæa, two or perhaps four great obelisks, one of which exists to the present day, and is the largest and most magnificent of all such monuments now extant. It stands in front of the Church of St. John Lateran at Rome, and has a height of a hundred and five feet, exclusive of the base, with a width diminishing from nine feet six inches to eight feet seven inches. It is estimated to weigh above four hundred and fifty tons, and is covered with well-cut hieroglyphics. No other obelisk approaches within twelve feet of its elevation, or within fifty tons of its weight. Yet, if we may believe an inscription of Thothmes, found on the spot,

SECTION OF PILLARED HALL OF THOTHMES III. AT KARNAK.

the pair of obelisks whereof this was one shrank into insignificance in comparison with another pair, also placed by him before his propylæa, the height of which was one hundred and eight cubits, or one hundred and sixty-two feet, and their weight consequently from seven hundred to eight hundred tons! As no trace has been found of these monsters, and as it seems almost impossible that they should have been removed, and highly improbable that they could have been broken up without leaving some indication of their existence, perhaps we may conclude that they were designed rather than executed, and that the inscription was set up in anticipation of an achievement contemplated but never effected.

Other erections of the Great Thothmes are the enclosure of the famous Temple of the Sun at Heliopolis, the temple of Phthah at Thebes, the small temple at Medinet-Abou, a temple to Kneph adorned with obelisks at Elephantine, and a series of temples and monuments erected at Ombos, Esneh, Abydos, Coptos, Denderah, Eileithyia, Hermonthis, and Memphis in Egypt, and at Amada, Corte, Talmis, Pselcis, Semneh, Koummeh, and Napata in Nubia. Extensive ruins of many of these buildings still remain, particularly at Koummeh, Semneh, Napata, Denderah, and Ombos. Altogether, Thothmes III. is pronounced to have left behind him more monuments than any other Pharaoh excepting Rameses II., and though occasionally showing himself, as a builder, somewhat capricious and whimsical, still, on the whole, to have worked in a pure style and proved that he was not deficient in good taste.[1]

It has happened, moreover, by a curious train of circumstances, that Thothmes III. is, of all the Pharaohs, the one whose great works are most widely diffused, and display Egyptian skill and taste to the largest populations, and in the most important cities, of the modern world. Rome, as we have seen, possesses his grandest obelisk, which is at the same time the greatest of all extant monoliths. The millions who have flocked to Rome in all ages have learnt the lesson of Egyptian greatness from the monument erected before the Church of St. John Lateran. Con-

[1] Wilkinson in Rawlinson's "Herodotus," vol. ii. p. 302.

stantinople holds an obelisk of Thothmes III., which is placed in the middle of the Atmeidan. London has put on its embankment, half-way between St. Paul's and the Palace and Abbey of Westminster, another obelisk of the same monarch, erected originally at Heliopolis, thence removed to Alexandria by Augustus, and now adorning the banks of the Thames, nearly in the centre of the most populous city that the world has ever seen. The companion monument, after having, similarly, stood at Heliopolis for fifteen centuries, and then at Alexandria for eighteen, has crossed the Atlantic Ocean, and now teaches the million residents, and the tens of thousands of visitors, of New York what great things could be done by the Egyptian engineers and artists of the time of the eighteenth dynasty.

Thothmes III. has been called "the Alexander of Egyptian history." The phrase is at once exaggerated and misleading. It is exaggerated as applied to his military ability; for, though beyond a doubt this monarch was by far the greatest of Egyptian conquerors, and possessed considerable military talent, much personal bravery, and an energy that has seldom been exceeded, yet, on the other hand, his task was trivial as compared with that of the Macedonian general, and his achievements insignificant. Instead of plunging with a small force into the midst of populous countries, and contending with armies ten or twenty times as numerous as his own, defeating them, and utterly subduing a vast empire, Thothmes marched at the head of a numerous disciplined army into thinly peopled regions, governed by petty chiefs jealous one of another, fought scarcely a single great battle, and succeeded in conquering two regions of a moderate size, Syria and Upper Mesopotamia, as far as the Khabour river. Alexander overran and subdued the entire tract between the Ægean and the Sutlej, the Persian Gulf and the Oxus. He conquered Egypt, and founded a dynasty there which endured for nearly three centuries. Thothmes subdued not a tenth part of the space, and the empire which he established did not endure for much more than a century. It is thus absurd to compare Thothmes III. to Alexander the Great as a conqueror.

Alexander was, besides, much more than a conqueror; he was a first-rate administrator. Had he lived twenty years' longer he would probably have built up a universal monarchy, which might have lasted for a millenium. As it was, he so organized the East that it continued for nearly three centuries mainly under Greek rule, in the hands of the monarchs who are known as his "successors." Thothmes III., on the contrary, organized nothing. He left his conquests in such a condition that they, all of them, revolted at his death. His successor had to reconquer all the countries that had submitted to his father, and to re-establish over them the Egyptian sovereignty.

In person the great Egyptian monarch was not remarkable. He had a long, well-shaped, and somewhat delicate nose, which was almost in line with his forehead, an eye prominent and larger than that of most Egyptians, a shortish upper lip, a resolute mouth with rather over-full lips, and a rounded, slightly retreating chin. The expression of his portrait statues is grave and serious, but lacks strength and determination. Indeed, there is something about the whole countenance that is a little womanish, though his character certainly presents no appearance of effeminacy. He died after a reign of fifty-four years, according to his own reckoning, having practically

BUST OF THOTHMES III.

exercised the sovereign power for about thirty-two of the fifty-four. His age at his death must have been about sixty.

During these stirring times, what were the children of Israel doing? We have supposed that Joseph was minister of the last of the Shepherd Kings, under whose reign his people had entered upon the peaceful occupation of the land of Goshen, where they were received with hospitality by a population of the same simple pastoral habits with themselves ; and it seems probable that, under Thothmes III., they were increasing abundantly and waxing mighty, and that the land between the Sebennytic and Pelusiac branches of the Nile was gradually being filled by them. Their period of severe oppression had not yet begun ; there had as yet arisen no sufficient reason for any measures of repression, such as were pursued by the new king who "knew not Joseph." The name and renown of the great minister seems still to have protected his kinsmen in the peaceful enjoyment of their privileges in the land that must by this time have lost for them most of its strangeness.

Thothmes III. was succeeded by his son, Amenhotep, whom historians commonly term Amenophis the Second. This king was a warrior like his father, and succeeded in reducing, without much difficulty, the various nations that had thrown off the authority of Egypt on receiving the news of his father's death. He even carried his arms, according to some, as far as Nineveh, which he claims to have besieged and taken ; he does not, however, mention the Assyrians as his opponents. His contests were with the Naïri, the Rutennu, and the Shasu (Arabs) in Asia, with the Tahennu (Libyans) and Nubians in Africa. On all sides victory crowned his arms ; but he stained the fair fame that his victories would have otherwise secured him by barbarous practices, and cruel and unnecessary bloodshed. He tells us that at Takhisa in northern Syria he killed seven kings with his own hand, and he represents himself in the act of destroying them with his war-club, not in the heat of battle, but after they have been taken prisoners. He further adds that, after killing them, he suspended their bodies from the prow of the vessel in which he returned to Egypt, and brought them, as trophies of victory, to Thebes, where he hung six of the seven outside the walls of the city, as the Philistines hung the bodies of Saul and Jonathan on the wall of Beth-shan (1 Sam. xxxi. 10, 12); while he had the seventh conveyed to Napata in Nubia, and there similarly exposed, to terrify his enemies in that quarter. It has been said of the Russians—not perhaps without some justice—"Grattez le Russe et vous trouverez le Tartare;" with far greater reason may we say of the ancient Egyptians, that, notwithstanding the veneer of civilization which they for the most part present to our observation, there was in their nature, even at the best of times, an underlying ingrained barbarism which could not be concealed, but was continually showing itself.

Amenôphis II. appears to have had a short reign; his seventh year is the last noted upon his monuments. As a builder he was unenterprizing. One temple at Amada, one hall at Thebes, and his tomb at Abd-el-Qurnah, form almost the whole of his known constructions. None of them is remarkable. Egypt under his sway had a brief rest before she braced herself to fresh efforts, military and architectural.

XIII.

AMENHOTEP III. AND HIS GREAT WORKS — THE VOCAL MEMNON.

THE fame of Amen-hotep the Third, the grandson of the great Thothmes, rests especially upon his Twin Colossi, the grandest, if not actually the largest, that the world has ever beheld. Imagine sitting figures, formed of a single solid block of sandstone, which have sat on for above three thousand years, mouldering gradually away under the influence of time and weather changes, yet which are still more than sixty feet high, and must originally, when they wore the tall crown of an Egyptian king, have reached very nearly the height of seventy feet! We think a statue vast, colossal, of magnificent dimensions, if it be as much as ten or twenty feet high—as Chantrey's statue of Pitt, or Phidias's chryselephantine statue of Jupiter. What, then, must these be, which are of a size so vastly greater? Let us hear how they impress an eye-witness of world-wide experience. "There they sit," says Harriet Martineau, "together, yet apart, in the midst of the plain, serene and vigilant, still keeping their untired watch over the lapse of ages and the eclipse of Europe. I can never believe that anything else so majestic as this pair has been

THE TWIN COLOSSI OF AMENHOTEP III. AT THEBES.

conceived of by the imagination of art. Nothing certainly, even in nature, ever affected me so unspeakably; no thunderstorms in my childhood, nor any aspect of Niagara, or the great lakes of America, or the Alps, or the Desert, in my later years. . . . The pair, sitting alone amid the expanse of verdure, with islands of ruins behind them, grew more striking to us every day. To-day, for the first time, we looked up to them from their base. The impression of sublime tranquillity which they convey when seen from distant points, is confirmed by a nearer approach. There they sit, keeping watch—hands on knees, gazing straight forward ; seeming, though so much of the face is gone, to be looking over to the monumental piles on the other side of the river, which became gorgeous temples, after these throne-seats were placed here—the most immovable thrones that have ever been established on this earth ! "[1]

The design of erecting two such colossi must be attributed to the monarch himself, and we must estimate, from the magnificence of the design, the grandeur of his thoughts and the wonderful depth of his artistic imagination ; but the skill to execute, the genius to express in stone such dignity, majesty, and repose as the statues possess, belongs to the first-rate sculptor, who turned the rough blocks of stone, hewn by the masons in a distant quarry, into the glorious statues that have looked down upon the plain for so many ages. The sculptors of Egyptian works are, in general, unknown ; but, by good fortune, in this particular case, the name of the artist has remained on

[1] " Eastern Life," vol. i. pp. 84, 289.

record, and he has himself given us an account of the feelings with which he saw them set up in the places where they still remain. The sculptor, who bore the same name as his royal master, *i.e.* Amenhotep or Amen-hept, declares in the exultation of his heart: " I immortalized the name of the king, and no one has done the like of me in my works. I executed two portrait-statues of the king, astonishing for their breadth and height; their completed form dwarfed the temple tower—forty cubits was their measure; they were cut in the splnndid sandstone mountain on either side, the eastern and the western. I caused to be built eight ships, whereon the statues were carried up the river; they were emplaced in their sublime temple; they will last as long as heaven. A joyful event was it when they were landed at Thebes and raised up in their place."

A peculiar and curious interest attaches to one—the more eastern—of the two statues. It was known to the Romans of the early empire as "The Vocal Memnon," and formed one of the chief attractions which drew travellers to Egypt, from the fact, which is quite indisputable, that at that time, for two centuries or perhaps more, it emitted in the early morning a musical sound, which was regarded as a sort of standing miracle. The fact is mentioned by Strabo, Pliny the elder, Pausanias, Tacitus, Juvenal, Lucian, Philostratus, and others, and is recorded by a number of ear-witnesses on the lower part of the colossus itself in inscriptions which may be seen at the present day. Amenhotep, identified by the idle fancy of some Greek or Roman scholar with the Memnon of Homer, son of Tithonus and *The Dawn*, who led an army of Ethiopians to the assistance of Priam of Troy against the Greeks, was regarded as a god, and to hear the sound was not only to witness a miracle, but to receive an assurance of the god's favourable regard. For the statue did not emit a sound—the god did not speak—every day. Sometimes travellers had to depart disappointed altogether, sometimes they had to make a second, a third, or a fourth visit before hearing the desired voice. But still it was a frequent phenomenon; and a common soldier has recorded the fact on the base of the statue, that he heard it no fewer than thirteen times. The origin of the sound, the time when it began to be heard, and the circumstances under which it ceased, are all more or less doubtful. Some of those exceedingly clever persons who find priestcraft everywhere, think that the musical sound was the effect of human contrivance, and explain the whole matter to their entire satisfaction by "the jugglery of the priests." The priests either found a naturally vocal piece of rock, and intentionally made the statue out of it; or they cunningly introduced a pipe into the interior of the figure, by which they could make musical notes issue from the mouth at their pleasure. It is against this view that in the palmy days of the Egyptian hierarchy, the vocal character of the statue was entirely unknown; we have no evidence of the sound having been heard earlier than the time of Strabo (B.C. 25-10), when Egypt was in the possession of the Romans, and the priests had little influence. Moreover, the theory is disproved by the fact that, during the two centuries of the continuance of the marvel, there were occasions when Memnon was obstinately silent, though the priests must have been most anxious that he should speak, while there were others when he spoke freely, though they must have been perfectly indifferent. The wife of a prefect of Egypt made two visits to the spot to no purpose ; and the Empress Sabina, wife of the Emperor Hadrian, was, on her first visit, also disappointed, so that "her venerable features were inflamed with anger." On the other hand, as already mentioned, a common Roman soldier heard the sound thirteen times.

With respect to the time when, and the circumstances under which, the phenomenon first showed itself, all that can be said is, that the earliest literary witness to the fact is Strabo (about B.C. 25); that the earliest of the inscriptions on the base that can be dated belongs to the reign of Nero, and that it is at least questionable whether the sound ever issued from the stone before B.C. 27. In that year there was an earthquake which wrought great havoc at Thebes ; and it is an acute suggestion, that it was this earthquake which at once shattered the upper part of the colossus, and so affected the remainder of the block of stone that it became vocal then for the first time. For centuries the figure remained a *torso*, and it was while a *torso* that it emitted the musical tone—

"*Dimidio* magicae resonabant Memnone chordae."

After a long interval of years, probably about A.D. 174, that restoration of the monument took place which is to be seen to the present day. Five blocks of stone, rudely shaped into a form like that of the unharmed colossus, were emplaced upon the *torso*, which was thus reconstructed. The intention was to do Memnon honour; but the effect was to strike him dumb. The peculiar condition of the stone, which the earthquake had superinduced, and which made it vocal, being changed by the new arrangement, the sound ceased, and has been heard no more.

It is a fact well known to scientific persons at the present day, that musical sounds are often given forth both by natural rocks and by quarried masses of stone, in consequence of a sudden change of temperature. Baron Humboldt, writing on the banks of the Oronooko, says: "The granite rock on which we lay is one of those where travellers have heard from time to time, towards sunrise, subterraneous sounds, resembling those of the organ. The missionaries call these stones *loxas de musica*. 'It is witchcraft,' said our young Indian pilot. . . . But the existence of a phenomenon that seems to depend on a certain state of the atmosphere cannot be denied. The shelves of rock are full of very narrow and deep crevices. They are heated during the day to about 50°. I often found their temperature during the night at 39°. It may easily be conceived that the difference of temperature between the subterraneous and the external air would attain its *maximum* about sunrise." Analogous phenomena occur among the sandstone rocks of El Nakous, in Arabia Petræa, near Mount Maladetta in the Pyrenees, and (perhaps) in the desert between Palestine and Egypt. "On the fifth day of my journey," says the accomplished author of 'Eothen,' "the sun growing fiercer and fiercer, . . . as I drooped my head under his fire, and closed my eyes against the glare that surrounded me, I slowly fell asleep—for how many minutes or moments I cannot tell—but after a while I was gently awakened by a peal of church bells—my native bells—the innocent bells of Marlen that never before sent forth their music beyond the Blagdon hills! My first idea naturally was that I still remained fast under the power of a dream. I roused myself, and drew aside the silk that covered my eyes, and plunged my bare face into the light. Then at least I was well enough awakened, *but still those old Marlen bells rang on*, not ringing for joy, but properly, prosily, steadily, merrily ringing 'for church.' *After a while the sound died away slowly;* it happened that neither I nor any of my party had a watch to measure the exact time of its lasting; but it seemed to me that about ten minutes had passed before the bells ceased."[1] The gifted writer proceeds to give a metaphysical explanation of the phenomena; but it may be questioned whether he did not hear actual musical sounds, emitted by the rocks that lay beneath the sands over which he was moving.

And similar sounds have been heard when the stones that sent them forth were quarried blocks, no longer in a state of nature, but shaped by human tools, and employed in architecture. Three members of the French Expedition, MM. Jomard, Jollois, and Devilliers, were together in the granite cell which forms the centre of the palace-temple of Karnak, when, according to their own account, they "heard a

---

[1] Kinglake, "Eothen," pp. 188, 189.

sound, resembling that of a chord breaking, issue from the blocks at sunrise." Exactly the same comparison is employed by Pausanias to describe the sound that issued from "the vocal Memnon."

On the whole, we may conclude that the musical qualities of his remarkable colossus were unknown alike to the artist who sculptured the monument and to the king whom it represented. To them, in its purpose and object, it belonged, not to Music, but wholly to the sister art of Architecture. "The Pair" sat at one extremity of an avenue leading to one of the great palace-temples reared by Amenhotep III.— a palace-temple which is now a mere heap of sandstone, "a little roughness in the plain." The design of the king was, that this grand edifice should be approached by a *dromos*, or paved way, eleven hundred feet long, which should be flanked on either side by nine similar statues, placed at regular intervals along the road, and all representing himself. The egotism of the monarch may perhaps be excused on account of the grandeur of his idea, which we nowhere else find repeated, avenues of sphinxes being common in Egypt, and avenues of sitting human *life-size* figures not unknown to Greece, but the history of art containing no other instance of an avenue of colossi.

Another of Amenhotep's palace-temples has been less unkindly treated by fortune than the one just mentioned. The temple of Luxor, or El-Uksur, on the eastern bank of the river, about a mile and a half to the south of the great temple of Karnak, is a magnificent edifice to this day; and though some portions of it, and some of its most remarkable features, must be assigned to Rameses II., yet still it is, in the main, a construction of Amenhotep's, and must be regarded as being, even if it stood alone, sufficient proof of his eminence as a builder. The length of the entire building is about eight hundred feet, the breadth varying from about one hundred feet to two hundred. Its general arrangement comprised, first, a great court, at a different angle from the rest, being turned so as to face Karnak. In front of this stood two colossal statues of the founder, together with two obelisks, one of which has been removed to France, and now adorns the centre of the Place de la Concorde at Paris. Behind this was a great pillared hall, of which only the two central ranges of columns are now standing. Still further back were smaller halls and numerous apartments, evidently meant for the king's residence, rather than for a temple or place exclusively devoted to worship. The building is remarkable for its marked affectation of irregularity. "Not only is there a considerable angle in the direction of the axis of the building, but the angles of the courtyards are hardly ever right angles; the pillars are variously spaced, and pains seem to have been gratuitously taken to make it as irregular as possible in nearly every respect."[1]

Besides this grand edifice, Amenhotep built two temples at Karnak to Ammon and Maut, embellished the old temple of Ammon there with a new propylon, raised temples to Kneph, or Khnum, at Elephantine and built a shrine to contain his own image at Soleb in Nubia, another shrine at Napata, and a third at

[1] Fergusson, "Handbook of Architecture," vol. i. p. 234.

Sedinga. He left traces of himself at Semneh, in the island of Konosso, on the rocks between Philæ and Assouan, at El-Kaab, at Toora near Memphis, at Silsilis, and at Sarabit-el-Khadim in the Sinaitic peninsula. He was, as M. Lenormant remarks, " un prince essentiellement batisseur." The scale and number of his works are such as to indicate unremitting attention to sculpture and building during the entire duration of his long reign of thirty-six years.

On the other hand, as a general he gained little distinction. He maintained, indeed, the dominion over Syria and Western Mesopotamia, which had been established by Thothmes III., and his cartouche has been found at Arban on the Khabour ; but there is no appearance of his having made any additional conquests in this quarter. The subjected peoples brought their tribute regularly, and the neighbouring nations, whether Hittites, Assyrians, or Babylonians, gave him no trouble. The dominion of Egypt over Western Asia had become " an accomplished fact," and was generally recognized by the old native kingdoms. It did not extend, however, beyond Taurus and Niphates towards the north, or beyond the Khabour eastward or southward, but remained fixed within the limits which it had attained under the Third Thothmes.

The only quarter in which Amenhotep warred was towards Ethiopia. He conducted in person several expeditions up the valley of the Nile, against the negro tribes of the Soudan. But these attacks were not so much wars as raids, or razzias. They were not made with the object of advancing the

Egyptian frontier, or even of extending Egyptian influence, but partly for the glorification of the monarch, who thus obtained at a cheap rate the credit of military successes, and partly—probably mainly—for the material gain which resulted from them through the capture of highly valuable slaves. The black races have always been especially sought for this purpose, and were in great demand in the Egyptian slave-market : ladies of rank were pleased to have for their attendants negro boys, whom they dressed in a fanciful manner; and the court probably indulged in a similar taste. Amenhotep's aim was certainly rather to capture than to kill. In one of his most successful raids the slain were only three hundred and twelve, while the captives consisted of two hundred and five men, two hundred and fifty women, and two hundred and eighty-five children, or a total of seven hundred and forty ; and the proportion in the others was similar. The trade of slave hunting was so lucrative that even a Great King could not resist the temptation of having a share in its profits.

When Amenhotep was not engaged in hunting men his favourite recreation was to indulge in the chase of the lion. On one of his scarabæi he states that between his first and his tenth year he slew with his own hand one hundred and ten of these ferocious beasts. Later on in his reign he presented to the priests who had the charge of the ancient temple of Karnak a number of live lions, which he had probably caught in traps. The lion was an emblem both of Horus and of Tum, and may, when tamed, have been assigned a part in religious processions. It is uncertain what was Amenhotep's hunting-ground; but the large number of his victims makes it probable that the scene of his exploits was Mesopotamia rather than any tract bordering on Egypt: since lions have always been scarce animals in North-Eastern Africa, but abounded in Mesopo-

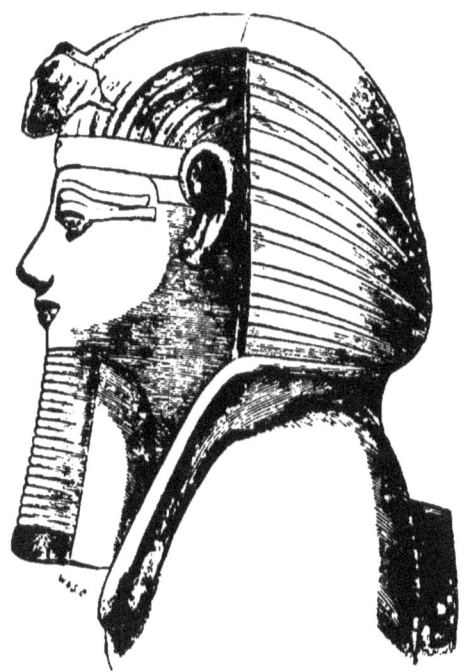

BUST OF AMENHOTEP III.

tamia even much later than the time of Amenhotep, and are "not uncommon" there even at the present day. We may suppose that he had a hunting pavilion at Arban, where one of his scarabs has been found, and from that centre beat the reed-beds and jungles of the Khabour.

In person, Amenhotep III. was not remarkable. His features were good, except that his nose was somewhat too much rounded at the end; his expression was pensive, but resolute; his forehead high, his upper lip short, his chin a little too prominent. He left behind him a character for affectionateness, kindliness, and generosity. Some historians have reproached him with being too much under female influence; and certainly in the earlier portion of his reign he deferred greatly to his mother, Mutemua, and in the latter portion to his wife, Tii or Taia; but there is no evidence that any evil result followed, or that these princesses did not influence him for good. It is too much taken for granted by many writers that female influence is corrupting. No doubt it is so in some cases; but it should not be forgotten that there are women whom to have known is "a liberal education." Mutemua and Tii may have been of the number.

XIV.

KHUENATEN AND THE DISK-WORSHIPPERS.

On the death of Amenhotep III., his son, Amenhotep IV., mounted the throne. Left by Amenhotep III. to the guardianship of his mother, Tii, who was of some entirely foreign race, he embraced a new form of religion, which she appears to have introduced, and shocked the Egyptians by substituting, so far as he found to be possible, this new creed for the old polytheism of the country. The heresy of Amenhotep IV. has been called " Disk-worship ; " and he, and the next two or three kings, are known in Egyptian history as "the Disk-worshippers." It is difficult to discover what exactly was the belief professed. Externally, it consisted, primarily, in a marked preference of a single one of the Egyptian gods over all the others, and a certain hatred or contempt for the great bulk of the deities composing the old Pantheon. Thus far it resembled the religion which Apepi, the last " Shepherd King," had endeavoured to introduce ; but the new differed from the old reformation in the matter of the god selected for special honour. Apepi had sought to turn the Egyptians away from all other worships except the worship of Set ; Amenhotep desired their universal adhesion to the worship of

Aten. Aten, in Egyptian theology, had hitherto represented a particular aspect or character of Ra, "the sun"—that aspect which is expressed by the phrase, "the solar disk." How it was possible to keep Aten distinct from the other sun-gods, Ra, Khepra, Tum, Shu, Mentu, Osiris, and Horus or Harmachis, is a puzzle to moderns; but it seems to have been a difficulty practically overcome by the Egyptians, to whom it did not perhaps even present itself as a difficulty at all. Disk-worship consisted then, primarily, in an undue exaltation of this god, who was made to take the place of Ammon-Ra in the Pantheon, and was ordinarily represented by a circle with rays proceeding from it, the rays mostly terminating in hands, which frequently presented the symbols of life and health and strength to the worshipper.

What was the inward essence of the religion? Was it simple sun-worship—the adoration of the visible material sun—considered as the ruling and vivifying power in the universe, whence heat and light, and so life, proceeded? Of all the forms of nature worship this was the most natural, and in the old world it was widely spread. Men adored the orb of day as the grandest object which nature presented to them, as the great quickener of all things upon the earth, the cause of germination and growth, of fruitage and harvest, the dispenser to man of ten thousand blessings, the sustainer of his life and health and happiness. With some the worship was purely and wholly material—the sun was viewed as a huge mass of fiery matter, uninformed by any animate life, unintelligent, impersonal; but with others, sun-worship was something higher than this: the orb of day was regarded as informed by a good, wise, bright, beneficent Spirit, which lived in it, and worked through it, and was the true benefactor of mankind and sustainer of life and

KHUENATEN WORSHIPPING THE SOLAR DISK.

of the universe. Sun-worship of this latter kind was no mean form of natural religion. If not purged from the debasing element of materialism, if not incompatible with a certain kind of polytheism, it is yet consistent with the firmest belief in the absolute supremacy of one God over all others, with the conception of that God as all-wise, all-powerful, pure, holy, kind, loving, and with the entire devotion of the worshipper to Him exclusively. And this latter form of sun-worship was, quite conceivably, the religion of the "Disk worshippers." "Aten" is probably the same as "Adon," the root of Adonis and Adonai, and has the signification of "Lord"—a term implying personality, and when used specially of one Being, implying absolute mastery and lordship, an exclusive right to worship, homage, and devotion. It is not unlikely that the "Disk-worshippers" were drawn on towards their monotheistic creed by the presence in Egypt at the time of a large monotheistic population, the descendants of Joseph and his brethren, who by this time had multiplied greatly, and must have attracted attention, from their numbers and from the peculiarity of their tenets. A historian of Egypt remarks that "curious parallels might be drawn between the external forms of the worship of the Israelites in the desert and those set up by the Disk-worshippers at Tel-el-Amarna ; portions of the sacred furniture, as the 'table of shewbread,' described in the Book of Exodus as placed within the Tabernacle, are repeated among the objects belonging to the worship of Aten, and do not occur among the representations of any other epoch." He further notes that the commencement of the persecution of the Israelites in Egypt coincides nearly with the downfall of the "Disk-worshippers" and the return of the Egyptians to their old creed, as if the captive race had been involved in the discredit and the odium which attached to Amenhotep and his immediate successors on account of their religious reformation.

The aversion of the " Disk-worshippers " to the old Egyptian religion was shown (1) in the change of his own name which the new monarch made soon after his accession, from Amenhotep to Khu-en-Aten, whereby he cleared himself from any connection with the old discarded head of the Pantheon, and associated himself with the new supreme god, Aten ; (2) in the obliteration of the name of Ammon from monuments ; and (3) in the removal of the seat of government from the site polluted by Ammon-worship and polytheism to a new site at Tel-el-Amarna, where Aten alone was worshipped and alone represented in the temples. The enmity, however, was not indiscriminate. Amenhotep took for one of his titles the epithet, " Mi-Harmakhu," or " beloved by Harmachis," probably because he could look on Harmachis, a purely sun-god, as a form of Aten ; and to this god he erected an obelisk at Silsilis. His monumental war upon the old religion seems also not to have been general, but narrowly circumscribed, being, in fact, confined to the erasure of Ammon's name, especially at Thebes, and the mutilation of his form in a few instances ; but there does not appear to have been any such general iconoclasm practised by the " Disk-worshippers " as by the " Shepherd Kings," or any such absolute requirement that " one god alone should be worshipped in all the land " as was put forth by Apepi. The " Disk-worshippers " did not so much attempt to change the religion of Egypt as to establish for themselves a peculiar court-religion of a pure and elevated character.

It has been remarked above that the motive power

which brought about the religious revolution is probably to be found in the powerful influence and the peculiar views of the queen mother, Tii or Taia. This princess was of foreign origin; her complexion was fair, her eyes blue, her hair flaxen, her cheeks rosy; she probably brought her "disk-worship" with her from her own country, whether it were Syria, or Arabia, or any other. Already in the lifetime of her husband, Amenhotep III., she had prevailed on him, as his wives prevailed on Solomon (1 Kings xi. 4-8), to allow her the free exercise of her own religion, and to provide her with the means of carrying it on with all proper pomp and ceremony. At her instance, Amenhotep III. constructed a great lake or basin, more than a mile long and a thousand feet broad, to be made use of for religious purposes on the queen's special festival day. It was proper on that festival day that "the barge of the most beautiful Disk" should perform a voyage on a sheet of water in the presence of his worshippers—a voyage probably representing the course of the sun through the heavens during the year. There is evidence that this festival was kept on the sixteenth day of the month Athor, in the eleventh year of Amenhotep III., and that the king himself took part in it.

So far, Queen Taia succeeded in introducing her religion into Egypt while her husband was alive. At his death she found herself regent for her son, or, at any rate, associated with him upon the throne, and saw that a fresh opportunity for pushing her religious views offered itself. Amenhotep IV. was of a most extraordinary *physique* and physiognomy. His appearance was rather that of a woman than of a man; he had a slanting forehead, a long aquiline nose, a flexible projecting mouth, and a strongly developed chin. His neck, which is represented as most unusually long, seems scarcely equal to the support of

HEAD OF AMENHOTEP IV. (KHUENATEN).

his head; and his spindle shanks seem ill adapted to sustain the weight of his over-corpulent frame. He readily yielded himself to his mother's influence, and completed her work in the manner which has been already described. As Thebes opposed itself to his reforms, he deserted it, withdrew his court to Tel-el-Amarna, and there raised the temples, palaces, and other monuments, in a "very advanced" style of art, which may be seen at the present day.

Amenhotep also introduced certain changes into the court ceremonial. He surrounded himself with officials of foreign race, probably kinsmen of his mother, and required from them an open display of submission and servility which Egyptian courts had not witnessed previously. An abject prostration was enforced on all, while the king posed before his courtiers as a benevolent god, who showered down his gifts upon them from a superior sphere, since his greatness did not permit a closer contact. He was himself the "Light of the Solar Disk," an *apaugasma*, or "Light proceeding from Light;" it behoved him to imitate the Sun-god, and perpetually bestow his gifts on men, but it behoved them to veil their faces from his radiance and receive his bounty prostrate in the dust beneath him.

The peculiar views of Khuen-Aten, or Amenhotep IV., were maintained by the two or three succeeding kings, who had short and disturbed reigns. After them there arose a king called Horus, or Har-em-hebi, who utterly swept away the "Disk-worshippers," ruined their new city, obliterated their names, mutilated their monuments, and restored the ancient religion of the Egyptians to its former place as the religion, not only of the people, but of the court. Henceforth, what was called "heresy" ceased to show itself in the land.

XV.

BEGINNING OF THE DECLINE OF EGYPT.

THE internal troubles connected with the "Diskworship" had for about forty years distracted the attention of the Egyptians from their Asiatic possessions; and this circumstance had favoured the development of a highly important power in Western Asia. The Hittites, whose motto was "reculer pour mieux sauter," having withdrawn themselves from Syria during the time of the Egyptian attacks, retaining, perhaps, their hold on Carchemish (Jerabus), but not seeking to extend themselves further southward, took heart of grace when the Egyptian expeditions ceased, and descending from their mountain fastnesses to the Syrian plains and vales, rapidly established their dominion over the regions recently conquered by Thothmes I. and Thothmes III. Without absorbing the old native races, they reduced them under their sway, and reigned as lords paramount over the entire region between the Middle Euphrates and the Mediterranean, the Taurus range and the borders of Egypt. The chief of the subject races were the Kharu, in the tract bordering upon Egypt; the Rutennu, in Central and Northern Palestine; and in Southern Cœlesyria, the Amairu or Amorites. The

Hittites themselves occupied the lower Cœlesyrian valley, and the tract reaching thence to the Euphrates. They were at this period so far centralized into a nation as to have placed themselves under a single monarch; and about the time when Egypt had recovered from the troubles caused by the "Disk-worshippers," and was again at liberty to look abroad, Saplal, Grand-Duke of Khita, a great and puissant sovereign, sat upon the Hittite throne.

Saplal's power, and his threatening attitude on the north-eastern border of Egypt, drew upon him the jealousy of Ramesses I., father of the great Seti, and (according to the prevalent tradition) founder of the "nineteenth dynasty." To defend oneself it is often best to attack, and Ramesses, taking this view, in his first or second year plunged into the enemy's dominions. He had the plea that Palestine and Syria, and even Western Mesopotamia, belonged of right to Egypt, which had conquered them by a long series of victories, and had never lost them by any defeat or disaster. His invasion was a challenge to Saplal either to fight for his ill-gotten gains, or to give them up. The Hittite king accepted the challenge, and a short struggle followed with an indecisive result. At its close peace was made, and a formal treaty of alliance drawn out. Its terms are unknown; but it was probably engraved on a silver plate in the languages of the two powers—the Egyptian hieroglyphics, and the now well-known Hittite picture-writing—and set up in duplicate at Carchemish and Thebes.

A brief pause followed the conclusion of the first

act of the drama. On the opening of the second act we find the *dramatis personæ* changed. Saplal and Ramesses have alike descended into the grave, and their thrones are occupied respectively by the son of the one and the grandson of the other. In Egypt, Seti - Menephthah I., the Sethos of Manetho, has succeeded his father, Ramesses I.; in the Hittite kingdom, Saplal has left his sceptre to his grandson Mautenar, the son of Marasar, who had probably died before his father. Two young and inexperienced princes confront one the other in the two neighbour lands, each distrustful of his rival, each covetous of glory, each hopeful of success if war should break out. True, by treaty the two kings were friends and allies — by treaty the two nations were bound to abstain from all aggression by the one upon the other: but such bonds are like the "green withes" that bound Samson, when the desire to burst them seizes those upon whom they have been placed. Seti and Mautenar were at war before the latter had been on the throne a year, and their swords were at one another's throats. Seti was, apparently, the aggressor. We find him at the head of a large army in the heart of Syria before we could have supposed that he had had time to settle himself comfortably in his father's seat.

Mautenar was taken unawares. He had not expected so prompt an attack. He had perhaps been weak enough to count on his adversary's good faith, or, at any rate on his regard for appearances. But Seti, as a god upon earth, could of course do no wrong, and did not allow himself to be trammelled by the moral laws that were binding upon ordinary mortals. He boldly rushed into war at the first possible moment, crossed the frontier, and having chastised the Shasu, who had recently made an invasion of his territory, fell upon the Kharu, or Southern Syrians, and gave them a severe defeat near Jamnia in the Philistine country. He then pressed forward into the country of the Rutennu, overcame them in several pitched battles, and, assisted by a son who fought constantly at his side, slaughtered them almost to extermination. His victorious progress brought him, after a time, to the vicinity of Kadesh, the important city on the Orontes which, a century earlier, had been besieged and taken by the Great Thothmes. Kadesh was at this time in possession of the Amorites, who were tributary to the Khita (Hittites) and held the great city as their subject allies. Seti, having carefully concealed his advance, came upon the stronghold suddenly, and took its defenders by surprise. Outside the city peaceful herdsmen were pasturing their cattle under the shade of the trees, when they were startled by the appearance of the Egyptian monarch, mounted on his war-chariot drawn by two prancing steeds. At once all was confusion: every one sought to save himself; the herds with their keepers fled in wild panic, while the Egyptians plied them with their arrows. But the garrison of the town resisted bravely: a portion sallied from the gates and met Seti in the open field, but were defeated with great slaughter; the others defended themselves behind the walls. But all was in vain. The disciplined troops of Egypt stormed the key of Northern Syria, and the whole Orontes valley lay open to the conqueror.

Hitherto the Hittites had not been engaged in the struggle. Attacked at a disadvantage, unprepared, they had left their subject allies to make such resistance as they might find possible, and had reserved themselves for the defence of their own country. Mautenar had, no doubt, made the best preparations of which circumstances admitted—he had organized his forces in three bodies, "on foot, on horseback, and in chariots." At the head of them, he gave battle to the invaders so soon as they attacked him in his own proper country, and a desperate fight followed, in which the Egyptians, however, prevailed at last. The Hittites received a "great overthrow." The song of triumph composed for Seti on the occasion declared: "Pharaoh is a jackal which rushes leaping through the Hittite land; he is a grim lion exploring the hidden ways of all regions; he is a powerful bull with a pair of sharpened horns. He has struck down the Asiatics; he has thrown to the ground the Khita; he has slain their princes; he has overwhelmed them in their own blood; he has passed among them as a flame of fire; he has brought them to nought."

The victory thus gained was followed by a treaty of peace. Mautenar and Seti agreed to be henceforth friends and allies, Southern Syria being restored to Egypt, and Northern Syria remaining under the dominion of the Hittites, probably as far as the sources of the Orontes river. A line of communication must, however, have been left open between Egypt and Mesopotamia, for Seti still exercised authority over the Naïri, and received tribute from their chiefs. He was also, by the terms of the treaty, at liberty to make war on the nations of the Upper Syrian coast, for we find him reducing the Tahai, who bordered on Cilicia, without any disturbance of his relations with Mautenar. The second act in the war between the Egyptians and the Hittites thus terminated with an advantage to the Egyptians, who recovered most of their Asiatic possessions, and had, besides, the prestige of a great victory.

The third act was deferred for a space of some thirty-five years, and fell into the reign of Ramesses II., Seti's son and successor. Before giving an account of it, we must briefly touch the other wars of Seti, to show how great a warrior he was, and mention one further fact in his warlike policy indicative of the commencement of Egypt's decline as a military power. Seti, then, had no sooner concluded his peace with the great power of the North, than he turned his arms against the West and South, invading, first of all, " the blue-eyed, fair-skinned nation of the Tahennu," who inhabited the North African coast from the borders of Egypt to about Cyrene, and engaging in a sharp contest with them. The Tahennu were a wild, uncivilized people, dwelling in caves, and having no other arms besides bows and arrows. For dress they wore a long cloak or tunic, open in front; and they are distinguished on the Egyptian monuments by wearing two ostrich feathers and having all their hair shaved excepting one large lock, which is plaited and hangs down on the right side of the head. This unfortunate people could make only a poor resistance to the Egyptian trained infantry and powerful chariot force. They were completely defeated in a pitched battle; numbers of the chiefs were made prisoners, while the people generally fled to their caves, where they remained hidden, "like jackals, through fear of the king's majesty." Seti, having struck terror into their hearts, passed on towards the south, and fiercely chastised the Cushites on the Upper Nile, who during the war with the Hittites had given trouble, and showed themselves inclined to shake off the Egyptian yoke. Here again he was successful; the negroes and Cushites submitted after a short struggle; and the Great King returned to his capital victorious on all sides—" on the south to the arms of the Winds, and on the north to the Great Sea."

Seti was not dazzled with his military successes. Notwithstanding his triumphs in Syria, he recognized the fact that Egypt had much to fear from her Asiatic neighbours, and could not hope to maintain for long her aggressive attitude in that quarter. Without withdrawing from any of the conquered countries, while still claiming their obedience and enforcing the payment of their tributes, he began to made preparation for the changed circumstances which he anticipated by commencing the construction of a long wall on his north-eastern frontier, as a security against invasion from Asia. This wall began at Pelusium, and was carried across the isthmus in a south-westerly direction by Migdol to Pithom, or Heroopolis, where the long line of lagoons began, which were connected with the upper end of the Red Sea. It recalls to the mind of the historical student the many ramparts raised by nations, in their decline, against aggressive foes—as the Great Wall of China, built to keep off the Tartars; the Roman wall between the Rhine and Danube, intended to restrain the advance of the German tribes; and the three Roman ramparts in Great Britain, built to protect the Roman province from its savage northern neighbours. Walls of this kind are always signs of weakness; and when Seti began, and Ramesses II. completed, the rampart of Egypt, it was a confession that the palmy days of the empire were past, and that henceforth she must look forward to having to stand, in the main, on the defensive.

Before acquiescing wholly in this conclusion, Ramesses II., who, after reigning conjointly with his father for several years, was now sole king, resolved on a desperate and prolonged effort to re-assert for Egypt that dominant position in Western Asia which she had held and obtained under the third Thothmes. Mautenar, the adversary of Seti, appears to have died, and his place to have been taken by his brother, Khita-sir, a brave and enterprizing monarch. Khita-sir, despite the terms of alliance on which the Hittites stood with Egypt, had commenced a series of intrigues with the nations bordering on Upper Syria, and formed a confederacy which had for its object to resist the further progress of the Egyptians, and, if possible, to drive them from Asia. This confederacy embraced the Naïri, or people of Western Mesopotamia, reckoned by the Egyptians among their subjects; the Airatu or people of Aradus; the Masu or inhabitants of the Mous Masius; the Leka, perhaps Lycians; the inhabitants of Carchemish, of Kadesh on the Orontes, of

Aleppo, Anaukasa, Akarita, &c.—all warlike races, and accustomed to the use of chariots. Khitasir's proceedings, having become known to Ramesses, afforded ample grounds for a rupture, and quite justified him in pouring his troops into Syria, and doing his best to meet and overcome the danger which threatened him. Unaware at what point his enemy would elect to meet him, he marched forward cautiously, having arranged his troops in four divisions, which might mutually support each other. Entering the Cœlesyrian valley from the south, he had proceeded as far as the lake of Hems, and neighbourhood of Kadesh, before he received any tidings of the position taken up by the confederate army. There his troops captured two of the enemy's scouts, and on questioning them were told that the Hittite army had been at Kadesh, but had retired on learning the Egyptian's advance and taken up a position near Aleppo, distant nearly a hundred miles to the north-east. Had Ramesses believed the scouts, and marched forward carelessly, he would have fallen into a trap, and probably suffered defeat; for the whole confederate army was massed just beyond the lake, and there lay concealed by the embankment which blocks the lake at its lower end. But the Egyptian king was too wary for his adversary. He ordered the scouts to be examined by scourging, to see if they would persist in their tale, whereupon they broke down and revealed the true position of the army. The battle had thus the character of a regular pitched engagement, without surprise or other accident on either side. Khitasir, finding himself foiled, quitted his ambush, and marched openly against the

Egyptians, with his troops marshalled in exact and orderly array, the Hittite chariots in front with their lines carefully dressed, and the auxiliaries and irregulars on the flanks and rear. Of the four divisions of the Egyptian army, one seems to have been absent, probably acting as a rear-guard; Ramesses, with one, marched down the left bank of the stream, while the two remaining divisions proceeded along the right bank, a slight interval separating them. Khitasir commenced the fight by a flank movement to the left, which brought him into collision with the extreme Egyptian right, "the brigade of Ra," as it was called, and enabled him to engage that division separately. His assault was irresistible. " Foot and horse of King Ramesses," we are told, "gave way before him," the " brigade of Ra " was utterly routed, and either cut to pieces or driven from the field. Ramesses, informed of this disaster, endeavoured to cross the river to the assistance of his beaten troops; but, before he could effect his purpose, the enemy had anticipated him, had charged through the Orontes in two lines, and was upon him. The adverse hosts met. The chariot of Ramesses, skilfully guided by his squire, Menna, seems to have broken through the front line of the Hittite chariot force; but his brethren in arms were less fortunate, and Ramesses found himself separated from his army, behind the front line and confronted by the second line of the hostile chariots, in a position of the greatest possible danger. Then began that Homeric combat, which the Egyptians were never tired of celebrating, between a single warrior on the one hand, and the host of the

BATTLE OF KADESH.

Hittites, reckoned at two thousand five hundred chariots, on the other, in which Ramesses, like Diomed or Achilles, carried death and destruction whithersoever he turned himself. "I became like the god Mentu," he is made to say; "I hurled the dart with my right hand, I fought with my left hand; I was like Baal in his fury against them. I had come upon two thousand five hundred pairs of horses; I was in the midst of them; but they were dashed in pieces before my steeds. Not one of them raised his hand to fight; their heart shrank within them; their limbs gave way, they could not hurl the dart, nor had they strength to thrust with the spear. As crocodiles fall into the water, so I made them fall; they tumbled headlong one over another. I killed them at my pleasure, so that not one of them looked back behind him, nor did any turn round. Each fell, and none raised himself up again."

The temporary isolation of the monarch, which is the main point of the heroic poem of Pentaour, and which Ramesses himself recorded over and over again upon the walls of his magnificent constructions, must no doubt be regarded as a fact; but it is not likely to have continued for more than a few minutes. The minutes may have seemed as hours to the king; and there may have been time for him to perform several exploits. But we may be sure that, when his companions found that he was lost to their sight, they at once made frantic efforts to recover him, dead or alive; they forced openings in the first Hittite chariot line, and sped to the rescue of their sovereign. He had, perhaps, already emptied many chariots of the second line, which was paralysed by his audacity ; and his companions found it easy to complete the work which he had begun. The broken second line turned and fled ; the confusion became general ; a headlong flight carried the entire host to the banks of the Orontes, into which some precipitated themselves, while others were forced into the water by their pursuers. The king of Khirabu (Aleppo) was among these, and was with great difficulty drawn out by his friends, exhausted and half dead, when he reached the eastern shore. But the great bulk of the Hittite army perished, either in the battle or in the river. Among the killed and wounded were Grabatasa, the charioteer of Khitasir ; Tarakennas, the commander of the cavalry; Rabsuna, another general ; Khirapusar, a royal secretary ; and Matsurama, a brother of the Hittite king.

On the next day the battle was renewed ; but, after a short time, Khitasir retired, and sent a humble embassy to the camp of his adversary to implore for peace. Ramesses held a council of war with his generals, and by their advice agreed to accept the submission made to him, and, without entering into any formal engagement, to withdraw his army and return to Egypt. It seems probable that his victory had cost him dear, and that he was not in a condition to venture further from his resources, or to affront new dangers in a difficult, and to him unknown, region.

Experience tells us that it is one thing to gain a battle, quite another to be successful in the result of a long war. Whatever glory Ramesses obtained by the battle of Kadesh, and the other victories which he claims to have won in the Syrian campaigns of several succeeding years, it is certain that he completely failed to break the power of the Hittites, and that he was led in course of time to confess his failure, and to adopt a policy of conciliation towards the people which he found himself unable to subdue. Sixteen years after the battle of Kadesh he concluded a solemn treaty with Khitasir, which was engraved on silver and placed under the most sacred sanctions, whereby an exact equality was established between the high contracting powers. Each nation bound itself under no circumstances to attack the other; each promised to give aid to the other, if requested, in case of its ally being attacked; each pledged itself to the extradition both of criminals flying from justice and of any other subjects wishing to change their allegiance; each stipulated for an amnesty of offences in the case of all persons thus surrendered. Thirteen years after the conclusion of the treaty the close alliance between the two powers was further cemented by a marriage, which, by giving the two dynasties common interests, greatly strengthened the previously existing bond. Ramesses requested and received in marriage a daughter of Khitasir in the thirty-fourth year of his sole reign, when he had borne the royal title for forty-six years. He thus became the son-in-law of his former adversary, whose daughter was thenceforth recognized as his sole legitimate queen.

A considerable change in the relations of Egypt to her still remaining Asiatic dependencies accompanied this alteration in the footing upon which she stood with the Hittites. "The bonds of their subjection became much less strict than they had been under Thothmes III. ; prudential motives constrained the Egyptians to be content with very much less—with such acknowledgments, in fact, as satisfied their vanity, rather than with the exercise of any real power." From and after the conclusion of peace and alliance between Ramesses and Khitasir, Egyptian influence in Asia grew vague, shadowy, and discontinuous. At long intervals monarchs of more enterprize than the ordinary run asserted it, and a brief success generally crowned their efforts ; but, speaking broadly, we may say that her Asiatic dominion was lost, and that Egypt became once more an African power, confined within nearly her ancient limits.

If, from a military point of view, the decline of Egypt is to be dated from the reigns, partly joint reigns, of Seti I. and Ramesses II., from the standpoint of art the period must be pronounced the very apogee of Egyptian greatness. The architectural works of these two monarchs transcend most decidedly all those of all other Pharaohs, either earlier or later. No single work, indeed, of either king equals *in mass* either the First or the Second Pyramid ; but in number, in variety, in beauty, in all that constitutes artistic excellence, the constructions of Seti and Ramesses are unequalled, not only among Egyptian monuments, but among those of all other nations. Greece is, of course, unapproachable in the matter of sculpture, whether in the way of statuary, or of high or low relief ; but, apart from this, Egypt in her architectural works will challenge comparison with any country that ever existed, or any people that ever gave itself to the embodiment of artistic conceptions in stone or marble. And Egyptian architecture culminated under Seti and his son Ramesses. The greatest of all Seti's works was his pillared hall at Karnak, the most splendid single chamber that has ever been built by any architect, and, even in its ruins, one of the grandest sights that the world contains. Seti's hall is three hundred and thirty feet long, by one hundred and seventy feet broad, having thus an internal area of fifty-six thousand square feet, and covers, together with its walls and pylons, an area of eighty-eight thousand such feet, or a larger space than that covered by the Dom of Cologne, the largest of all the cathedrals north of the Alps. It was supported by one hundred and sixty-four massive stone columns, which were divided into three groups—twelve central ones, each sixty-six feet high and thirty-three feet in circumference, formed the main avenue down its midst; while on either side, two groups of sixty-one columns, each forty-two feet high and twenty-seven round, supported the huge wings of the chamber, arranged in seven rows of seven each, and two rows of six. The whole was roofed over with solid blocks of stone, the lighting being, as in the far smaller hall of Thothmes III., by means of a clerestory. The roof and pillars and walls were everywhere covered with painted bas-reliefs and hieroglyphics, giving great richness of effect, and constituting the whole building the most magnificent on which the eye of man has ever rested. Fergusson, the best modern authority on architecture, says of it : " No language can convey an idea of its beauty, and no artist has yet been able to reproduce its form so as to convey to those who have not seen it an idea of its grandeur. The mass of its central piers, illumined by a flood of light from the clerestory, and the smaller pillars of the wings gradually fading into obscurity, are so arranged and lighted as to convey an idea of infinite space ; at the same time the beauty and massiveness of the forms, and the brilliancy of their coloured decorations, all combine to stamp this as *the greatest of man's architectural works*, but such a one as it would be impossible to reproduce, except in such a climate, and in that individual style, in which and for which it was created."[1]

As Seti constructed the most wonderful of all the palatial buildings which Egypt produced, so he also constructed what is, on the whole, the most wonderful of the tombs. The pyramids impose upon us by their enormity, and astonish by the engineering skill shown in their execution ; but they embody a single simple idea ; they have no complication of parts, no elaboration of ornament ; they are taken in at a glance ; they do not gradually unfold themselves, or furnish a succession of surprises. But it is otherwise with the rock-tombs, whereof Seti's is the most magnificent. The rock-tombs are " gorgeous palaces, hewn out of the rock, and painted with all the decorations that could have been seen in palaces." They contain a succession of passages, chambers, corridors, staircases, and pillared halls, each further removed from the entrance than the last, and all covered with an infinite variety of the most finished and brilliant paintings. The tomb of Seti contains three pillared halls, respec-

[1] " History of Architecture," vol. i. pp. 119, 120.

tively twenty-seven feet by twenty-five, twenty-eight feet by twenty-seven, and forty-three feet by seventeen and a half; a large saloon with an arched roof, thirty feet by twenty-seven; six smaller chambers of different sizes; three staircases, and two long corridors. The whole series of apartments, from end to end of the tomb, is continuously ornamented with painted bas-reliefs. "The idea is that of conducting the king to the world of death. The further you advance into the tomb, the deeper you become involved in endless processions of jackal-headed gods, and monstrous forms of genii, good and evil; and the goddess of Justice, with her single ostrich feather; and barges carrying mummies, raised aloft over the sacred lake; and mummies themselves; and, more than all, everlasting convolutions of serpents in every possible form and attitude—human-legged, human-headed, crowned, entwining mummies, enwreathing or embraced by processions, extending down whole galleries, so that meeting the head of a serpent at the top of a staircase, you have to descend to its very end before you reach his tail. At last you arrive at the close of all—the vaulted hall, in the centre of which lies the immense alabaster sarcophagus, which ought to contain the body of the king. Here the processions, above, below, and around, reach their highest pitch—meandering round and round—white, and black, and red, and blue—legs and arms and wings spreading in enormous forms over the ceilings; and below lies the sarcophagus itself." [1]

[1] Adapted from Dean Stanley's "Sinai and Palestine," Introduction, p. xl.

The greatest of the works of Ramesses are of a different description, and are indicative of that inordinate vanity which is the leading feature of his character. They are colossal images of himself. Four of these, each seventy feet in height, form the façade of the marvellous rock-temple of Ipsambul—"the finest of its class known to exist anywhere"—and constitute one of the most impressive sights which the world has to offer. There stands the Great King, four times repeated, silent, majestic, superhuman—with features marked by profound repose and tranquillity, touched perhaps with a little scorn, looking out eternally on the grey-white Nubian waste, which stretches far away to a dim and distant horizon. Here, as you sit on the deep pure sand, you seem to see the monarch, who did so much, who reigned so long, who covered, not only Egypt, but Nubia and Ethiopia with his memorials. "You can look at his features inch by inch, see them not only magnified to tenfold their original size, so that ear and mouth and nose, and every link of his collar, and every line of his skin, sinks into you with the weight of a mountain; but those features are repeated exactly the same three times over—four times they once were, but the upper part of the fourth statue is gone. Look at them as they emerge—the two northern figures—from the sand which reaches up to their throats; the southernmost, as he sits unbroken, and revealed from the top of his royal helmet to the toe of his enormous foot."[1] Look at them, and remember that you have here portrait-statues of one of the greatest of the kings of the Old

---

[1] Stanley, "Sinai and Palestine," p. xlvii.

World, of the world that was "old" when Greece and Rome were either unborn or in their swaddling clothes; portrait-statues, moreover, of the king who, if either tradition or chronology can be depended on, was the actual great oppressor of Israel—the king who sought the life of Moses—the king from whom Moses fled, and until whose death he did not dare to return out of the land of Midian.

According to the almost unanimous voice of those most conversant with Egyptian antiquities, the "great oppressor" of the Hebrews was this Ramesses. Seti may have been the originator of the scheme for crushing them by hard usage, but, as the oppression lasted close upon eighty years (Ex. ii. 1 ; vii. 7), it must have covered at least two reigns, so that, if it began under Seti, it must have continued under his son and successor. The bricks found at Tel-el-Maskoutah show Ramesses as the main builder of Pithom (Pa-Tum), and the very name indicates that he was the main builder of Raamses (Pa-Ramessu). We must thus ascribe to him, at any rate, the great bulk of that severe and cruel affliction, which provoked Moses (Ex. ii. 12), which made Israel "sigh" and "groan" (ib. 23, 24), and on which God looked down with compassion (ib. iii. 7). It was he especially who "made their lives bitter in mortar, and in brick, and in all manner of service in the field"—service which was "with rigour." Ramesses was a builder on the most extensive scale. Without producing any single edifice so perfect as the "Pillared Hall of Seti," he was indefatigable in his constructive efforts, and no Egyptian king came up to him in this respect. The monuments show that he erected his buildings chiefly by forced labour, and that those employed on them were chiefly foreigners. Some have thought that the Hebrews are distinctly mentioned as employed by him on his constructions under the term "Aperu," or

HEAD OF SETI I.

"Aperiu"; but this view is not generally accepted. Still, "the name is so often used for foreign bondsmen engaged in the very work of the Hebrews, and especially during the oppression, that it is hard not to believe it to be a general term in which they are included, though it does not actually describe them."[1]

[1] Stuart Poole, "Cities of Egypt," p. 105.

The physiognomies of Seti I. and Ramesses II., as represented on the sculptures,[1] offer a curious con

BUST OF RAMESSES II.

[1] The mummy of Seti I. has been recently uncovered. It was in good condition, and is said to have revealed a face very closely resembling that of Ramesses II., with fine delicate features, and altogether of an elevated type. "The nose, mouth, chin, in short all the features," says M. Maspero, "are the same; but in the father they are more refined, more intelligent, more spiritual, than when reproduced in the son. Seti I. is, as it were, the idealized type of Ramesses II." (Letter of M. Maspero in *The Times* of July 23, 1886.) It may perhaps be doubted whether the shrunken mummy, 3300 years old, is better evidence of the living reality than the contemporary sculptures

trast. Seti's face is thoroughly African, strong, fierce, prognathous, with depressed nose, thick lips, and a heavy chin. The face of Ramesses is Asiatic. He has a good forehead, a large, well-formed, slightly aquiline nose, a well-shaped mouth, with lips that are not too full, a small delicate chin, and an eye that is thoughtful and pensive. We may conclude that Seti was of the true Egyptian race, with perhaps an admixture of more southern blood; while Ramesses, born of a Semitic mother, inherited through her Asiatic characteristics, and, though possessing less energy and strength of character than his father, had a more sensitive temperament, a wider range of taste, and a greater inclination towards peace and tranquillity. His important wars were all concluded within the limit of his twenty-first year, while his entire reign was one of sixty-seven years, during fifty of which he held the sole sovereignty. Though he left the fame of a great warrior behind him, his chief and truest triumphs seem to have been those of peace—the Great Wall for the protection of Egypt towards the east, with its strong fortresses and "store-cities," the canal which united the Nile with the Red Sea, and the countless buildings, excavations, obelisks, colossal statues, and other great works, with which he adorned Egypt from one end to the other.

CHAPTER XVI.

MENEPHTHAH I., THE PHARAOH OF THE EXODUS.

MENEPHTHAH, the thirteenth son and immediate successor of Ramesses II., came to the throne under circumstances which might at first sight have seemed favourable. Egypt was on every side at peace with her neighbours. The wall of Ramesses, and his treaty with the Hittites, cemented as it had been by a marriage, secured the eastern frontier. No formidable attack had ever yet fallen upon Egypt from the west or from the south, and so no danger could well be apprehended from those quarters. Internal tranquillity might not be altogether assured, so long as there was within the limits of Egypt a large subject population, suffering oppression and bitterly discontented with its lot. But this population was quite unwarlike, and had hitherto passively submitted itself to the will of its rulers, without giving any indication that it might become actively hostile. Menephthah, who was perhaps not more than five and twenty, may have been justified in looking forward to a long, quiet, and uneventful reign, during which he might indulge the natural apathy of his temper, or dream away life, like his fabled neighbours, the Lotus-Eaters.

Menephthah's features were soft and womanly. He

had a full but sleepy eye, a slightly aquiline nose, an extremely short upper-lip, a broad cheek, and a rounded chin. In character he was weak, irresolute, wanting in physical courage, yet, as so often happens with weak characters, harsh, oppressive, and treacherous. The monuments depict him as neither a soldier nor an administrator, but as "one whose mind was turned almost exclusively towards the chimeras of sorcery and magic," which he regarded as of the utmost importance. Still, had the times been quiet, had the prospect of tranquillity which seemed to lie before him on his accession been realized, he might perhaps have so conducted affairs as to bring neither discredit nor injury upon his country. But the circumstances of the period were against him. The unclouded prospect of his early years gave place, after a brief interval, to storm and tempest of the most fearful kind ; a terrible invasion carried fire and sword into the heart of his dominions ; and he had scarcely escaped this danger by meeting it in a way not very honourable to himself, when internal troubles broke out : a subject race, highly valued for services which it was compelled to render, insisted on quitting the land ; a great loss was incurred in an attempt to compel it to remain ; then open rebellion broke out in the weakened state ; and the reign, which had commenced under such fair auspices, terminated in calamity and confusion. Menephthah was quite incompetent to deal with the difficulties and complications wherewith he found himself surrounded ; he hesitated, temporized, made concessions, retracted them, and finally conducted Egypt to a catastrophe from which she did not recover for a generation.

LIBYAN INVASION OF EGYPT. 255

The first great trouble which disturbed the tranquillity of his reign was an invasion of his territories from the north-west. Hitherto, though no serious danger had ever threatened from this quarter, there had been frequent raids into Egypt on the part of the native Africans, and most of the more warlike of the

HEAD OF MENEPHTHAH.

Egyptian monarchs had regarded it as incumbent on them to lead from time to time expeditions into the region, for the purpose of weakening the wild tribes, Tahennu, Maxyes, and others, and inspiring them with a wholesome dread of the Egyptian power. Ramesses II. had on one occasion warred in this quarter, as already related, and had met with a certain amount of success. But since that time many years had passed. A new generation had grown up, which the Egyptians had allowed to remain unmolested, and which felt no fear of its quiet, peaceful, and industrious neighbours. Population had probably multiplied in the region, and the tribes began to feel stinted for room. Above all, new relations had been contracted between the old inhabitants of the tract and some other races, now for the first time heard of in authentic history, who had been brought into contact with them. A league of nations had become possible; and the force of the united league must have been considerable. Might not an actual conquest be effected, and the half-starved nomads of Marmarica and the Cyrenaica become the lords and masters of the rich plain, so long coveted, which adjoined upon their eastern frontier?

The leading spirit of the combination was a native African prince, Marmaiu, the son of Deid. Having determined on a serious invasion of Egypt, for the purpose of conquest, not of plunder, he first of all collected his native forces, Lubu, Tahennu, Mashuash, Kahaka, to the number of twenty-five or thirty thousand, and then purchased the services of a number of auxiliaries, who raised his force probably to a total of thirty-five or forty thousand men. A peculiar interest attaches to these auxiliaries. They consisted of contingents from five nations, whose names are read as Akausha, Luku, Tursha, Shartana or Shardana, and Sheklusha, and whom most modern historians of Egypt identify with the Achæans,

Laconians, Tyrsenians, Sardinians, and Sicilians. If these identifications are accepted—and they are at least plausible—we shall have to suppose that, as early as the fourteenth century B.C., the nations of Southern Europe were so far advanced as to launch fleets upon the Mediterranean, to enter into a regular league with an African prince, and in conjunction with him to make an attack on one of the chief civilized monarchies of the world, the old kingdom of the Pharaohs. We shall have to imagine the Achæans of the Peloponnese, a century before the time of Agamemnon, braving the perils of the Levant in their cockle-shells of ships, and not merely plundering the coasts, but landing large bodies of men on the North African shore to take part in a regular campaign. We shall have to picture to ourselves the Laconians—the people of Menelaüs— about the time of his grandfather, Atreus, or his great-grandfather, Pelops, similarly employed, and contending with the Pharaoh of the Exodus on the soil of the Delta. Nay, we shall have to antedate the rise of the Tyrsenians to naval greatness by about seven hundred years, and to suppose that the Sicels and Sardi, whom the Greeks and Romans found living the life of savages in Sicily and Sardinia, when they first visited their shores, about B.C. 750-600, were flourishing peoples and skilful navigators half a millennium earlier. The picture which we thus obtain of the ancient world is very surprising, and quite unlike anything that could be gathered from the literature of the Greeks; but it is not to be regarded as beyond the range of possibility, since nations are quite as apt to lapse from civilization into barbarism as to emerge out of barbarism into civilization. It is quite conceivable that the nations of South-Eastern Europe were more advanced in civilization and the arts of life about B.C. 1400–1300 than they are found to have been six centuries later, the false dawn having been succeeded by a time of darkness before the true dawn came.

However this may have been, it is certain that Menephthah, in the fifth year of his reign, had to meet a formidable, and apparently unprovoked, attack from a combination of nations, the like of which we do not again meet with in Egyptian history, either earlier or later. Marmaiu, son of Deid, led against him a confederate army, consisting of three principal tribes of the Tahennu—the Lubu (Libyans), the Mashuash (Maxyes), and the Kahaka—together with auxiliaries from five other tribes or peoples, the Akausha, the Luku, the Tursha, the Shartana, and the Sheklusha. The entire number of the army, as already stated, was probably not less than forty thousand; they had numerous chariots, and were armed with bows and arrows, cuirasses, and bronze or copper swords. They had skin tents, and brought with them their wives and children, with the intention of settling in Egypt, as the Hyksôs had done five hundred years earlier. They had also with them a considerable number of cattle, as bulls, oxen, and goats. The chiefs came provided with thrones, and both they and their officers had numerous drinking vessels of bronze, of silver, and of gold.

The attack was made on the western side of Egypt, towards the apex of the Delta. It was at first completely successful. The small frontier towns were taken by assault, and " turned into heaps of rubbish ;" the Delta was entered upon, and a position taken up in the nome of Paari-sheps, or Prosopis, which lay between the Canobic and Sebennytic branches of the Nile, commencing at the point of their separation. From this position Memphis and Heliopolis were alike menaced. Menephthah hastily fortified these cities, or rather, we must suppose, strengthened their existing defences. Meanwhile the Libyans and their allies ravaged the open country. " The like had not been seen," as the native scribe observes, "even in the times of the kings of Lower Egypt, when the plague (*i.e.* the Hyksôs power) was in the land, and the kings of Upper Egypt were unable to drive it out." Egypt was desolated ; its people " trembled like geese ;" the fertile lands were overrun and wasted ; the cities were pillaged ; even the harbours were in some cases ruined and destroyed. Menephthah for a time remained on the defensive, shut up within the walls of Memphis, whose god Phthah he viewed as his special protector. He made, however, strenuous efforts to gather together a powerful force ; his captains collected the native troops from the various provinces of Egypt, while he sent a number of emissaries into Asia, who were instructed to raise a large body of mercenaries in that quarter. At last all was ready, and Menephthah appointed the fourteenth day as that on which he would place himself at the head of his army and lead them in person against the enemy ; but, before the day came, his courage failed him. He " saw in a dream "—at least so he himself declares—"as it were a figure of the god Phthah, standing so as to prevent his advance;" and the figure said to him, "Stay where thou art, and let thy troops proceed against the enemy." So the pious king, in obedience to this convenient vision, remained secure behind the walls of Memphis, and sent his forces, native and mercenary, into the nome of Prosopis against the Libyans. The two armies joined battle on the 3rd of Epiphi (May 18), and a desperate engagement took place, in which, after six hours of hard fighting, the Egyptians were victorious, and the confederates suffered a severe defeat. Menephthah charges the Libyan chief with cowardice, but only because, after the battle was lost, he precipitately quitted the field, leaving behind him, not only his camp-equipage, but his throne, the ornaments of his wives, his bow, his quiver, and his sandals. The reproaches uttered recoil upon himself. Whose conduct is the more cowardly, that of the man who fights at the head of his troops for six hours against an enemy, probably more numerous, certainly better armed and better disciplined, and only quits the field when his forces are utterly overthrown and put to flight ; or that of one who avoids exposing himself to danger, and lurks behind the walls of a fortress while his soldiers are affronting wounds and death in the battlefield ? There is no evidence that Marmaiu, son of Deid, in the battle of Prosopis, conducted himself otherwise than as became a prince and a general ; there is abundant evidence that Menephthah, son of Ramesses, who declined to be present at the engagement, showed the white feather.

The defeat of Prosopis was decisive. Marmaiu lost in slain between eight thousand and nine thousand of his troops, or, according to another estimate, between twelve thousand and thirteen thousand. Above nine thousand were made prisoners. The tents, camp-equipage, and cattle, fell into the hands of the enemy. The expedition at once broke up and dispersed. Marmaiu returned into his own land with a shattered remnant of his grand army, and devoted himself to peaceful pursuits, or at any rate abstained from any further collision with the Egyptians. The mercenaries, whatever the races to which they in reality belonged, learned by experience the wisdom of leaving the Libyans to fight their own battles, and are not again found in alliance with them. The Akaiusha and Luku appear in Egyptian history no more. The Tursha and Sheklusha do not wholly disappear, but receive occasional mention among the races hostile to Egypt. As for the Shartana or Shardana, they were struck with so much admiration of the Egyptian courage and conduct, that they shortly afterwards entered the Egyptian service, and came to hold a place among the most trusted of the Egyptian troops.

Despite his cowardice in absenting himself from the battle of Prosopis under the transparent device of a divine vision, Menephthah took to himself the whole credit of the victory, and gloried in it as much as if he had really had a hand in bringing about the result. "The Lubu," he says, "were meditating to do evil in Egypt; they were as grasshoppers; every road was blocked by their hosts. Then I vowed to lead them captive. Lo, I vanquished them ; I slaughtered them, making a spoil of their country. I made the land of Egypt traversable once more ; I gave breath to those who were in the cities." Egyptian generals, like Roman poets, had to content themselves with complaining secretly, " Sic vos non vobis."

So far as we can tell, no long period elapsed between the expedition of Marmaiu, son of Deid, and the second great trouble in which Menephthah was involved. Moses must have returned to Egypt from his sojourn in Midian within a year or two of the death of Ramesses II., and cannot have allowed any very long time to elapse before he proffered the demand which he was divinely commissioned to make. Still, as he was timid, and a somewhat unwilling messenger, he may have delayed both his return and his first address to Pharaoh as long as he dared (Ex. iv. 19) ; and if the invasion of Marmaiu had begun before he had summoned courage to address Pharaoh a second time, he would then naturally wait until the danger was past, and the king could again be approached without manifest impropriety. In this case, the severe oppression of the Israelites, which followed the first application of Moses (Ex. v. 5-23) may have lasted longer than has generally been supposed ; and it may not have been till Menephthah's sixth or seventh year that the divine messenger became urgent, and began to press his request, and to show the signs and wonders which alone, as he had been told (Ex. vii. 2–4), would break the spirit of the king. The signs then followed each other at moderately short intervals, the entire series of the plagues not covering a longer space than about six months, from October till April. None of the plagues affected the king greatly except the last, through which he lost his own eldest son, a bereavement mentioned in an inscription. This loss, combined with the dread power shown in the infliction during one night of not less than a million of deaths, produced a complete revolution in the mind of the king, and made him as anxious at the moment to get rid of the Israelites out of his country as he had previously been anxious to retain them. So he called for Moses and Aaron by night and said, " Rise up, get you forth from among my people, both ye and the children of Israel, and go, serve the Lord, as ye have said. Also take your flocks and your herds, as ye have said, and be gone; and bless me also" (Ex. xii. 31, 32). Moses was prepared for the event, and had prepared his people. All were ready, with their loins girded, their sandals on their feet, and their staves in their hands; the word was given, and the exodus began. "The children of Israel journeyed from Rameses to Succoth, about six hundred thousand on foot that were men, beside children; and a mixed multitude went up also with them; and flocks, and herds, even very much cattle."

Hereupon the king's mind underwent another change. "Unstable as water," he was certain not to "excel." Learning that the Israelites, instead of marching away into the desert, had after reaching its edge turned southward, and were "entangled" in a corner of his territory, between high mountains on the one hand, and on the other the Red Sea, which then stretched far further to the north than at present, perhaps to Lake Timseh, at any rate as far as the "Bitter Lakes," he thought he saw an opportunity of following and recovering the fugitives, whose services as bondsmen he highly valued. Rapidly calling together such troops as were tolerably near at hand, he collected a considerable force of infantry and chariots—of the latter more than six hundred—and following upon the steps of the Hebrews, he caught them on the western shore of the Red Sea, encamped "between Migdol and the sea, over against Baal-Zephon." The exact spot cannot be fixed, on account of the alterations in the bed of the Red Sea, and the uncertainty of the ancient geography of Egypt, in which names so often repeat themselves ; but it was probably some part of the region that is now dry land, between Suez and the southern extremity of the Bitter Lakes. Here in high tides the sea and the lakes communicated ; but on the evening of Menephthah's arrival, an unusual ebb of the tide, co-operating with a "strong east wind" which held back the water of the Bitter Lakes, left the bed of the sea bare for a certain space ; and the Israelites were thus able to cross during the night from one side of the sea to the other. As morning dawned, Menephthah, once more carefully guarding his own person, sent his chariots in pursuit. The force entered on the slippery and dangerous ground, and advanced half-way ; but its progress was slow ; the chariot-wheels sank into the soft ooze, the horses slipped and floundered ; all was disorder and confusion. Before the troops could extricate themselves, the waters returned on either hand ; a high flow of the tide, the necessary consequence of a low ebb, brought in the whelming flood from the south-east ; a strong wind from the Mediterranean, drove down upon them the pent up waters of the Bitter Lakes from the north-west. The channel, which had lately been dry land, became once more sea, and the entire force that had entered it in pursuit of the Israelites perished. Safe on the opposite shore, the Israelites saw the utter destruction of their adversaries, whose dead bodies, driven before the gale, were cast up in hundreds upon the coast where they sate encamped. (Ex. xiv. 30).

The disaster paralyzed the monarch, and he made no further effort. If the loss was not great numerically, it affected the most important arm of the service, and it was the destruction of the very *élite* of the Egyptian troops. It was a blow in which the anger of the Egyptian gods may well have been seen by some, while others may have regarded it as a revelation of the incompetence of the monarch. The blow seems to have been followed, within a short time, by revolt. Menephthah's last monumental year is his eighth. A pretender to the crown arose in a certain Amon-mes, or Amon-meses, who contested the throne with Seti II., Menephthah's son, and succeeded in establishing himself as king ; but for many years there raged in Egypt, as so often happens when a state is suddenly weakened, civil war, bloodshed, and confusion.

The two dynasties that have last occupied us constitute the most brilliant period of Egyptian architecture ; for, as Fergusson, the latest historian of architecture, has said, the hall of Seti at Karnak is "the greatest of man's architectural works," the building to which it belongs is "the noblest effort of architectural magnificence ever produced by the hand of man," and the rock-cut temple of Ipsambul is "the finest of its class known to exist anywhere." These works combine enormous mass and size with a profusion of elaborate ornamentation. Covering nearly as much ground as the greatest of the pyramids, and containing equally enormous blocks of stone, the Theban palace-temples unite a wealth of varied ornamentation almost unparalleled among the edifices erected by man. Here are long avenues of sphinxes and colossi, leading to tall, tapering obelisks which shoot upwards like the pinnacles, towers, and spires of a modern cathedral, while beyond the obelisks are vistas of gateways and courts, of colonnades and pillared halls, that impress the beholder with a deep sense of the constructive imagination of the architect who could design them, no less than with admiration of the ruler whose resources were sufficient to make them realities.

Truly the Egyptians were, as Mr. Fergusson enthusiastically asserts, "the most essentially a building people of all those we are acquainted with, and the most generally successful in all that they attempted in this way. The Greeks, it is true, surpassed them in refinement and beauty of detail, and in the class of sculpture with which they ornamented their buildings, while the Gothic architects far excelled them in constructive cleverness; but with these exceptions, no other styles can be put into competition with them. At the same time, neither Grecian nor Gothic architects understood more perfectly all the gradations of art, and the exact character that should be given to every form and every detail. . . . They understood also better than any other nation, how to use sculpture in combination with architecture, and to make their colossi and avenues of sphinxes group themselves into parts of one great design, and at the same time to use historical paintings, fading by insensible degrees into hieroglyphics on the one hand, and into sculpture on the other, linking the whole together with the highest class of phonetic utterance. With the most brilliant colouring, they thus harmonized all these arts into one great whole, unsurpassed by anything the world has seen during the thirty centuries of struggle and aspiration that have elapsed since the brilliant days of the great kingdom of the Pharaohs."

Not only did architecture and the glyphic art reach such perfection during this period, but the arts of life made considerable progress. The royal costumes became suddenly most elaborate ; brilliant colours, costly armlets and bracelets, many-hued collars, complicated head-dresses, elegant sandals, jewels of price, gay sashes, and wigs with conventional adornment, came into vogue. Luxury was exhibited in the designs of the dwellings of the wealthy ; the grounds were laid out with formal courts and alleys, palms and vines adorned them, ponds and reservoirs gave freshness to the summer temperature, irrigation clothed the lawns with verdure. Inside, there was richly carved furniture covered with cushions of delicate stuffs, and adding the harmony of colour to the luxurious scene.

The horse, which had been introduced from Asia, helped in the march of extravagance and refinement; the chariot took the place of the palanquin, and there was a new opportunity for adornment in the trappings, as well as in the construction of light or heavy vehicles.

At the same time, letters made equal progress; men of wisdom devoted themselves to the preservation of the knowledge of the past, and to the composition of original works in history, divinity, poetry, correspondence, and practical philosophy, for the preservation of which a public library was established at Thebes under a competent director. The highest perfection thus reached in the arts of peace seems to have been coincident with an advance in sensualism; indecency in apparel was common, polygamy increased, woman lost her former degree of purity; cruelty and barbarism were more and more common in war; taxation bore heavily and without pity upon the lower orders, and the wretched fellahin were beaten by the severest of tyrants, the irresponsible tax-gatherer; women as well as men were stripped for the indignity and pain of the terrible bastinado; and even dead enemies were mutilated for the purpose of preserving evidence of their numbers.

XVII.

THE DECLINE OF EGYPT UNDER THE LATER RAMESSIDES.

THE troublous period which followed the death of Menephthah issued finally in complete anarchy. Egypt broke up into nomes, or cantons, the chiefs of which acknowledged no superior. It was as though in England, after centuries of centralized rule, the Heptarchy had suddenly returned and re-established itself. But even this was not the worst. The suicidal folly of internal division naturally provokes foreign attack; and it was not long before Aarsu, a Syrian chieftain, took advantage of the state of affairs in Egypt to extend his own dominion over one nome after another, until he had made almost the whole country subject to him. Then, at last, the spirit of patriotism awoke. Egypt felt the shame of being ruled by a foreigner of a race that she despised; and a prince was found after a time, a descendant of the Ramesside line, who unfurled the national banner, and commenced a war of independence. This prince, who bore the name of Set-nekht, or "Set the victorious," is thought by some to have been a son of Seti II., and so a grandson of Menephthah; but the evidence is insufficient to establish any such relationship. There is reason to believe that the blood of the nineteenth dynasty, of Seti I. and Ramesses II., ran in his veins; but no particular relationship to any former monarch can be made out. And certainly he owed his crown less to his descent than to his strong arm and his stout heart. It was by dint of severe fighting that he forced his way to the throne, defeating Aarsu, and gradually reducing all Egypt under his power.

Set-nekht's reign must have been short. He set himself to " put the whole land in order, to execute the abominables, to set up the temples, and re-establish the divine offerings for the service of the gods, as their statutes prescribed." But he was unable to effect very much. He could not even discharge properly the main duty of a king towards himself, which was to prepare a fitting receptacle for his remains when he should quit the earth. To excavate a rock-tomb in the style fashionable at the day was a task requiring several years for its due accomplishment; Set-nekht felt that he could not look forward to many years—perhaps not even to many months— of life. In this difficulty, he felt no shame in appropriating to himself a royal tomb recently constructed by a king, named Siphthah, whom he looked upon as a usurper, and therefore as unworthy of consideration. In this sepulchre we see the names of Siphthah and his queen, Taouris, erased by the chisel from their cartouches, and the name of Set-nekht substituted in their place. By one and the same act the king punished an unworthy predecessor, and provided himself with a ready-made tomb befitting his dignity.

It was also, probably, on account of his advanced age at his accession, that he almost immediately associated in the kingdom his son Ramesses, a prince of much promise, whom he made "Chief of On," and viceroy over Lower Egypt, with Heliopolis (On) for his residence and capital. Ramesses the Third, as he is commonly called, was one of the most distinguished of Egyptian monarchs, and the last who acquired any great glory until we come down to the time of the Ethiopians, Shabak and Tirhakah. He reigned as sole monarch for thirty-one years, during the earlier portion of which period he carried on a number of important wars, while during the later portion he employed himself in the construction of those magnificent buildings, which have been chiefly instrumental in carrying his name down to posterity, and in other works of utility. Lenormant calls him "the last of the great sovereigns of Egypt," and observes with reason, that though he never ceased, during the whole time that he occupied the throne, to labour hard to re-establish the integrity of the empire abroad, and the prosperity of the country at home, yet his wars and his conquests had a character essentially defensive ; his efforts, like those of the Trajans, the Marcus Aurelius's and the Septimius Severus's of history, were directed to making head against the ever rising flood of barbarians, which had already before his time burst the dykes that restrained it, and though once driven back, continued to dash itself on every side against the outer borders of the empire, and to presage its speedy overthrow. His efforts were, on the whole, successful ; he was able to uphold and preserve for some considerable time longer the territorial greatness which the nineteenth dynasty had built up a second time. The monumental temple of Medinet-Abou, near Thebes, is the Pantheon erected to the glory of this great Pharaoh. Every pylon, every gateway, every chamber, relates to us the exploits which he accomplished. Sculptured compositions of large dimensions represent his principal battles.

There are times in the world's history when a restless spirit appears to seize on the populations of large tracts of country, and, without any clear cause that can be alleged, uneasy movements begin. Subdued mutterings are heard; a tremor goes through the nations, expectation of coming change stalks abroad; the air is rife with rumours; at last there bursts out an eruption of greater or less violence—the destructive flood overleaps its barriers, and flows forth, carrying devastation and ruin in one direction or another, until its energies are exhausted, or its progress stopped by some obstacle that it cannot overcome, and it subsides reluctantly and perforce. Such a time was that on which Ramesses III. was cast. Wars threatened him on every side. On his north-eastern frontier the Shasu or Bedouins of the desert ravaged and plundered, at once harrying the Egyptian territory and threatening the mining establishments of the Sinaitic region. To the north-west the Libyan tribes, Maxyes, Asbystæ, Auseis, and others, were exercising a continuous pressure, to which the Egyptians were forced to yield, and gradually a foreign population was "squatting" on the fertile lands, and driving the former possessors of the soil back upon the more eastern portion of the Delta. "The Lubu and Mashuash," says Ramesses, "were *seated* in Egypt ; they took the cities on the western side from Memphis as far as Karbana, reaching the Great River along its entire course (from Memphis northwards), and capturing the city of Kaukut. For many years had they been in Egypt." Ramesses began his warlike operations by a campaign against the Shasu, whose country he invaded and overran, spoiling and destroying their cabins, capturing their cattle, slaying all who resisted him, and carrying back into Egypt a vast number of prisoners, whom he attached to the various temples as "sacred slaves." He then turned against the Libyans, and coming upon them unexpectedly in the tract between the Sebennytic branch of the Nile and the Canopic, he defeated in a great battle the seven tribes of the Mashuash, Lubu, Merbasat, Kaikasha, Shai, Hasa, and Bakana, slaughtering them with the utmost fury, and driving them before him across the western branch of the river. "They trembled before him," says the native historian, "as the mountain goats tremble before a bull, who stamps with his foot, strikes with his horns, and makes the mountains shake as he rushes on whoever opposes him." The Egyptians gave no·quarter that memorable day. Vengeance had free course: the slain Libyans lay in heaps upon heaps—the chariot wheels passed over them—the horses trampled them in the mire. Hundreds were pushed and forced into the marshes and into the river itself, and, if they escaped the flight of missiles which followed, found for the most part a watery grave in the strong current. Ramesses portrays this flight and carnage in the most graphic way. The slain enemy strew the ground, as he advances over them with his prancing steeds and in his rattling war-car, plying them moreover with his arrows as they vainly seek to escape. His chariot force and his infantry have their share in the pursuit, and with sword, or spear, or javelin, strike down alike the resisting and the unresisting. No one seeks to take a prisoner. It is a day of vengeance and of down-treading, of fury allowed to do its worst, of a people drunk with passion that has cast off all self-restraint.

Even passion exhausts itself at last, and the arm grows weary of slaughtering. Having sufficiently revenged themselves in the great battle, and the pursuit that followed it, the Egyptians relaxed somewhat from their policy of extreme hostility. They made a large number of the Libyans prisoners, branded them with a hot iron, as the Persians often did their prisoners, and forced them to join the naval service and serve as mariners on board the Egyptian fleet. The chiefs of greater importance they confined in fortresses. The women and children became the slaves of the conquerors; the cattle, "too numerous to count," was presented by Ramesses to the Priest-College of Ammon at Thebes.

So far success had crowned his arms; and it may well be that Ramesses would have been content with the military glory thus acquired, and have abstained from further expeditions, had not he been forced within a few years to take the field against a powerful combination of new and partly unheard-of enemies. The uneasy movement among the nations, which has been already noticed, had spread further afield, and now agitated at once the coasts and islands of South-Eastern Europe, and the more western portion of Asia Minor. Seven nations banded themselves together, and resolved to unite their forces, both naval and military, against Egypt, and to attack her both by land and sea, not now on the north-western frontier, where some of them had experienced defeat before, but in exactly the opposite quarter, by way of Syria and Palestine. Of the seven, three had been among her former adversaries in the time of Menephthah, namely, the Sheklusha, the Shartana, and the Tursha ; while four were new antagonists, unknown at any former period. There were, first, the Tânauna, in whom it is usual to see either the Danai of the Peloponnese, so celebrated in Homer, or the Daunii of south-eastern Italy, who bordered on the Iapyges ; secondly, the Tekaru, or Teucrians, a well-known people of the Troad ; thirdly, the Uashasha, who are identified with the Oscans or Ausones, neighbours of the Daunians; and fourthly, the Purusata, whom some explain as the Pelasgi, and others as the Philistines. The lead in the expedition was taken by these last. At their summons the islands and shores of the Mediterranean gave forth their piratical hordes—the sea was covered by their light galleys and swept by their strong oars—Tânauna, Shartana, Sheklusha, Tursha, and Uashasha combined their squadrons into a powerful fleet, while Purusata and Tekaru advanced in countless numbers along the land. The Purusata were especially bent on effecting a settlement; they marched into Northern Syria from Asia Minor accompanied by their wives and children, who were mounted upon carts drawn by oxen, and formed a vast unwieldy crowd. The other nations sent their sailors and their warriors without any such encumbrances. Bursting through the passes of Taurus, the combined Purusata and Tekaru spread themselves over Northern Syria, wasting and plundering the entire country of the Khita, and proceeding eastward as far as Carchemish "by Euphrates," while the ships of the remaining confederates coasted along the Syrian shore. Such resistance as the Hittites and Syrians made was wholly ineffectual. "No people stood before their arms." Aradus and Kadesh fell. The conquerors pushed on towards Egypt, anticipating an easy victory. But their fond hopes were doomed to disappointment.

Ramesses had been informed of the designs and approach of the enemy, and had had ample time to make all needful preparations. He had strengthened his frontier, called out all his best-disciplined troops and placed the mouths of the Nile in a state of defence by means of forts, strong garrisons, and flotillas upon the stream and upon the lakes adjacent. He had selected an eligible position for encountering the advancing hordes on the coast route from Gaza to Egypt, about half-way between Raphia and Pelusium, where a new fort had been built by his orders. At this point he took his stand, and calmly awaited his enemies, not having neglected the precaution to set an ambush or two in convenient places. Here, as he kept his watch, the first enemy to arrive was the land host of the Purusata, encumbered with its long train of slowly moving bullock-carts, heavily laden with women and children. Ramesses instantly attacked them—his ambushes rose up out of their places of concealment—and the enemy was beset on every side. They made no prolonged resistance. Assaulted by the disciplined and seasoned troops of the Egyptians, the entire confused mass was easily defeated. Twelve thousand five hundred men were slain in the fight; the camp was taken; the army shattered to pieces. Nothing was open to the survivors but an absolute surrender, by which life was saved at the cost of perpetual servitude.

The danger, however, was as yet but half overcome—the snake was scotched but not killed. For as yet the fleet remained intact, and might land its thousands on the Egyptian coasts and carry fire and sword over the broad region of the Delta. The Tânauna and their confederates—Sheklusha, Shartana, and Tursha — made rapidly for the nearest mouth of the Nile, which was the Pelusiac, and did their best to effect a landing. But the precautions taken by Ramesses, before he set forth on his march, proved sufficient to frustrate their efforts. The Egyptian fleet met the combined squadrons of the enemy in the shallow waters of the Pelusiac lagoon, and contended with them in a fierce battle, which Ramesses caused to be represented in his sculptures — the earliest representation of a sea-fight that has come down to us. Both sides have ships propelled at once by sails and oars, but furl their sails before engaging

Each ship has a single yard, constructed to carry a single large square-sail, and hung across the vessel's single mast at a short distance below the top. The mast is crowned by a bell-shaped receptacle, large enough to contain a man, who is generally a slinger or an archer, placed there to gall the enemy with stones or arrows, and so to play the part of our own sharpshooters in the main-tops. The rowers are from sixteen to twenty-two in number, besides whom each vessel carries a number of fighting men, armed with shields, spears, swords, and bows. The fight is a promiscuous *melée*, the two fleets being intermixed, and each ship engaging that next to it, without a thought of combined action or of manœuvres. One of the enemy's vessels is represented as capsized and sinking; the rest continue the engagement. Several are pressing towards the shore of the lagoon, and the men-at-arms on board them are endeavouring to effect a landing; but they are met by the land-force under Ramesses himself, who greet them with such a hail of arrows as renders it impossible for them to carry out their purpose.

It would seem that Ramesses had no sooner defeated and destroyed the army of the Purusata and Tekaru than he set off in haste for Pelusium, and marched with such speed as to arrive in time to witness the naval engagement, and even to take a certain part in it. The invading fleet was so far successful as to force its way through the opposing vessels of the Egyptians, and to press forward towards the shore; but here its further progress was arrested. "A wall of iron," says Ramesses, "shut them in upon

SEA-FIGHT IN THE TIME OF RAMESSES III.

the lake." The best troops of Egypt lined the banks of the lagoon, and wherever the invaders attempted to land they were foiled. Repulsed, dashed to the ground, hewn down or shot down at the edge of the water, they were slain "by hundreds of heaps of corpses." "The infantry," says the monarch in his vainglorious inscription, set up in memory of the event, "all the choicest troops of the army of Egypt, stood upon the bank, furious as roaring lions; the chariot force, selected from among the heroes that were quickest in battle, was led by officers confident in themselves. The war-steeds quivered in all their limbs, and burned to trample the nations under their feet. I myself was like the god Mentu, the warlike; I placed myself at their head, and they saw the achievements of my hands. I, Ramesses the king, behaved as a hero who knows his worth, and who stretches out his arm over his people in the day of combat. The invaders of my territory will gather no more harvests upon the earth, their life is counted to them as eternity. . . . Those that gained the shore, I caused to fall at the water's edge, they lay slain in heaps; I overturned their vessels; all their goods sank in the waves." After a brief combat, all resistance ceased. The empty ships, floating at random upon the still waters of the lagoon, or stuck fast in the Nile mud, became the prize of the victors, and were found to contain a rich booty. Thus ended this remarkable struggle, in which nations widely severed and of various bloods—scarcely, as one would have thought, known to each other, and separated by a diversity of interests—united in an attack upon the foremost power of the known world, traversed several hundreds of miles of land or sea successfully, neither quarrelling among themselves nor meeting with disaster from without, and reached the country which they had hoped to conquer, but were there completely defeated and repulsed in two engagements—one by land, the other partly by land and partly by sea—so that "their spirit was annihilated, their soul was taken from them." Henceforth no one of the nations which took part in the combined attack is found in arms against the power that had read them so severe a lesson.

It was not long after repulsing this attack upon the independence of Egypt that Ramesses undertook his "campaign of revenge." Starting with a fleet and army along the line that his assailants had followed, he traversed Palestine and Syria, hunting the lion in the outskirts of Lebanon, and re-establishing for a time the Egyptian dominion over much of the region which had been formerly held in subjection by the great monarchs of the eighteenth and nineteenth dynasties. He claims to have carried his arms to Aleppo and Carchemish, in which case we must suppose that he defeated the Hittites, or else that they declined to meet him in the field; and he gives a list of thirty-eight conquered countries or tribes, which are thought to belong to Upper Syria, Southern Asia Minor, and Cyprus. In some of his inscriptions he even speaks of having recovered Naharaina, Kush, and Punt; but there is no evidence that he really visited—much less conquered—these remote regions.

The later life of Ramesses III. was, on the whole,

a time of tranquillity and repose. The wild tribes of North Africa, after one further attempt to establish themselves in the western Delta, which wholly failed, acquiesced in the lot which nature seemed to have assigned them, and, leaving the Egyptians in peace, contented themselves with the broad tract over which they were free to rove between the Mediterranean and the Sahara Desert. On the south Ethiopia made no sign. In the east the Hittites had enough to do to rebuild the power which had been greatly shattered by the passage of the hordes of Asia Minor through their territory, on their way to Egypt and on their return from it. The Assyrians had not yet commenced their aggressive wars towards the north and west, having probably still a difficulty in maintaining their independence against the attacks of Babylon. Egypt was left undisturbed by her neighbours for the space of several generations, and herself refrained from disturbing the peace of the world by foreign expeditions. Ramesses turned his attention to building, commerce, and the planting of Egypt with trees. He constructed and ornamented the beautiful temple of Ammon at Medinet-Abou, built a fleet on the Red Sea and engaged in trade with Punt, dug a great reservoir in the country of Aina (Southern Palestine), and "over the whole land of Egypt planted trees and shrubs, to give the inhabitants rest under their cool shade."

The general decline of Egypt must, however, be regarded as having commenced in his reign. His Eastern conquests were more specious than solid, resulting in a nominal rather than a real subjection of Palestine and

Syria to his yoke. His subjects grew unaccustomed to the use of arms during the last twenty, or five and twenty, years of his life. Above all, luxury, intrigue, and superstition invaded the court, where the eunuchs and concubines exercised a pernicious influence. Magic was practised by some of the chief men in the State, and the belief was widely spread that it was possible by charms, incantations, and the use of waxen images, to bewitch men, or paralyse their limbs, or even to cause their deaths. Hags were to be found about the court as wicked as Canidia, who were willing to sell their skill in the black art to the highest bidder. The actual person of the monarch was not sacred from the plottings of this nefarious crew, who planned assassinations and hatched conspiracies in the very purlieus of the royal palace. Ramesses himself would, apparently, have fallen a victim to a plot of the kind, had not the parties to it been discovered, arrested, tried by a Royal Commission, and promptly executed.

The descendants of Ramesses III. occupied the throne from his death (about B.C. 1280) to B.C. 1100. Ten princes of the name of Ramesses, and one called Meri-Tum, bore sway during this interval, each of them showing, if possible, greater weakness than the last, and all of them sunk in luxury, idle, effeminate, sensual. Ramesses III. provoked caricature by his open exhibition of harem-scenes on the walls of his Medinet-Abou palace. His descendants, content with harem life, scarcely cared to quit the precincts of the royal abode, desisted from all war, and even devolved the task of government on other shoulders. The

RAPID DECLINE OF THE ARTS. 285

Pharaohs of the twentieth dynasty bcame absolute *fainéants*, and devolved their duties on the highpriests of the great temple of Ammon at Thebes, who "set themselves to play the same part which at a distant period was played by the Mayors of the Palace under the later French kings of the Merovingian line."

In an absolute monarchy, the royal authority is the mainspring which controls all movements and all actions in every part of the State. Let this source of energy grow weak, and decline at once shows itself throughout the entire body politic. It is as when a fatal malady seizes on the seat of life in an individual —instantly every member, every tissue, falls away, suffers, shrinks, decays, perishes. Egyptian architecture is simply non-existent from the death of Ramesses III. to the age of Sheshonk; the "grand style" of pictorial art disappears; sculpture in relief becomes a wearisome repetition of the same stereotyped religious groups; statuary deteriorates and is rare; above all, literature declines, undergoing an almost complete eclipse. A galaxy of literary talent had, as we have seen, clustered about the reigns of Ramesses II. and Menephthah, under whose encouragement authors had devoted themselves to history, divinity, practical philosophy, poetry, epistolary correspondence, novels, travels, legend. From the time of Ramesses III.—nay, from the time of Seti II. —all is a blank: " the true poetic inspiration appears to have vanished," literature is almost dumb; instead of the masterpieces of Pentaour, Kakabu, Nebsenen, Enna, and others, which even moderns can peruse

286 EGYPT UNDER THE LATER RAMESSIDES.

CARICATURE OF THE TIME OF RAMESSES III.

with pleasure, we have only documents in which "the dry official tone" prevails — abstracts of trials, lists of functionaries, tiresome enumerations in the greatest detail of gifts made to the gods, together with fulsome praises of the kings, written either by themselves or by others, which we are half inclined to regret the lapse of ages has spared from destruction. At the same time morals fall off. Sensuality displays itself in high places. Intrigue enters the charmed circle of the palace. The monarch himself is satirized in indecent drawings. Presently, the whole idea of a divinity hedging in the king departs; and a "thieves' society" is formed for rifling the royal tombs, and tearing the jewels, with which they have been buried, from the monarchs' persons. The king's life is aimed at by conspirators, who do not scruple to use magical arts; priests and high judicial functionaries are implicated in the proceedings. Altogether, the old order seems to be changed, the old ideas to be upset; and no new principles, possessing any vital efficacy, are introduced. Society gradually settles upon its lees; and without some violent application of force from without, or some strange upheaval from within, the nation seems doomed to fall rapidly into decay and dissolution.

XVIII.

THE PRIEST-KINGS—PINETEM AND SOLOMON.

THE position of the priests in Egypt was, from the first, one of high dignity and influence. Though not, strictly speaking, a caste, they formed a very distinct order or class, separated by important privileges, and by their habits of life, from the rest of the community, and recruited mainly from among their own sons, and other near relatives. Their independence and freedom was secured by a system of endowments. From a remote antiquity a considerable portion of the land of Egypt—perhaps as much as one-third—was made over to the priestly class, large estates being attached to each temple, and held as common property by the "colleges," which, like the chapters of our cathedrals, directed the worship of each sacred edifice. These priestly estates were, we are told, exempt from taxation of any kind ; and they appear to have received continual augmentation from the piety or superstition of the kings, who constantly made over to their favourite deities fresh "gardens, orchards, vineyards, fields," and even " cities."

The kings lived always in a considerable amount of awe of the priests. Though claiming a certain qualified divinity themselves, they yet could not but be aware that there were divers flaws and imperfections in their own divinity—"little rifts within the lute"—which made it not quite a safe support to trust to, or lean upon, entirely. There were other greater gods than themselves—gods from whom their own divinity was derived; and they could not be certain what power or influence the priests might not have with these superior beings, in whose existence and ability to benefit and injure men they had the fullest belief. Consequently, the kings are found to occupy a respectful attitude towards the priests throughout the whole course of Egyptian history, from first to last; and this respectful attitude is especially maintained towards the great personages in whom the hierarchy culminates, the head officials, or chief priests, of the temples which are the principal centres of the national worship—the temple of Ra, or Tum, at Heliopolis, that of Phthah at Memphis, and that of Ammon at Thebes. According to the place where the capital was fixed for the time being, one or other of these three high-priests had the pre-eminence; and, in the later period of the Ramessides, Thebes having enjoyed metropolitan dignity for between five and six centuries, the Theban High-Priest of Ammon was recognized as beyond dispute the chief of the sacerdotal order, and the next person in the kingdom after the king.

It had naturally resulted from this high position, and the weight of influence which it enabled its possessor to exercise, that the office had become hereditary. As far back as the reign of Ramesses IX., we find that the holder of the position has succeeded his father in it, and regards himself as high-priest rather by natural right than by the will of the king. The priest of that time, Amenhotep by name, the son of Ramesses-nekht, undertakes the restoration of the Temple of Ammon at Thebes of his own proper motion, "strengthens its walls, builds it anew, makes its columns, inserts in its gates the great folding-doors of acacia wood." Formerly, the kings were the builders, and the high-priests carried out their directions and then in the name of the gods gave thanks to the kings for their pious munificence. Under the ninth Ramesses the order was reversed—"now it is the king who testifies his gratitude to the High-Priest of Ammon for the care bestowed on his temple by the erection of new buildings and the improvement and maintenance of the older ones." The initiative has passed out of the king's hands into those of his subject; he is active, the king is passive; all the glory is Amenhotep's; the king merely comes in at the close of all, as an ornamental person, whose presence adds a certain dignity to the final ceremony.

Under the last of the Ramessides the High-Priest of Ammon at Thebes was a certain Her-hor. He was a man of a pleasing countenance, with features that were delicate and good, and an expression that was mild and agreeable. He had the art so to ingratiate himself with his sovereign as to obtain at his hands at least five distinct offices of state besides his sacred dignity. He was "Chief of Upper and Lower Egypt," " Royal son of Cush," " Fanbearer on the right hand of the King," " Principal Architect," and " Administrator of the Granaries." Some of these offices may have been honorary; but the duties of others must have been important, and their proper discharge would have required a vast amount of varied ability. It is not likely that Herhor possessed all the needful

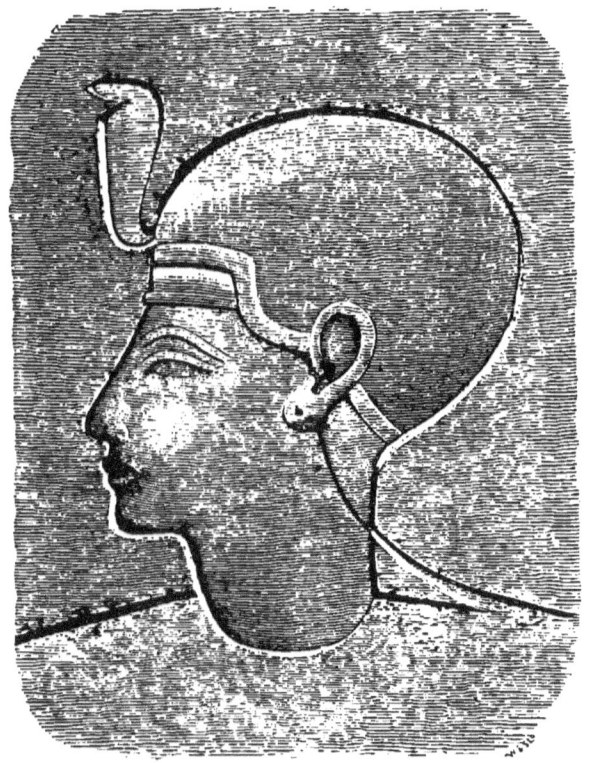

HEAD OF HER-HOR.

qualifications; rather we must presume that he grasped at the multiplicity of appointments in order to accumulate power, so far as was possible, in his own hands, and thereby to be in a better position to seize the royal authority on the monarch's demise. If Ramesses III. died without issue, his task must have been facilitated; at any rate, he seems to have had the skill to accomplish it without struggle or disturbance; and if, as some suppose, he banished the remaining descendants of Ramesses III. to the Great Oasis, at any rate he did not stain his priestly hands with bloodshed, or force his way to the throne through scenes of riot and confusion. Egypt, so far as appears, quietly acquiesced in his rule, and perhaps rejoiced to find herself once more governed by a prince of a strong and energetic nature.

For some time after he had mounted the throne, Herhor did not abandon his priestly functions. He bore the title of High-Priest of Ammon regularly on one of his royal escutcheons, while on the other he called himself "Her-Hor Si-Ammon," or "Her-Hor, son of Ammon," following the example of former kings, who gave themselves out for sons of Ra, or Phthah, or Mentu, or Horus. But ultimately he surrendered the priestly title to his eldest son, Piankh, and no doubt at the same time devolved upon him the duties which attached to the high-priestly office. There was something unseemly in a priest being a soldier, and Herhor was smitten with the ambition of putting himself at the head of an army, and reasserting the claim of Egypt to a supremacy over Syria. He calls himself "the conqueror of the Ruten," and there is no reason to doubt that he was successful in a Syrian campaign, though to what distance he penetrated must remain uncertain. The Egyptian monarchs are not very exact in their geographical nomenclature, and Herhor may have spoken of Ruten, when his adversaries were really the Bedouins of the desert between Egypt and Palestine. The fact that his expedition is unnoticed in the Hebrew Scriptures renders it tolerably certain that he did not effect any permanent conquest, even of Palestine.

Herhor's son, Piankh, who became High-Priest of Ammon on his father's abdication of the office, does not appear to have succeeded him in the kingdom. Perhaps he did not outlive his father. At any rate, the kingly office seems to have passed from Herhor to his grandson, Pinetem, who was a monarch of some distinction, and had a reign of at least twenty-five years. Pinetem's right to the crown was disputed by descendants of the Ramesside line of kings; and he thought it worth while to strengthen his title by contracting a marriage with a princess of that royal stock, a certain Ramaka, or Rakama, whose name appears on his monuments. But compromise with treason has rarely a tranquillizing effect; and Pinetem's concession to the prejudices which formed the stock-in-trade of his opponents only exasperated them and urged them to greater efforts. The focus of the conspiracy passed from the Oasis to Thebes, which had grown disaffected because Pinetem had removed the seat of government to Tanis in the Delta, which was the birthplace of his grandfather, Herhor. So threatening had become the general aspect of affairs, that the king thought it prudent to send his son, Ra-men-khepr or Men-khepr-ra, the existing high-priest of the Temple of Ammon at

Thebes, from Tanis to the southern capital, in order that he should make himself acquainted with the secret strength, and with the designs of the disaffected, and see whether he could not either persuade or coerce them. It was a curious part for the Priest of Ammon to play. Ordinarily an absentee from Thebes and from the duties of his office, he visits the place as Royal Commissioner, entrusted with plenary powers to punish or forgive offenders at his pleasure. His fellow-townsmen are in the main hostile to him; but the terror of the king's name is such that they do not dare to offer him any resistance, and he singles out those who appear to him most guilty for punishment, and has them executed, while he grants the royal pardon to others without any let or hindrance on the part of the civic authorities. Finally, having removed all those whom he regarded as really dangerous, he ventured to conclude his commission by granting a general amnesty to all persons implicated in the conspiracy, and allowing the political refugees to return from the Oasis to Thebes and to live there unmolested.

Men-khepr-ra soon afterwards became king. He married a wife named Hesi-em-Kheb, who is thought to have been a descendant of Seti I., and thus gave an additional legitimacy to the dynasty of Priest-Kings. He also adorned the city of Kheb, the native place of his wife, with public buildings; but otherwise nothing is known of the events of his reign. As a general rule, the priest-kings were no more active or enterprizing than their predecessors, the Ramessides of the twentieth dynasty. They were content to rule

Egypt in peace, and enjoy the delights of sovereignty, without fatiguing themselves either with the construction of great works or the conduct of military expeditions. If the people that has no history is rightly pronounced happy, Egypt may have prospered under their rule ; but the historian can scarcely be expected to appreciate a period which supplies him with no materials to work upon.

The inaction of Egypt was favourable to the growth and spread of other kingdoms and empires. Towards the close of the Ramesside period Assyria had greatly increased in power, and extended her authority beyond the Euphrates as far as the Mediterranean. After this, causes that are still obscure had caused her to decline, and, Syria being left to itself, a new power grew up in it. In the later half of the eleventh century, probably during the reign of Men-khepr-ra in Egypt, David began that series of conquests by which he gradually built up an empire, uniting in one all the countries and tribes between the river of Egypt (Wady-el-Arish) and the Euphrates. Egypt made no attempt to interfere with his proceedings ; and Assyria, after one defeat (1 Chron. xix. 16-19), withdrew from the contest. David's empire was inherited by Solomon (1 Kings iv. 21-24); and Solomon's position was such as naturally brought him into communication with the great powers beyond his borders, among others with Egypt. A brisk trade was carried on between his subjects and the Egyptians, especially in horses and chariots (ib. x. 28, 29) : and diplomatic intercourse was no doubt established between the courts of Tanis and

Jerusalem. It is a little uncertain which Egyptian prince was now upon the throne; but Egyptologers incline to Pinetem II., the second in succession after Men-khepr-ra, and the last king but one of the dynasty. The Hebrew monarch having made overtures through his ambassador, this prince, it would seem, received them favourably; and, soon after his accession (1 Kings iii. 1), Solomon took to wife his daughter, an Egyptian princess, receiving with her as a dowry the city and territory of Gezer, which Pinetem had recently taken from its independent Canaanite inhabitants (ib. ix. 16). The new connection had advantages and disadvantages. The excessive polygamy, which had been affected by the Egyptian monarchs ever since the time of Ramesses II., naturally spread into Judea, and " King Solomon loved many strange women, together with the daughter of Pharaoh, women of the Moabites, Ammonites, Edomites, Zidonians, and Hittites . . . . and he had seven hundred wives, princesses, and three hundred concubines; and his wives turned away his heart" (ib. xi. 1, 3). On the other hand, commerce was no doubt promoted by the step taken, and much was learnt in the way of art from the Egyptian sculptors and architects. The burst of architectural vigour which distinguishes Solomon's reign among those of other Hebrew kings, is manifestly the direct result of ideas brought to Jerusalem from the capital of the Pharaohs. The plan of the Temple, with its open court in front, its porch, its Holy Place, its Holy of Holies, and its chambers, was modelled after the Egyptian pattern. The two pillars, Jachin and Boaz, which stood in front of the porch, took the place of the twin obelisks, which in every finished example of an Egyptian temple stood just in front of the principal entrance. The lions on the steps of the royal throne (ib. x. 20) were imitations of those which in Egypt often supported the seat of the monarch on either side; and "the house of the forest of Lebanon" was an attempt to reproduce the effect of one of Egypt's "pillared halls." Something in the architecture of Solomon was clearly learnt from Phœnicia, and a little—a very little—may perhaps have been derived from Assyria; but Egypt gave at once the impulse and the main bulk of the ideas and forms.

The line of priest-kings terminated with Hor-pa-seb-en-sha, the successor of Pinetem II. They held the throne for about a century and a quarter; and if they cannot be said to have played a very important part in the "story of Egypt," or in any way to have increased Egyptian greatness, yet at least they escape the reproach, which rests upon most of the more distinguished dynasties, of seeking their own glory in modes which caused their subjects untold suffering.

XIX.

SHISHAK AND HIS DYNASTY.

THE rise of the twenty-second resembles in many respects that of the twenty-first dynasty. In both cases the cause of the revolution is to be found in the weakness of the royal house, which rapidly loses its pristine vigour, and is impotent to resist the first assault made upon it by a bold aggressor. Perhaps the wonder is rather that Egyptian dynasties continued so long as they did, than that they were not longer-lived, since there was in almost every instance a rapid decline, alike in the *physique* and in the mental calibre of the holders of sovereignty; so that nothing but a little combined strength and audacity was requisite in order to push them from their pedestals. Shishak was an official of a Semitic family long settled in Egypt, which had made the town of Bubastis its residence. We may suspect, if we like, that the family had noble—shall we say royal?—blood in its veins, and could trace its descent to dynasties which had ruled at Nineveh or Babylon. The connexion is possible, though scarcely probable, since no *éclat* attended the first arrival of the Shishak family in Egypt, and the family names, though Semitic, are decidedly neither Babylonian nor Assyrian. It is tempting to adopt the sensational views of writers, who, out of half a dozen names, manufacture an Assyrian conquest of Egypt, and the establishment on the throne of the Pharaohs of a branch derived from one or other of the royal Mesopotamian houses ; but "facts are stubborn things," and the imagination is scarcely entitled to mould them at its will. It is necessary to face the two certain facts—(1) that no one of the dynastic names is the natural representative of any name known to have been borne by any Assyrian or Babylonian ; and (2) that neither Assyria nor Babylonia was at the time in such a position as to effect, or even to contemplate, distant enterprizes. Babylonia did not attain such a position till the time of Nabopolassar ; Assyria had enjoyed it about B.C. 1150–1100, but had lost it, and did not recover it till B.C. 890. Moreover, Solomon's empire blocked the way to Egypt against both countries, and required to be shattered in pieces before either of the great Mesopotamian powers could have sent a *corps d'armée* into the land of the Pharaohs.

Sober students of history will therefore regard Shishak (Sheshonk) simply as a member of a family which, though of foreign extraction, had been long settled in Egypt, and had worked its way into a high position under the priest-kings of Herhor's line, retaining a special connection with Bubastis, the place which it had from the first made its home. Sheshonk's grandfather, who bore the same name, had had the honour of intermarrying into the royal house, having taken to wife Meht-en-hont, a princess of the blood, whose exact parentage is unknown to us. His father,

Namrut, had held a high military office, being commander of the Libyan mercenaries, who at this time formed the most important part of the standing army. Sheshonk himself, thus descended, was naturally in the front rank of Egyptian court-officials. When we first hear of him he is called " His Highness," and given the title of " Prince of the princes," which is thought to imply that he enjoyed the first rank among all the chiefs of mercenaries, of whom there were many. Thus he held a position only second to that occupied by the king, and when his son became a suitor for the hand of a daughter of the reigning sovereign, no one could say that etiquette was infringed, or an ambition displayed that was excessive and unsuitable. The match was consequently allowed to come off, and Sheshonk became doubly connected with the royal house, through his daughter-in-law and through his grandmother. When, therefore, on the death of Hor-pa-seb-en-sha, he assumed the title and functions of king, no opposition was offered : the crown seemed to have passed simply from one member of the royal family to another.

In monarchies like the Egyptian, it is not very difficult for an ambitious subject, occupying a certain position, to seize the throne; but it is far from easy for him to retain it Unless there is a general impression of the usurper's activity, energy, and vigour, his authority is liable to be soon disputed, or even set at nought. It behoves him to give indications of strength and breadth of character, or of a wise, far-seeing policy, in order to deter rivals from attempting to undermine his power. Sheshonk early let it be seen that he possessed both caution and far-reaching views by his treatment of a refugee who, shortly after his accession, sought his court. This was Jeroboam, one of the highest officials in the neighbouring kingdom of Israel, whom Solomon, the great Israelite monarch, regarded with suspicion and hostility, on account of a declaration made by a prophet that he was at some future time to be king of Ten Tribes out of the Twelve. To receive Jeroboam with favour was necessarily to offend Solomon, and thus to reverse the policy of the preceding dynasty, and pave the way for a rupture with the State which was at this time Egypt's most important neighbour. Sheshonk, nevertheless, accorded a gracious reception to Jeroboam; and the favour in which he remained at the Egyptian court was an encouragement to the disaffected among the Israelites, and distinctly foreshadowed a time when an even bolder policy would be adopted, and a strike made for imperial power. The time came at Solomon's demise. Jeroboam was at once allowed to return to Palestine, and to foment the discontent which it was foreseen would terminate in separation. The two kings had, no doubt, laid their plans. Jeroboam was first to see what he could effect unaided, and then, if difficulty supervened, his powerful ally was to come to his assistance. For the Egyptian monarch to have appeared in the first instance would have roused Hebrew patriotism against him. Sheshonk waited till Jeroboam had, to a certain extent, established his kingdom, had set up a new worship blending Hebrew with Egyptian notions, and had sufficiently tested the affection or disaffection towards his rule of the various classes of his subjects. He then marched out to his assistance. Levying a force of twelve hundred chariots, sixty thousand horse (? six thousand), and footmen "without number" (2 Chron. xii. 3), chiefly from the Libyan and Ethiopian mercenaries which now formed the strength of the Egyptian armies, he proceeded into the Holy Land, entering it "in three columns," and so spreading his troops far and wide over the southern country. Rehoboam, Solomon's son and successor, had made such preparation as was possible against the attack. He had anticipated it from the moment of Jeroboam's return, and he had carefully guarded the main routes whereby his country could be approached from the south, fortifying, among other cities, Shoco, Adullam, Azekah, Gath, Mareshah, Ziph, Tekoa, and Hebron (2 Chron. xi. 6-10). But the host of Sheshonk was irresistible. Never before had the Hebrews met in battle the forces of their powerful southern neighbour —never before had they been confronted with huge masses of disciplined troops, armed and trained alike, and soldiers by profession. The Jewish levies were a rude and untaught militia, little accustomed to warfare, or even to the use of arms, after forty years of peace, during which "every man had dwelt safely under the shade of his own vine and his own fig-tree" (1 Kings iv. 25). They must have trembled before the chariots, and cavalry, and trained footmen of Egypt. Accordingly, there seems to have been no battle, and no regularly organized resistance. As the host of Sheshonk advanced along the chief roads that led to the Jewish capital, the cities, fortified with so much care by Rehoboam, either opened their gates to him, or fell after brief sieges (2 Chron. xii. 4). Sheshonk's march was a triumphal progress, and in an incredibly short space of time he appeared before Jerusalem, where Rehoboam and "the princes of Judah" were tremblingly awaiting his arrival. The son of Solomon surrendered at discretion; and the Egyptian conqueror entered the Holy City, stripped the Temple of its most valuable treasures, including the shields of gold which Solomon had made for his body-guard, and plundered the royal palace (2 Chron xii. 9). The city generally does not appear to have been sacked; nor was there any massacre. Rehoboam's submission was accepted; he was maintained in his kingdom; but he had to become Sheshonk's "servant" (2 Chron. xii. 8), *i.e.*, he had to accept the position of a tributary prince, owing fealty and obedience to the Egyptian monarch.

The objects of Sheshonk's expedition were not yet half accomplished. By the long inscription which he set up on his return to Egypt, we find that, after having made Judea subject to him, he proceeded with his army into the kingdom of Israel, and there also took a number of towns which were peculiarly circumstanced. The Levites of the northern kingdom had from the first disapproved of the religious changes effected by Jeroboam; and the Levitical cities within his dominions were regarded with an unfriendly eye by the Israelite monarch, who saw in them hotbeds of rebellion. He had not ventured to make a direct attack upon them himself, since he would thereby have lighted the torch of civil war within his own borders; but, having now an Egyptian army at his beck and call, he used the foreigners as an instrument at once to free him from a danger and to execute his vengeance upon those whom he looked upon as traitors. Sheshonk was directed or encouraged to attack and take the Levitical cities of Rehob, Gibeon, Mahanaim, Beth-horon, Kedemoth, Bileam or Ibleam, Alemoth, Taanach, Golan, and Anem, to plunder them and carry off their inhabitants as slaves; while he was also persuaded to reduce a certain number of Canaanite towns, which did not yield Jeroboam a very willing obedience. We may trace the march of Sheshonk by Megiddo, Taanach, and Shunem, to Beth-shan, and thence across the Jordan to Mahanaim and Aroer; after which, having satisfied his vassal, Jeroboam, he proceeded to make war on his own account with the Arab tribes adjoining on Trans-Jordanic Israel, and subdued the Temanites, the Edomites, and various tribes of the Hagarenes. His dominion was thus established from the borders of Egypt to Galilee, and from the Mediterranean to the Great Syrian Desert.

On his return to Egypt from Asia, with his prisoners and his treasures, it seemed to the victorious monarch that he might fitly follow the example of the old Pharaohs who had made expeditions into Palestine and Syria, and commemorate his achievements by a sculptured record. So would he best impress the mass of the people with his merits, and induce them to put him on a par with the Thothmeses and the Amenhoteps of former ages. On the southern external wall of the great temple of Karnak, he caused himself to be represented twice—once as holding by the hair of their heads thirty-eight captive Asiatics, and threatening them with uplifted mace; and a second time as leading captive one hundred and thirty-three cities or tribes, each specified by name and personified in an individual form, the form, however, being incomplete. Among these representa-

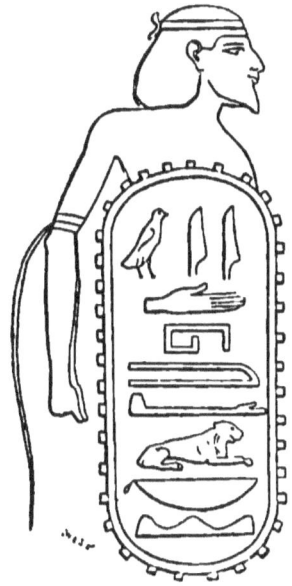

FIGURE RECORDING THE CONQUEST OF JUDÆA BY SHISHAK.

tions is one which bears the inscription "Yutch Malek," and which must be regarded as figuring the captive Judæan kingdom.

Thus, after nearly a century and a half of repose, Egypt appeared once more in Western Asia as a conquering power, desirious of establishing an empire. The political edifice raised with so much trouble by

David, and watched over with such care by Solomon, had been shaken to its base by the rebellion of Jeroboam; it was shattered beyond all hope of recovery by Shishak. Never more would the fair fabric of an Israelite empire rear itself up before the eyes of men; never more would Jerusalem be the capital of a State as extensive as Assyria or Babylonia, and as populous as Egypt. After seventy years, or so, of union, Syria was broken up—the cohesion effected by the warlike might of David and the wisdom of Solomon ceased—the ill-assimilated parts fell asunder; and once more the broad and fertile tract intervening between Assyria and Egypt became divided among a score of petty States, whose weakness invited a conqueror.

Sheshonk did not live many years to enjoy the glory and honour brought him by his Asiatic successes. He died after a reign of twenty-one years, leaving his crown to his second son, Osorkon, who was married to the Princess Keramat, a daughter of Sheshonk's predecessor. The dynasty thus founded continued to occupy the Egyptian throne for the space of about two centuries, but produced no other monarch of any remarkable distinction. The Asiatic dominion, which Sheshonk had established, seems to have been maintained for about thirty years, during the reigns of Osorkon I., Sheshonk's son, and Takelut I., his grandson; but in the reign of Osorkon II., the son of Takelut, the Jewish monarch of the time, Asa, the grandson of Rehoboam, shook off the Egyptian yoke, re-established Judæan independence, and fortified himself against attack by restoring the defences of all those cities which Sheshonk had dismantled, and "making about them walls, and towers, gates, and bars" (2 Chron. xiv. 7). At the same time he placed under arms the whole male population of his kingdom, which is reckoned by the Jewish historian at 580,000

HEAD OF SHISHAK.

men. The "men of Judah" bore spears and targets, or small round shields; the "men of Benjamin" had shields of a larger size, and were armed with the bow (ib. ver. 8). "All these," says the historian, "were mighty men of valour." It was not to be supposed that Egypt would bear tamely this defiance, or submit to the entire loss of her Asiatic dominion, which was necessarily involved in the revolt of Judæa, without an effort to retain it. Osorkon II., or whoever was king at the time, rose to the occasion. If it was to be a contest of numbers, Egypt should show that she was certainly not to be outdone numerically; so more mercenaries than ever before were taken into pay, and an army was levied, which is reckoned at "a thousand thousand" (ib. ver. 9), consisting of Cushites or Ethiopians, and of Lubim (ib. xvi. 8), or natives of the North African coast-tract. With these was sent a picked force of three hundred war-chariots, probably Egyptian; and the entire host was placed under the command of an Ethiopian general, who is called Zerah. The host set forth from Egypt, confident of victory, and proceeded as far as Mareshah in Southern Judæa, where they were met by the undaunted Jewish king. What force he had brought with him is uncertain, but the number cannot have been very great. Asa had recourse to prayer, and, in words echoed in later days by the great Maccabee (1 Mac. iii. 18, 19), besought Jehovah to help him against the Egyptian "multitude." Then the two armies joined battle; and, notwithstanding the disparity of numbers, Zerah was defeated. "The Ethiopians and the Lubim, a huge host, with very many chariots and horsemen" (2 Chron. xvi. 8) fled before Judah—they were "overthrown that they could not recover themselves, and were destroyed before Jehovah and before His host" (ib. xiv. 13). The Jewish troops pursued them as far as Gerar, smiting them with a great slaughter, taking their camp, and loading themselves with spoil.

What became of Zerah we are not told. Perhaps he fell in the battle ; perhaps he carried the news of his defeat to his Egyptian master, and warned him against any further efforts to subdue a people which could defend itself so effectually.

The direct effect of the victory of Asa was to put an end, for three centuries, to those dreams of Asiatic dominion which had so long floated before the eyes of Egyptian kings, and dazzled their imaginations. If a single one of the petty princes between whose rule Syria was divided could defeat and destroy the largest army that Egypt had ever brought into the field, what hope was there of victory over twenty or thirty of such chieftains ? Henceforth, until the time of the great revolution brought about in Western Asia through the destruction of the Assyrian Empire by the Medes, the eyes of Egypt were averted from Asia, unless when attack threatened her. She shrank from provoking the repetition of such a defeat as Zerah had suffered, and was careful to abstain from all interference with the affairs of Palestine, except on invitation. She learnt to look upon the two Israelite kingdoms as her bulwarks against attack from the East, and it became an acknowledged part of her policy to support them against Assyrian aggression. If she did not succeed in rendering them any effective assistance, it was not for lack of good-will. She was indeed a "bruised reed" to lean upon, but it was because her strength was inferior to that of the great Mesopotamian power.

From the time of Osorkon II., the Sheshonk dynasty rapidly declined in power. A system of constituting appanages for the princes of the reigning house grew up, and in a short time conducted the country to the verge of dissolution. "For the purpose of avoiding usurpations analogous to that of the High-Priests of Ammon," says M. Maspero, "Sheshonk and his descendants made a rule to entrust all positions of importance, whether civil or military, to the princes of the blood royal. A son of the reigning Pharaoh, most commonly his eldest son, held the office of High-Priest of Ammon and Governor of Thebes; another commanded at Sessoun (Hermopolis); another at Hakhensu, others in all the large towns of the Delta and of Upper Egypt. Each of them had with him several battalions of those Libyan soldiers—Matsiou and Mashuash—who formed at this time the strength of the Egyptian army, and on whose fidelity it was always safe to count. Ere long these commands became hereditary, and the feudal system, which had anciently prevailed among the chiefs of nomes or cantons, re-established itself for the advantage of the members of the reigning house. The Pharaoh of the time continued to reside at Memphis, or at Bubastis, to receive the taxes, to direct as far as was possible the central administration, and to preside at the grand ceremonies of religion, such as the enthronement or the burial of an Apis-Bull; but, in point of fact, Egypt found itself divided into a certain number of principalities, some of which comprised only a few towns, while others extended over several continuous cantons. After a time the chiefs of these principalities were emboldened to reject the sovereignty of the Pharaoh altogether; relying on their bands of Libyan mercenaries, they usurped, not only the functions of royalty, but even the title of king, while the legitimate dynasty, cooped up in a corner of the Delta, with difficulty preserved a certain remnant of authority."

Upon disintegration followed, as a natural consequence, quarrel and disturbance. In the reign of Takelut II., the grandson of Osorkon II., troubles broke out both in the north and in the south. Takelut's eldest son, Osorkon, who was High-Priest of Ammon, and held the government of Thebes and the other provinces of the south, was only able to maintain the integrity of the kingdom by means of perpetual civil wars. Under his successors, Sheshonk III., Pamai, and Sheshonk IV., the revolts became more and more serious. Rival dynasties established themselves at Thebes, Tanis, Memphis, and elsewhere. Ethiopia grew more powerful as Egypt declined, and threatened ere long to establish a preponderating influence over the entire Nile valley. But the Egyptian princes were too jealous of each other to appreciate the danger which threatened them. A very epidemic of decentralization set in; and by the middle of the eighth century, just at the time when Assyria was uniting together and blending into one all the long-divided tribes and nations of Western Asia, Egypt suicidally broke itself up into no fewer than twenty governments!

Such a condition of things was, of course, fatal to literature and art. Art, as has been said, "did not so much decline as disappear." After Sheshonk I. no monarch of the line left any building or sculpture of the slightest importance. The very tombs became unpretentious, and merely repeated antique forms

without any of the antique spirit. Each Apis, indeed, had, in his turn, his arched tomb cut for him in the solid rock of the Serapeum at Memphis, and was laid to rest in a stone sarcophagus, formed of a single block. A stela, moreover, was in every case inscribed and set up to his memory: but the stelæ were rude memorials, devoid of all artistic taste; the tombs were mere reproductions of old models; and the inscriptions were of the dullest and most prosaic kind. Here is one, as a specimen: " In the year 2, the month Mechir, on the first day of the month, under the reign of King Pimai, the god Apis was carried to his rest in the beautiful region of the west, and was laid in the grave, and deposited in his everlasting house and his eternal abode. He was born in the year 28, in the time of the deceased king, Sheshonk III. His glory was sought for in all places of Lower Egypt. He was found after some months in the city of Hashed-abot. He was solemnly introduced into the temple of Phthah, beside his father—the Memphian god Phthah of the south wall—by the high-priest in the temple of Phthah, the great prince of the Mashuash, Petise, the son of the high-priest of Memphis and great prince of the Mashuash, Takelut, and of the princess of royal race, Thes-bast-per, in the year 28, in the month of Paophi, on the first day of the month. The full lifetime of this god amounted to twenty-six years." Such is the historical literature of the period. The only other kind of literature belonging to it which has come down to us, consists of what are called " Magical Texts." These are to the following effect:—
" When Horus weeps, the water that falls from his

DECLINE OF ART AND LITERATURE.

eyes grows into plants producing a sweet perfume. When Typhon lets fall blood from his nose, it grows into plants changing to cedars, and produces turpentine instead of the water. When Shu and Tefnut weep much, and water falls from their eyes, it changes into plants that produce incense. When the Sun weeps a second time, and lets water fall from his eyes, it is changed into working bees; they work in the flowers of each kind, and honey and wax are produced instead of the water. When the Sun becomes weak, he lets fall the perspiration of his members, and this changes to a liquid." Or again—"To make a magic mixture: Take two grains of incense, two fumigations, two jars of cedar-oil, two jars of *tas*, two jars of wine, two jars of spirits of wine. Apply it at the place of thy heart. Thou art protected against the accidents of life; thou art protected against a violent death; thou art protected against fire; thou art not ruined on earth, and thou escapest in heaven."

XX.

THE LAND SHADOWING WITH WINGS—EGYPT UNDER THE ETHIOPIANS

The name of Ethiopia was applied in ancient times, much as the term Soudan is applied now, vaguely to the East African interior south of Egypt, from about lat. 24° to about lat. 9°. The tract was for the most part sandy or rocky desert, interspersed with oases, but contained along the course of the Nile a valuable strip of territory; while, south and south-east of the point where the Nile receives the Atbara, it spread out into a broad fertile region, watered by many streams, diversified by mountains and woodlands, rich in minerals, and of considerable fertility. At no time did the whole of this vast tract—a thousand miles long by eight or nine hundred broad—form a single state or monarchy. Rather, for the most part, was it divided up among an indefinite number of states, or rather of tribes, some of them herdsmen, others hunters or fishermen, very jealous of their independence, and frequently at war one with another. Among the various tribes there was a certain community of race, a resemblance of physical type, and a similarity of language. Their neighbours, the Egyptians, included them all under a single ethnic name, speaking of them as Kashi or Kushi—a term manifestly identical with the Cush or Cushi of the Hebrews. They were a race cognate with the Egyptians, but darker in complexion and coarser in feature —not by any means negroes, but still more nearly allied to the negro than the Egyptians were. Their best representatives in modern times are the purebred Abyssinian tribes, the Gallas, Wolaïtzas, and the like, who are probably their descendants.

The portion of Ethiopia which lay nearest to Egypt had been from a very early date penetrated by Egyptian influence. Wars with "the miserable Kashi" began as far back as the time of Usurtasen I.; and Usurtasen III. carried his arms beyond the Second Cataract, and attached the northern portion of Ethiopia to Egypt. The great kings of the eighteenth dynasty, Thothmes III., Amenhotep II., and Amenhotep III., proceeded still further southward ; and the last of these monarchs built a temple to Ammon at Napata, near the modern Gebel Berkal. The Ethiopians of this region, a plastic race, adopted to a considerable extent the Egyptian civilization, worshipped Egyptian gods in Egyptian shrines, and set up inscriptions in the hieroglyphic character and in the Egyptian tongue. Napata, and the Nile valley both below it and above it, was already half Egyptianized, when, on the establishment of the Sheshonk dynasty in Egypt, the descendants of Herhor resolved to quit their native country, and remove themselves into Ethiopia, where they had reason to expect a welcome. They were probably already connected by marriage with some of the leading chiefs of

Napata, and their sacerdotal character gave them a great hold on a peculiarly superstitious people. The "princes of Noph" received them with the greatest favour, and assigned them the highest position in the state. Retaining their priestly office, they became at once Ethiopian monarchs, and High-Priests of the Temple of Ammon which Amenhotep III. had erected at Napata. Napata, under their government, flourished greatly, and acquired a considerable architectural magnificence. Fresh temples were built, in which the worship of Egyptian was combined with that of Ethiopian deities; avenues of sphinxes adorned the approaches to these new shrines; the practice of burying the members of the royal house in pyramids was reverted to; and the necropolis of Napata recalled the glories of the old necropolis of Memphis.

Napata was also a place of much wealth. The kingdom, whereof it was the capital, reached southward as far as the modern Khartoum, and eastward stretched up to the Abyssinian highlands, including the valleys of the Atbara and its tributaries, together with most of the tract between the Atbara and the Blue Nile. This was a region of great natural wealth, containing many mines of gold, iron, copper, and salt, abundant woods of date-palm, almond-trees, and ilex, some excellent pasture-ground, and much rich meadow-land suitable for the growth of *doora* and other sorts of grain. Fish of many kinds, and excellent turtle, abounded in the Atbara and the other streams; while the geographical position was favourable for commerce with the tribes of the interior, who were able to furnish an almost inexhaustible supply of ivory, skins, and ostrich feathers.

The first monarch of Napata, whose name has come down to us, is a certain Piankhi, who called himself Mi-Ammon, or Meri-Ammon—that is to say, " beloved of Ammon." He is thought to have been a descendant of Herhor, and to have begun to reign about B.C. 755. At this time Egypt had reached the state of extreme disintegration described in the last section. A prince named Tafnekht, probably of Libyan origin, ruled in the western Delta, and held Saïs and Memphis ; an Osorkon was king of the eastern Delta, and held his court at Bubastis ; Petesis was king of Athribis, near the apex of the Delta ; and a prince named Aupot, or Shupot, ruled in some portion of the same region. In Middle Egypt, the tract immediately above Memphis formed the kingdom of Pefaabast, who had his residence in Sutensenen, or Heracleopolis Magna, and held the Fayoum under his authority ; while further south the Nile valley was in the possession of a certain Namrut, whose capital was Sesennu, or Hermopolis. Bek-en-nefi, and a Sheshonk, had also principalities, though in what exact position is uncertain ; and various towns, including Mendes, were under the government of chiefs of mercenaries, of whom it is reckoned that there were more than a dozen. Thebes and Southern Egypt from about the latitude of Hermopolis had already been absorbed into the kingdom of Napata, and were ruled directly by Piankhi.

Such being the state of affairs when he came to the throne, Piankhi contrived between his first and his twenty-first year (about B.C. 755-734) gradually to extend his authority over the other kings, and to reduce them to the position of tributary princes or feudatories. It is uncertain whether he used force to effect his purpose. Perhaps the fear of the Assyrians, who, under Tiglath-pileser II., were about this time (B.C. 745-730) making great advances in Syria and Palestine, may have been sufficiently strong to induce the princes voluntarily to adopt the protection of Piankhi, whom they may have regarded as an Egyptian rather than a foreigner. At any rate, we do not hear of violence being used until revolt broke out. In the twenty-first year of Piankhi, news reached him that Tafnekht, king of Memphis and Saïs, had rebelled, and, not content with throwing off his allegiance, had commenced a series of attacks upon the princes that remained faithful to their suzerain, and was endeavouring to make himself master of the whole country. Already had he fallen upon Pafaabast, and forced him to surrender at discretion; he was advancing up the river; Namrut had joined him; and he would soon threaten Thebes, unless a strenuous resistance were offered. Piankhi seems at first to have despised his enemy. He thought it enough to send two generals, at the head of a strong body of troops, down the Nile, with orders to suppress the revolt, and bring the arch-rebel into his presence. The expedition left Thebes. On its way down the river, it fell in with the advancing fleet of the enemy, and completely defeated it. The rebel chiefs, who now included Petesis, Osorkon, and Aupot, as well as Tafnekht, Pefaabast, and Namrut, abandoning Hermopolis and the Middle Nile, fell back upon Sutensenen or Heracleopolis Magna, where they concentrated their forces, and awaited a second attack. This was not long delayed. Piankhi's fleet and army, having besieged and taken Hermopolis, descended the river to Sutensenen, gave the confederates a second naval defeat, and disembarking, followed up their success with another great victory on land, completely routing the rebels, and driving them to take refuge in Lower Egypt, or in the towns on the river bank below Heracleopolis. But now a strange reverse of fortune befell them. Namrut, the Hermopolitan monarch, hearing of the occupation of his capital by Piankhi's army, resolved on a bold attempt to retake it ; and, having collected a number of ships and troops, quitted his confederates, sailed up the Nile, besieged the Ethiopian garrison which had been left to hold the place, overpowered them, and recovered his city.

This unexpected blow roused Piankhi from his inaction. Having collected a fresh army, he quitted Napata in the first month of the year, and reached Thebes in the second, where he stopped awhile to perform a number of religious ceremonies ; at their close, he descended the Nile to Hermopolis, invested it, and commenced its siege. Moveable towers were brought up against the walls, from which machines threw stones and arrows into the city ; the defenders suffered terribly, and after a short time insisted on a surrender. Namrut made his peace with his offended sovereign through the intercession of his wife with Piankhi's wives, sisters, and daughters, and was allowed once more to do homage to his lord in the temple of Thoth, leading his war-horse in one hand and holding a sistrum, the instrument wherewith it was usual to approach a god, in the other. Piankhi entered Hermopolis, and examined the treasury, store-houses, and stables, finding in the last a number of horses, which had been reduced almost to starvation by the siege. Either on this account, or for some other reason, Piankhi treated the Hermopolitan prince with

PIANKHI RECEIVING THE SUBMISSION OF NAMRUT AND OTHERS.

coldness, and did not for some time reinstate him in his kingdom.

Continuing his triumphal march towards the north Piankhi received the submission of Heracleopolis the capital of Pefaabast, and of various other cities on either bank of the Nile, and in a short time appeared before Memphis and summoned it to surrender; but his summons was set at nought. Tafnekht had recently visited the city, had strengthened its defences, augmented its supplies, and reinforced its garrison with an addition of eight thousand men, thereby greatly inspiriting them. It was resolved to resist to the uttermost. So the gates were shut, the walls manned, and Piankhi challenged to do his worst. "Then was His Majesty furious against them, like a panther." Piankhi attacked the city fiercely, both by land and water. Taking the command of the fleet in person, he sailed down the Nile, and, bringing his vessels close up to the walls and towers on the riverside, made use of the masts and yards as ladders, and so scaled the fortifications; then after slaughtering thousands on the ramparts, he forced an entrance into the town. Memphis, upon this, surrendered. Piankhi entered the town, and sacrificed to the god Phthah A number of the princes, including Aupot and Merkaneshu, a leader of mercenaries, came in and made their submission; but two of the principal rebels still remained unsubdued—Tafnekht, the leader of the revolt, and Osorkon, king of Bubastis. Piankhi proceeded against the latter. Advancing first on Heliopolis, instead of resistance he was received with acclamations, the people, priests, and soldiery having gone over to his side. "Nothing succeeds like success." Egypt was as prone as other countries to "worship the rising sun;" and Piankhi's victories had by this time marked him out in the eyes of the Egyptians as the favourite of Heaven, their predestined monarch and ruler. Accordingly, Heliopolis received him gladly, hailing him as "the indestructible Horus"—he was allowed to bathe in the sacred lake within the precincts of the great temple, to offer sacrifice to Ra, and to enter through the folding-doors into the central shrine, where were laid up the sacred boats of Ra and Tum. After this surrender, Osorkon thought it vain to attempt further resistance. He quitted Bubastis, and, seeking the presence of the victorious Piankhi, submitted himself and renewed his homage. At the same time, Petisis, king of Athribis, made his submission.

The only prince who still remained unsubdued was Tafnekht, the original rebel. Tafnekht had fled after the fall of Memphis, and had taken refuge either in one of the islands of the Delta, or beyond the seas, in Aradus or Cyprus. But he saw that further resistance was vain; and that, if he was to rule an Egyptian principality, it must be as a secondary monarch. Accordingly he, too, submitted himself, and was restored to his former kingdom. Piankhi returned up the Nile to his own city of Napata amid songs and rejoicings—whether sincere or feigned, who shall say? His own account of the matter is the following: "When His Majesty sailed up the river, his heart was glad; all its banks resounded with music. The inhabitants of the west and of the east betook themselves to making melody at His Majesty's approach. To the notes of the music they sang, 'O king, thou conqueror! O Piankhi, thou conquering king! Thou hast come and smitten Lower Egypt; thou madest the men as women. The heart of the mother rejoices who bare such a son, for he who begat thee dwells in the vale of death. Happiness be to thee, O cow that hast borne the Bull! Thou shalt live for ever in after ages. Thy victory shall endure, O king and friend of Thebes!'"

This happy condition of things did not, however, continue long. Piankhi, soon after his return to his capital, died without leaving issue; and the race of Herhor being now extinct, the Ethiopians had to elect a king from the number of their own nobles. Their choice fell on a certain Kashta, a man of little energy, who allowed Egypt to throw off the Ethiopian sovereignty without making any effort to prevent it. Bek-en-ranf, the son of Tafnekht, was the leader of this successful rebellion, and is said to have reigned over all Egypt for six years. He got a name for wisdom and justice, but he could not alter that condition of affairs which had been gradually brought about by the slow working of various more or less occult causes, whereby Ethiopia had increased and Egypt diminished in power, their relative strength, as compared with former times, having become inverted. Ethiopia, being now the stronger, was sure to reassert herself, and did so in Bek-en-ranf's seventh year. Shabak, the son of Kashta, whose character was cast in a far stronger mould than that of his father, having mounted the Ethiopian throne, lost no time in swooping down upon Egypt from the upper region, and, carrying all before him, besieged and took Saïs, made Bek-en-ranf a prisoner, and barbarously burnt him alive for his rebellion. His fierce and sensuous physiognomy is quite in keeping with this bloody deed, which was well calculated to strike terror into the Egyptian nation, and to ensure a general submission.

The rule of the Ethiopians was now for some fifty years firmly established. Shabak founded a dynasty which the Egyptians themselves admitted to be legitimate, and which the historian Manetho declared to have consisted of three kings—Sabacos (or Shabak), Sevechus (or Shabatok), and Taracus (or Tehrak), the Hebrew Tirhakah. The extant monuments confirm the names, and order of succession, of these monarchs. They were of a coarser and ruder fibre than the native Egyptians, but they did not rule Egypt in any alien or hostile spirit. On the contrary, they were pious worshippers of the old Egyptian gods; they repaired and beautified the old Egyptian temples; and, instead of ruling Egypt, as a conquered province, from Napata, they resided permanently, or at any rate occasionally, at the Egyptian capitals, Thebes and Memphis. There are certain indications which make it probable that to some extent they pursued the policy of Piankhi, and governed Lower Egypt by means of tributary kings, who held their courts at Saïs, Tanis, and perhaps Bubastis. But they kept a jealous watch over their subject princes, and allowed none of them to attain a dangerous pre-eminence.

By a curious coincidence the Ethiopic sway, or extension of influence over Egypt by the great monarchy of the south, exactly synchronized with the development of Assyrian power in south-western Asia, which bordered Egypt upon the north; and thus were brought into hostile collision, the two greatest military powers of the then known world who fought over the prostrate Egypt, like Achilles a..d Hector over the corpse of Patroclus. Shabak's conquest of the Lower Nile valley took place about B.C. 725 or 724. Exactly at that time Shalmaneser IV. was proceeding to extremities against the kingdom of Israel, and was thus threatening to sweep away one of the last two feeble barriers which had hitherto been interposed between the Assyrian territory and the Egyptian. Shabak, entreated by Hoshea, the last Israelite monarch, to lend him aid, consented to take the kingdom of Israel under his protection (2 Kings xvii. 4),

HEAD OF SHABAK (SABACO).

actuated no doubt by an enlightened view of his own interest. But when Samaria was besieged (B.C. 723) and the danger became pressing, he had not the courage to act up to his engagements. The stout resistance offered by the Israelite capital for more than two years (2 Kings xvii. 5) drew forth no corresponding effort on the part of the Ethiopic king. Hoshea was left to his own resources, and in B.C. 722 was forced to succumb. His capital was taken by storm, its inhabitants seized and carried off by the conqueror, the whole territory absorbed into that of Assyria, and the cities occupied by Assyrian colonists (2 Kings xvii. 24). Assyria was brought one step nearer to Egypt, and it became more than ever evident that contact and collision could not be much longer deferred.

The collision came in B.C. 720. In that year Sargon, the founder of the last and greatest of the Assyrian dynasties, who had succeeded Shalmaneser IV. in B.C. 722, having arranged matters in Samaria and taken Hamath, pressed on against Philistia, the last inhabited country on the route which led to Egypt. Shabak, having made alliance with Hanun, king of Gaza, marched to his aid. The opposing hosts met at Ropeh, the Raphia of the Greeks, on the very borders of the desert. Sargon commanded in person on the one side, Shabak and Hanun on the other. A great battle was fought, which was for a long time stoutly contested; but the strong forms, the superior arms, and the better discipline of the Assyrians, prevailed. Asia proved herself, as she has generally done, stronger than Africa; the Egyptians and Philistines fled away in disorder; Hanun was made a prisoner; Shabak with difficulty escaped. Negotiations appear to have followed, and a convention to have been drawn up, to which the Ethiopian and Assyrian monarchs attached their seals. The lump of clay which received the impressions was found by Sir A. Layard at Nineveh, and is now in the British Museum.

Shortly afterwards, about B.C. 712, Shabak died, and was succeeded in Egypt by his son Shabatok, in Ethiopia by a certain Tehrak, who appears to have been his nephew. Tehrak exercised the paramount authority over the whole realm, but resided at Napata, while Shabatok held his court at Memphis and ruled Lower Egypt as Tehrak's representative. Assyrian

SEAL OF SHABAK.

aggression still continued. In B.C. 711 Sargon took Ashdod, and threatened an invasion of Egypt, which Shabatok averted by sending a submissive embassy with presents.

Six years afterwards Sargon died, and his son, Sennacherib, mounted the Assyrian throne. At once south-western Asia was in a ferment. The Phœnician and Philistine kings recently subjected by Tiglath-Pileser and Sargon, broke out in open revolt. Hezekiah, king of Judah, joined the malcontents. The aid of Egypt was implored, and certain promises of support and assistance received, in part from Tehrak, in part from Shabatok and other native rulers of nomes and cities. Sennacherib, in B.C. 701, led his army into Syria to suppress the rebellion, reduced Phœnicia, received the submission of Ashdod, Ammon, Moab, and Edom; took Ascalon, Hazor, and Joppa, and was proceeding against Ekron, when for the first time he encountered an armed force in the field. A large Egyptian and Ethiopian contingent had at last reached Philistia, and, having united itself with the Ekronites, stood prepared to give the Assyrians battle near Eltekeh. The force consisted of chariots, horsemen, and footmen, and was so numerous that Sennacherib calls it "a multitude that no man could number." Once more, however, Africa had to succumb. Sennacherib at Eltekeh defeated the combined forces of Egypt and Ethiopia with as much ease and completeness as Sargon at Raphia; the multitudinous host was entirely routed, and fled from the field, leaving in the hands of the victors the greater portion of their war-chariots and several sons of one of their kings.

After this defeat, it is not surprising that Tehrak made no further effort. Hezekiah, the last rebel unsubdued, was left to defend himself as he best might. The Egyptians retreated to their own borders, and there awaited attack. It seemed as if the triumph of Assyria was assured, and as if her yoke must almost immediately be imposed alike upon Judea, upon Egypt, and upon the kingdom of Napata; but an extraordinary catastrophe averted the immediate danger, and gave to Egypt and Ethiopia a respite of thirty-four years. Sennacherib's army, of nearly two

SENNACHERIB, HEZEKIAH, AND TIRHAKAH. 329

hundred thousand men, was almost totally destroyed in one night. "The angel of the Lord went forth," says the contemporary writer, Isaiah, "and smote in the camp of the Assyrians a hundred and fourscore and five thousand; and when they arose early in the morning, behold, they were all dead corpses" (Isa. xxxvii. 36). Whatever the agency employed in this remarkable destruction—whether it was caused by a simoon, or a pestilence, or by a direct visitation of the Almighty,

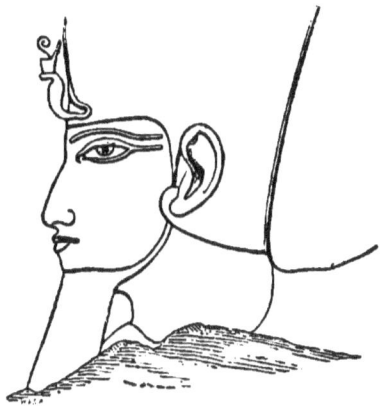

HEAD OF TEHRAK (TIRHAKAH).

as different writers have explained it—the event is certain. Its truth is written in the undeniable facts of later history, which show us a sudden cessation of Assyrian attack in this quarter, the kingdom of Judea saved from absorption, and the countries on the banks of the Nile left absolutely unobstructed by Assyria for the third part of a century. As the destruction happened on their borders, the Egyptians naturally enough ascribed it to their own gods, and made a boast of it centuries after. Everything marks, as one of the most noticeable facts in history, this annihilation of so great a portion of the army of the greatest of all the kings of Assyria.

The reign of Tirhakah (Tehrak) during this period appears to have been glorious. He was regarded by Judea as its protector, and exercised a certain influence over all Syria as far as Taurus, Amanus, and the Euphrates. In Africa, he brought into subjection the native tribes of the north coast, carrying his arms, according to some, as far as the Pillars of Hercules. He is exhibited at Medinet-Abou in the dress of a warrior, smiting with a mace ten captive foreign princes. He erected monuments in the Egyptian style at Thebes, Memphis, and Napata. Of all the Ethiopian sovereigns of Egypt he was undoubtedly the greatest; but towards the close of his life reverses befell him, which require to be treated of in another section.

XXI.

THE FIGHT OVER THE CARCASE—ETHIOPIA v. ASSYRIA.

THE miraculous destruction of his army was accepted by Sennacherib as a warning to desist from all further attempts against the independence of Judea, and from all further efforts to extend his dominions towards the south-west. He survived the destruction during a period of seventeen years, and was actively engaged in a number of wars towards the east, the north, and the north-west, but abstained carefully from further contact with either Palestine or Egypt. His son Esarhaddon succeeded him on the throne in B.C. 681, and at once, to a certain extent, modified this policy. He re-established the Assyrian dominion over Upper Syria, Phœnicia, and even Edom ; but during the first nine years of his reign the memory of his father's disaster caused him to leave Judea and Egypt unattacked. At last, however, in B.C. 672, encouraged by his many military successes, by the troubled state of Judea under the idolatrous Manasseh, who "shed innocent blood very much from one end of Jerusalem to the other" (2 Kings xxi. 16), and by the advanced age of Tehrak, which seemed to render him a less formidable antagonist now than formerly, he resumed the designs on Egypt which his father and grandfather had entertained, swept Manasseh from his path by seizing him and carrying him off a prisoner to Babylon, marched his troops from Aphek along the coast of Palestine to Raphia, and there made the dispositions which seemed to him best calculated to effect the conquest of the coveted country. As Tirhakah, aware of his intentions, had collected all his available force upon his north-east frontier, about Pelusium and its immediate neighbourhood, the Assyrian monarch took the bold resolution of proceeding southward through the waste tract, known to the Hebrews as "the desert of Shur," in such a way as to turn the flank of Tirhakah's army, to reach Pithom (Heroopolis) and to attack Memphis along the line of the Old Canal. The Arab Sheikhs of the desert were induced to lend him their aid, and facilitate his march by conveying the water necessary for his army on the backs of their camels in skins. The march was thus made in safety, though the soldiers are said to have suffered considerably from fatigue and thirst, and to have been greatly alarmed by the sight of numerous serpents.

Tehrak, on his part, did all that was possible. On learning Esarhaddon's change of route, he broke up from Pelusium, and, by a hasty march across the eastern Delta succeeded in interposing his army between Memphis and the host of the Assyrians, which had to follow the line taken by Sir Garnet Wolseley in 1884, and encountered the enemy, probably, not far from the spot where the British general completely defeated the troops of Arabi. Here for

TEHRAK DEFEATED BY ESARHADDON. 333

the third time Asia and Africa stood arrayed the one against the other. Assyria brought into the field a host of probably not fewer than two hundred thousand men, including a strong chariot force, a powerful cavalry, and an infantry variously armed and appointed—some with huge shields and covered by almost complete panoplies, others lightly equipped with targe and dart, or even simply with slings. Egypt opposed to her a force, probably, even more numerous, but consisting chiefly of a light-armed infantry, containing a large proportion of mercenaries whose hearts would not be in the fight, deficient in cavalry, and apt to trust mainly to its chariots. In the flat Egyptian plains lightly accoutred troops fight at a great disadvantage against those whose equipment is of greater solidity and strength; cavalry are an important arm, since there is nothing to check the impetus of a charge; and personal strength is a most important element in determining the result of a conflict. The Assyrians were more strongly made than the Egyptians; they had probably a better training; they certainly wore more armour, carried larger shields and longer spears, and were better equipped both for offence and defence. We have, unfortunately, no description of the battle; but it is in no way surprising to learn that the Assyrians prevailed; Tehrak's forces suffered a complete defeat, were driven from the field in confusion, and hastily dispersed themselves.

Memphis was then besieged, taken, and given up to pillage. The statues of the gods, the gold and silver, the turquoise and lapis lazuli, the vases, censers, jars, goblets, amphoræ, the stores of ivory, ebony, cinnamon, frankincense, fine linen, crystal, jasper, alabaster, embroidery, with which the piety of kings had enriched the temples—especially the Great Temple of Phthah—during fifteen or twenty centuries, were ruthlessly carried off by the conquerors, who destined them either for the adornment of the Ninevite shrines or for their own private advantage. Tehrak's wife and concubines, together with several of his children and numerous officers of his court, left behind in consequence of his hurried flight, fell into the enemy's hands. Tehrak himself escaped, and fled first to Thebes, and then to Napata; while the army of Esarhaddon, following closely on his footsteps, advanced up the valley of the Nile, scoured the open country with their cavalry, stormed the smaller towns, and after a siege of some duration took "populous No," or Thebes, "that was situate among the rivers, that had the waters round about it, whose rampart was the great deep" (Nahum iii. 8). All Egypt was overrun from the Mediterranean to the First Cataract; thousands of prisoners were taken and carried away captive; the Assyrian monarch was undisputed master of the entire land of Mizraïm from Migdol to Syene and from Pelusium to the City of Crocodiles.

Upon conquest followed organization. The great Assyrian was not content merely to overrun Egypt; he was bent upon holding it. Acting on the Roman principle, "*Divide et impera,*" he broke up the country into twenty distinct principalities, over each of which he placed a governor, while in the capital of each he put an Assyrian garrison. Of the governors, by far the greater number were native Egyptians; but in

EGYPT SUBDUED AND DIVIDED UP. 335

one or two instances the command was given to an Assyrian. For the most part, the old divisions of the nomes were kept, but sometimes two or more nomes were thrown together and united under a single governor. Neco, an ancestor of the great Pharaoh who bore the same name (2 Kings xxiii. 29-35), had Saïs, Memphis, and the nomes that lay between them; Mentu-em-ankh had Thebes and southern Egypt as far as Elephantine. Satisfied with these arrangements,

FIGURE OF ESAR-HADDON AT THE NAHR-EL-KELB.

the conqueror returned to Nineveh, having first, however, sculptured on the rocks at the mouth of the Nahr-el-Kelb a representation of his person and an account of his conquests.

Egypt lay at the feet of Assyria for about three or four years (B.C. 672-669). Then the struggle was renewed. Tehrak, who had bided his time, learning that Esarhaddon was seized with a mortal malady, issued (B.C. 669) from his Ethiopian fastnesses, descended the valley of the Nile, expelled the governors whom Esarhaddon had set up, and possessed himself of the disputed territory. Thebes received him with enthusiasm, as one attached to the worship of Ammon ; and the priests of Phthah opened to him the gates of Memphis, despite the efforts of Neco and the Assyrian garrison. The religious sympathy between Ethiopia and Egypt was an important factor in the as yet undecided contest, and helped much to further the Ethiopic cause. But in war sentiment can effect but little. Physical force, on the whole, prevails, unless in the rare instances where miracle intervenes, or where patriotic enthusiasm is exalted to such a pitch as to strike physical force with impotency

In the conflict that was now raging patriotism had little part. Ethiopia and Assyria were contending, partly for military pre-eminence, partly for the prey that lay between them, inviting a master—the rich and now weak Egyptian kingdom. Tehrak's success, communicated to the Assyrian Court by the dispossessed governors, drew forth almost immediately a counter effort on the part of Assyria, which did not intend to relinquish without a struggle the important addition that Esarhaddon had made to the empire. In B.C. 668, Asshur-bani-pal, the Sardanapalus of the Greeks, having succeeded his father Esarhaddon, put the forces of Assyria once more in motion, and swooping down upon the unhappy Egypt, succeeded in carrying all before him, defeated Tehrak at Karbanit in the Delta, recovered Memphis and Thebes, forced Tehrak to take refuge at Napata, re-established in power the twenty petty kings, and restored the country in all respects to the condition into which it had been brought four years previously by Esarhaddon. Egypt thus passed under the Assyrians for the second time, Ethiopia relinquishing her hold upon the prey as soon as Assyria firmly grasped it.

Still the matter was not yet settled, the conflict was not yet ended. The petty kings themselves began now to coquet with Tehrak, and to invite his co-operation in an attempt, which they promised they would make, to throw off the yoke of the Assyrians. Detected in this intrigue, Neco and two others were arrested by the Assyrian commandants, loaded with chains, and sent as prisoners to Nineveh. But their arrest did not check the movement. On the contrary, the spirit of revolt spread. The commandants tried to stop it by measures of extreme severity: they sacked the great cities of the Delta—Saïs, Mendes, and Tanis or Zoan ; but all was of no avail. Tehrak once more took the field, descended the Nile valley, recovered Thebes, and threatened Memphis. Asshurbani-pal upon this hastily sent Neco from Nineveh at the head of an Assyrian army to exert his influence on the Assyrian side—which he was content to do, since the Ninevite monarch had made him chief of the petty kings, and conferred the principality of Athribis on his son, Psamatik. Tehrak, in alarm, retreated from his bold attempt, evacuated Thebes, and returned to his own dominions, where he shortly afterwards died (B.C. 667).

It might have been expected that the death of the aged warrior-king would have been the signal for Ethiopia to withdraw from the struggle so long maintained, and relinquish Egypt to her rival; but the actual result was the exact contrary. Tehrak was succeeded at Napata by his step-son, Rut-Ammon, a young prince of a bold and warlike temper. Far from recoiling from the enterprize which Tehrak had adjudged hopeless, he threw himself into it with the utmost ardour. Once more an Ethiopian army descended the Nile valley, occupied Thebes, engaged and defeated a combined Egyptian and Assyrian force near Memphis, took the capital, made its garrison prisoners, and brought under subjection the greater portion of the Delta. Neco, having fallen into the hands of the Ethiopians, was cruelly put to death. His son, Psamatik, saved himself by a timely flight.

History now "repeated itself." In B.C. 666 Asshur-bani-pal made, in person, a second expedition into Egypt, defeated Rut-Ammon upon the frontier, recovered Memphis, marched upon Thebes, Rut-Ammon retiring as he advanced, stormed and sacked the great city, inflicted wanton injury on its temples, carried off its treasures, and enslaved its population. The triumph of the Assyrian arms was complete. Very shortly all resistance ceased. The subject princes were replaced in their principalities. Asshur-bani-pal's sovereignty was universally acknowledged, and Ethiopia, apparently, gave up the contest.

One more effort was, however, made by the southern power. On the death of Rut-Ammon, Mi-Ammon-Nut, probably a son of Tirhakah's, became king of Ethiopia, and resolved on a renewal of the war. Egyptian disaffection might always be counted on, whichever of the two great powers held temporary possession of the country; and Mi-Ammon-Nut further courted the favour of the Egyptian princes, priests, and people, by an ostentatious display of zeal for their religion. Assyria had allowed the temples to fall into decay; the statues of the gods had in some instances been cast down, the temple revenues confiscated, the priests restrained in their conduct of the religious worship. Mi-Ammon-Nut proclaimed himself the chosen of Ammon, and the champion of the gods of Egypt. On entering each Egyptian town he was careful to visit its chief temple, to offer sacrifices and gifts, to honour the images and lead them in procession, and to pay all due respect to the college of priests. This prudent policy met with complete success. As he advanced down the Nile valley, he was everywhere received with acclamations. " Go onward in the peace of thy name," they shouted, " go onward in the peace of thy name. Dispense life throughout all the land—that the temples may be restored which are hastening to ruin ; that the statues of the gods may be set up after their manner ; that their revenues may be given back to the gods and goddesses, and the offerings of the dead to the deceased; that the priest may be established in his place, and all things be fulfilled according to the Holy Ritual." In many places where it had been intended to oppose his advance in arms, the news of his pious acts produced a complete revulsion of feeling, and "those whose intention it had been to fight were moved with joy." No one opposed him until he had nearly reached the northern capital, Memphis, which was doubtless held in force by the

Assyrians, to whom the princes of Lower Egypt were still faithful. A battle, accordingly, was fought before the walls, and in this Mi-Ammon-Nut was victorious; the Egyptians probably did not fight with much zeal, and the Assyrians, distrusting their subject allies, may well have been dispirited. After the victory, Memphis opened her gates, and soon afterwards the princes of the Delta thought it best to make their submission—the Assyrians, we must suppose, retired—Mi-Ammon-Nut's authority was acknowledged, and the princes, having transferred their allegiance to him, were allowed to retain their governments.

The consequences of this last Ethiopian invasion of Egypt appear to have been transient. Mi-Ammon-Nut did not live very long to enjoy his conquest, and in Egypt he had no successor. He was not even recognized by the Egyptians among their legitimate kings. Egypt at his death reverted to her previous position of dependence upon Assyria, feeling herself still too weak to stand alone, and perhaps not greatly caring, so that she had peace, which of the two great powers she acknowledged as her suzerain. She had now (about B.C. 650) for above twenty years been fought over by the two chief kingdoms of the earth—each of them had traversed with huge armies, as many as five or six times, the Nile valley from one extremity to the other; the cities had been half ruined, harvest after harvest destroyed, trees cut down, temples rifled, homesteads burnt, villas plundered. Thebes, the Hundred-gated, probably for many ages quite the most magnificent city in the world, had become a by-word for desolation (Nahum iii. 8, 9) ; Memphis, Heliopolis, Tanis, Saïs, Mendes, Bubastis, Heracleopolis, Hermopolis, Crocodilopolis, had been taken and retaken repeatedly; the old buildings and monuments had been allowed to fall into decay ; no king had been firmly enough established on his throne to undertake the erection of any but insignificant new ones. Egypt was "fallen, fallen, fallen—fallen from her high estate;" an apathy, not unlike the stillness of death, brooded over her ; literature was silent, art extinct ; hope of recovery can scarcely have lingered in many bosoms. As events proved, the vital spark was not actually fled ; but the keenest observer would scarcely have ventured to predict, at any time between B.C. 750 and B.C. 650, such a revival as marked the period between B.C. 650 and B.C. 530.

XXII.

THE CORPSE COMES TO LIFE AGAIN—PSAMATIK I. AND HIS SON NECO.

WHEN a country has sunk so gradually, so persistently, and for so long a series of years as Egypt had now been sinking, if there is a revival, it must almost necessarily come from without. The corpse cannot rise without assistance—the expiring patient cannot cure himself. All the vital powers being sapped, all the energies having departed, the Valley of the Shadow of Death having been entered, nothing can arrest dissolution but some foreign stock, some blood not yet vitiated, some " saviour " sent by Divine providence from outside the nation (Isa. xix. 20), to recall the expiring life, to revivify the paralyzed frame, to infuse fresh energy into it, and to make it once more live, breathe, act, think, assert itself. Yet the saviour must not be altogether from without. He must not be a conqueror, for conquest necessarily weakens and depresses ; he must not be too remote in blood, or he will lack the power fully to understand and sympathize with the nation which he is to restore, and without true understanding and true sympathy he can effect nothing ; he must not be a stranger to the nation's recent history, or he will make mistakes that will be irremediable. What is wanted is a scion of a foreign stock, connected by marriage and otherwise with the nation that he is to regenerate, and well acquainted with its circumstances, character, position, history, virtues, weaknesses. No entirely new man can answer to these requirements; he must be found, if he is to be found at all, among the principal men of the time, whose lot has for some considerable period been cast in with the State which is to be renovated.

In Egypt, at the time of which we are speaking, exactly this position was occupied by Psamatik, son of Neco. He was, according to all appearance, of Libyan origin; his stock was new; his name and his father's name are unheard of hitherto in Egyptian history; etymologically, they are non-Egyptian; and Psamatik has a non-Egyptian countenance. He was probably of the same family as "Inarus the Libyan," whose father was a Psamatik. He belonged thus to a Libyan stock, which had, however, been crossed, more than once, with the blood of the Egyptians. The family was one of those Libyan families which had long been domiciled at Saïs, and had intermarried with the older Saites, who were predominantly Egyptian. He had also for twenty years or more been an important unit in the Egyptian political system, having shared the vicissitudes of his father's fortunes from B.C. 672 to B.C. 667, and having then been placed at the head of one of the many principalities into which Egypt was divided. In the same, or the next, year he seems to have succeeded his father: and he had reigned at Saïs for sixteen or seventeen years before he felt himself called upon to take any step that was at all abnormal, or attempt in any way to change his position.

Familiar with the politics and institutions of Egypt, yet, as a semi-Libyan, devoid of Egyptian prejudices,

HEAD OF PSAMATIK I.

and full of the ambition which naturally inspires young princes of a vigorous stock, Psamatik had at once the desire to shake off the yoke of Assyria, and reunite Egypt under his own sway, and also a willingness to adopt any means, however new and strange, by which such a result might be accomplished. He had probably long watched for a favourable moment at which to give his ambition vent, and found it at last in the circumstances that ushered in the second half of the seventh century. Assyria was, about B.C. 651, brought into a position of great difficulty, by the revolt of Babylon in alliance with Elam, and was thus quite unable to exercise a strict surveillance over the more distant parts of the Empire. The garrison by which she held Egypt had probably been weakened by the withdrawal of troops for the defence of Assyria Proper; at any rate, it could not be relieved or strengthened under the existing circumstances. At the same time a power had grown up in Asia Minor, which was jealous of Assyria, having lately been made to tremble for its independence. Gyges of Lydia had, in a moment of difficulty, been induced to acknowledge himself Assyria's subject; but he had emerged triumphant from the perils surrounding him, had reasserted his independent authority, and was anxious that the power of Assyria should be, as much as possible, diminished. Psamatik must have been aware of this. Casting his eyes around the political horizon in search of any ally at once able and willing to lend him aid, he fixed upon Lydia as likely to be his best auxiliary, and dispatched an embassy into Asia Minor. Gyges received his application favourably, and sent him a strong Asiatic contingent, chiefly composed of Ionians and Carians. Both races were at this time warlike, and wore armour of much greater weight and strength than any which the Egyptians were accustomed to carry. It was in reliance, mainly, on these foreigners, that Psamatik ventured to proclaim himself "King of the Two Countries," and to throw out a gage of defiance at once to his Assyrian suzerain and to his nineteen fellow-princes.

The gage was not taken up by Assyria. Immersed in her own difficulties, threatened in three quarters, on the south, on the south-east, and on the east by Babylonia, by Elam, and by Media, she had enough to do at home in guarding her own frontiers, and seeking to keep under her immediate neighbours, and was therefore in no condition to engage in distant expeditions, or even to care very much what became of a remote and troublesome dependency. Thus Assyria made no sign. But the petty princes took arms at once. To them the matter was one of life or death; they must either crush the usurper or be themselves swept out of existence. So they gathered together in full force. Pakrur from Pisabtu, and Petubastes from Tanis, and Sheshonk from Busiris, and Tafnekht from Prosopitis, and Bek-en-nefi from Athribis, and Nakh-he from Heracleopolis, and Pimai from Mendes, and Lamentu from Hermopolis, and Mentu-em-ankh from Thebes, and other princes from other cities, met and formed their several contingents into a single army, and stood at bay near Momemphis, the modern Menouf, in the western Delta, on the borders of the Libyan Desert. Here a great battle was fought, which was for some time doubtful; but the valour of the Greco-Carians, and the superiority of their equipment, prevailed. The victory rested with Psamatik; his adversaries were defeated and dispersed; following up his first success, he proceeded to attack city after city, forcing all to submit, and determined that he would nowhere tolerate even the shadow of a rival. Disintegration had been the curse of Egypt for the space of above a century ; Psamatik put an end to it. No more princes of Bubastis, or of Tanis, or of Saïs, or of Mendes, or of Heracleopolis, or of Thebes ! No more eikosiarchies, dodecarchies, or heptarchies even ! Monarchy pure, the absolute rule of one and one only sovereign over the whole of Egypt, from the cataracts of Syene to the shores of the Mediterranean, and from Pelusium and Migdol to Momemphis and Marea, was established, and henceforth continued, as long as Egyptian rule endured. The lesson had been learnt at a tremendous cost, but it had now at last been thoroughly learnt, that only in unity is there strength —that the separate sticks of the faggot are impotent to resist the external force which the collective bundle might without difficulty have defied and scorned.

Psamatik had gained the object of his ambition— sovereignty over all Egypt ; he had now to consider how it might best be kept. And first, as that which is won by the sword must be kept by the sword, he made arrangements with the troops sent to his aid by Gyges, that they should take permanent service under his banner, and form the most important element in his standing army. His native troops were quartered at Elephantine, in the extreme south, and in Marea and Daphnæ, at the two extremities of the Delta towards the west and east. The new accession to his military strength he stationed at no great distance from the capital, settling them in permanent camps on either side of the Pelusiac branch of the Nile, near the city of Bubastis. We are told that this exaltation of the new corps to the honourable position of keeping watch upon the capital, greatly offended the native troops, and induced 200,000 of them to quit Egypt and seek service with the Ethiopians. The facts have probably been exaggerated, for Ethiopia certainly does not gain, or Egypt lose, in strength, either at or after this period.

Psamatik, further, for the better securing of his throne against pretenders, thought it prudent to contract a marriage with the descendant of a royal stock held in honour by many of his subjects. The princess, Shepenput, was the daughter of a Piankhi, who claimed descent from the unfortunate Bek-en-ranf, the king burnt alive by Shabak, and who had also probably some royal Ethiopian blood in his veins. By his nuptials with this princess, Psamatik assured to his crown the legitimacy which it had hitherto lacked. Uniting henceforth in his own person the rights of the twenty-fourth and twenty-fifth dynasties, those of the Saïtes and those of the Ethiopians, he became the one and only legal king, and no competitor could possibly arise with a title to sovereignty higher or better than his own.

Being now personally secure, he could turn his attention to the restoration and elevation of the nationality of which he had taken it upon him to assume the direction. He could cast his eyes over the unhappy Egypt — depressed, down-trodden, well-nigh trampled to death — and give his best consideration to the question what was to be done to restore her to her ancient greatness. There she lay before his eyes in a deplorable state of misery and degradation. All the great cities, her glory and her boast in former days, had suffered more or less in the incessant wars; Memphis had been besieged and pillaged half a dozen times; Thebes had been sacked and burnt twice; from Syene to Pelusium there was not a town which had not been injured in one or other of the many invasions. The canals and roads, carefully repaired by Shabak, had since his decease met with entire neglect; the cultivable lands had been devastated, and the whole population decimated periodically. Out of the ruins of the old Egypt, Psamatik had to raise up a new Egypt. He had to revivify the dead corpse, and put a fresh life into the stiff and motionless limbs. With great energy and determination he set himself to accomplish the task. Applying himself, first of all, to the restoration of what was decayed and ruined, he re-established the canals and the roads, encouraged agriculture, favoured the development of the population. The ruined towns were gradually repaired and rebuilt, and vast efforts made everywhere to restore, and even to enlarge and beautify the sacred edifices. At Memphis, Psamatik built the great southern portal which gave completeness to the ancient temple of the god Phthah, and also constructed a grand court for the residence of the Apis-Bulls, surrounded by a colonnade, against the piers of which stood colossal figures of Osiris, from eighteen to twenty feet in height. At Thebes he re-erected the portions of the temple of Karnak, which had been thrown down by the Assyrians; at Saïs, Mendes, Heliopolis, and Philæ he undertook extensive works. The entire valley of the Nile became little more than one huge workshop, where stone-cutters and masons, bricklayers and carpenters, laboured incessantly. Under the liberal encouragement of the king and of his chief nobles, the arts recovered themselves and began to flourish anew. The engraving and painting of the hieroglyphics were resumed with success, and carried out with a minuteness and accuracy that provokes the admiration of the beholder. Bas-reliefs of extreme beauty and elaboration characterize the period. There rests upon some of them "a gentle and almost feminine tenderness, which has impressed upon the imitations of living creatures the stamp of an incredible delicacy both of conception and execution." Statues and statuettes of merit were at the same time produced in abundance. The "Saïtie art," as that of the revival under the Psamatiks has been called, is characterized by an extreme neatness of manipulation in the drawings and lines, the fineness of which often reminds us of the performances of a seal-engraver, by grace, softness, tenderness, and elegance. It is not the broad, but somewhat realistic style of the Memphitic period, much less the highly imaginative and vigorous style of the Ramesside kings; but it is a style which has quiet merits of its own, sweet and pure, full of refinement and delicacy.

Egypt was thus rendered flourishing at home; her magnificent temples and other edifices put off their look of neglect; her cities were once more busy seats of industry and traffic; her fields teemed with rich harvests; her population increased; her whole aspect changed. But the circumstances of the time led Psamatik to attempt something more. His employ-

ENCOURAGEMENT OF FOREIGNERS. 351

ment of Greek and Carian mercenaries naturally led him on into an intimacy with foreigners, and into a regard and consideration for them quite unknown to previous Pharaohs, and in contradiction to ordinary Egyptian prejudices. Egypt was the China of the Old World, and had for ages kept herself as much as

BAS-RELIEFS OF THE TIME OF PSAMATIK I.

possible aloof from foreigners, and looked upon them with aversion. Foreign vessels were, until the time of Psamatik, forbidden to enter any of the Nile mouths, or to touch at an Egyptian port. Psamatik saw that the new circumstances required an extensive change. The mercenaries, if they were to be content with their position, must be allowed to communicate freely with the cities and countries from which they came, and intercourse between Greece and Egypt must be encouraged rather than forbidden. Accordingly the Greeks were invited to make settlements in the Delta, and Naucratis, favourably situated on the Canopic branch of the Nile, was specially assigned to them as a residence. Most of the more enterprizing among the commercial states of the time took advantage of the opening, and Miletus, Phocæa, Rhodes, Samos, Chios, Mytilene, Halicarnassus, and Ægina established factories at the locality specified, built temples there to the Greek gods, and sent out a body of colonists. A considerable trade grew up between Egypt and Greece. The Egyptians of the higher classes especially appreciated the flavour and quality of the Greek wines, which were consequently imported into the country in large quantities. Greek pottery and Greek glyptic art also attracted a certain amount of favour. On her side Egypt exported corn, alum, muslin and linen fabrics, and the excellent paper which she made from the *Cyperus Papyrus*.

The trade thus established was carried on mainly, if not wholly, in Greek bottoms, the Egyptians having a distaste to the sea, and regarding commerce with no great favour. Nevertheless, the life and stir which foreign commerce introduced among them, the familiarity with strange customs and manners, engendered by daily intercourse with the Greeks, the acquisition (on the part of some) of the Greek language, the sight of Greek modes of worship, of Greek painting and Greek sculpture, the insight into Greek habits of thought, which could not but follow, produced no inconsiderable effect upon the national character of the Egyptians, shaking them out of their accustomed groove, and awakening curiosity and inquiry. The effect was scarcely beneficial. Egyptian national life had been eminently conservative and unchanging. The introduction of novelty in ten thousand shapes unsettled and disturbed it. The old beliefs were shaken, and a multitude of superstitions rushed in. The corruptions introduced by the Greeks were more easy of adoption and imitation than the sterling points of their character, their intelligence, their unwearied energy, their love of truth. Egypt was awakened to a new life by the novel circumstances of the Psamatik period; but it was a fitful life, unquiet, unnatural, feverish. The character of the men lost in dignity and strength by the discontinuance of military training consequent upon the substitution for a native army of an army of mercenaries. The position of the women sank through the adoption of those ideas concerning them which their contact with orientals had engrained into the minds of the Asiatic Greeks. The national spirit of the people was sapped by the concentration of the royal favour on a race of foreigners whose manners and customs were abhorrent to them, and whom they regarded with envy and dislike. If some improvement is to be seen on the surface of Egyptian life under the Psamatiks, some greater activity and enterprise, some increased intellectual stir, some improved methods in art, these ameliorations scarcely compensate for the indications of decline which lie deeper, and which in the sequel determined the actual fate of the nation.

The later years of the reign of Psamatik were coincident with a time of extreme trouble and confusion in Asia, in the course of which the Assyrian Monarchy came to an end, and south-western Asia was partitioned between the Medes and the Babylonians. A tempting field was laid open for an ambitious prince, who might well have dreamt of Syrian or even Mesopotamian conquest, and of recalling the old glories of Seti, Thothmes, and Amenhotep. Psamatik did go so far as to make an attack upon Philistia, but met with so little success that he was induced to restrain any grander aspirations which he may have cherished, and to leave the Asiatic monarchs to settle Asiatic affairs as it pleased them. Ashdod, we are told, resisted the Egyptian arms for twenty-nine years; and though it fell at last, the prospect of half-a-dozen such sieges was not encouraging. Psamatik, moreover, was an old man by the time that the Assyrian Empire fell to pieces, and we can understand his shrinking from a distant and dangerous expedition. He left the field open for his son, Neco, having in no way committed him, but having secured for him a ready entrance into Asia by his conquest of the Philistine fortress.

Neco, the son of Psamatik I., from the moment that he ascended the throne, resolved to make the bold stroke for empire from which his father had held back. Regarding his mercenary army as a sufficient land-force, he concentrated his energies on the enlargement and improvement of his navy, which was weak in numbers and of antiquated construction. Naval architecture had recently made great strides, first by the inventiveness of the Phœnicians, who introduced the bireme, and then by the skill of the Greeks, who, improving on the hint furnished them, constructed the trireme. Neco, by the help of Greek artificers, built two fleets, both composed of triremes, one in the ports which opened on the Red Sea, the other in those upon the Mediterranean. He then, with the object of uniting

HEAD OF NECO.

the two fleets into one, when occasion should require, made an attempt to re-open the canal between the Nile and the Red Sea, which had been originally constructed by Seti I. and Ramesses II., but had been allowed to fall into disrepair. The Nile mud and the desert sand had combined to silt it up. Neco commenced excavations on a large scale, following the line of the old cutting, but greatly widening it, so that triremes might meet in it and pass each other, without shipping their oars. After a time, however, he felt compelled to desist, without effecting his purpose, owing to an extraordinary mortality among the labourers. According to Herodotus, 120,000 of them perished. At any rate, the suffering and loss of life, probably by epidemics, was such as induced him to relinquish his project, and to turn his thoughts toward gaining his end in another way.

Might not Nature have herself established a water communication between the two seas by which Egypt was washed? It was well known that the Mediterranean and the Red Sea both communicated with an open ocean, and it was the universal teaching of the Greek geographers, that the ocean flowed round the whole earth. Neco determined to try whether Africa was not circumnavigable. Manning some ships with Phœnician mariners, as the boldest and most experienced, accustomed to brave the terrors of the Atlantic outside the Pillars of Hercules, he dispatched them from a port on the Red Sea, with orders to sail southwards, keeping the coast of Africa on their right, and see if they could not return to Egypt by way of the Mediterranean. The enterprise succeeded. The ships, under the skilful guidance of the Phœnicians, anticipated the feat of Vasco di Gama—rounded the Cape of Storms, and returned by way of the Atlantic, the Straits of Gibraltar, and the Mediterranean to the land from which they had set out. But they did not reach Egypt *till the third year.* The success obtained was thus of no practical value, so far as the Pharaoh's warlike projects were concerned. He had to relinquish the idea of uniting his two fleets in one, owing to the length of the way and the dangers of the navigation. He had, however, no mind to relinquish his warlike projects. Syria, Phœnicia, and Palestine were still in an unsettled state, the yoke of Assyria being broken, and that of Babylon not yet firmly fixed on them. Josiah was taking advantage of the opportunity to extend his authority over Samaria. Phœnicia was hesitating whether to submit to Nabopolassar or to assert her freedom. The East generally was in a ferment. Neco in B.C. 608, determined to make his venture. At the head of a large army, consisting mainly of his mercenaries, he took the coast route into Syria, supported by his Mediterranean fleet along the shore, and proceeding through the low tracts of Philistia and Sharon, prepared to cross the ridge of hills which shuts in on the south the great plain of Esdraëlon; but here he found his passage barred by an army. Josiah, either because he feared that, if Neco were successful, his own position would be imperilled, or because he had entered into engagements with Nabopolassar, had resolved to oppose the further progress of the Egyptian army, and had occupied a strong position near Megiddo, on the southern verge of the plain. In vain did Neco seek to persuade him to retire, and leave the passage free. Josiah was obstinate, and a battle became unavoidable. As was to be expected, the Jewish army suffered complete defeat ; Neco swept it from his path, and pursued his way, while Josiah, mortally wounded, was conveyed in his reserve chariot to Jerusalem. The triumphant Pharaoh pushed forward into Syria and carried all before him as far as Carche mish on the Euphrates. The whole country submitted to him. After a campaign which lasted three months, Neco returned in triumph to his own land, carrying with him Jehoahaz, the second son of Josiah, as a prisoner, and leaving Jehoiakim, the eldest son, as tributary monarch, at Jerusalem.

For three years Egypt enjoyed the sense of triumph, and felt herself once more a conquering power, capable of contending on equal terms with any state or kingdom that the world contained. But then Nemesis swooped down on her. In B.C. 605 Nabopolassar of Babylon woke up to a consciousness of his loss of prestige, and determined on an effort to retrieve it. Too old to undertake a distant campaign in person, he placed his son, Nebuchadnezzar, at the head of his troops, and sent him into Syria to recover the lost provinces. Neco met him on the Euphrates. A great battle was fought at Carchemish between the forces of Egypt and Babylon, in which the former suffered a terrible defeat. We have no historical account of it, but may gratefully accept, instead, the prophetic description of Jeremiah :—

"Order ye the buckler and the shield, and draw ye near to battle;
Harness the horses; and get up, ye horsemen, and stand forth with
 your helmets;
Furbish the spears, and put on the brigandines.
Wherefore have I seen them dismayed, and turned away backward?
And their mighty ones are beaten down, and fled apace, and look not
 behind them;
For fear is round about, saith Jehovah.
Let not the swift flee away, nor the mighty men escape;
They shall stumble and fall toward the north by the river Euphrates.
Who is this that cometh up as a flood [like the Nile], whose waters are
 moved as the rivers?

Egypt rises up as a flood [like the Nile], and his waters are moved as
the rivers;
And he saith, I will go up, and I will cover the earth;
I will destroy the city, with its inhabitants.
Come up, ye horses; and rage, ye chariots; and let the mighty men
come forth;
Cush and Phut, that handle the shield, and Lud that handles and bends
the bow.
For this is the day of the Lord, the Lord of hosts, a day of vengeance,
that he may smite his foes;
And the sword shall devour, and be made satiate and drunk with blood;
For the Lord, the Lord of Hosts hath a sacrifice in the north country,
by the river Euphrates.
Go up into Gilead, and take balm, O virgin daughter of Egypt!
In vain shalt thou use many medicines; to thee no cure shall come.
The nations have heard of thy shame, and thy cry hath filled the land;
For the mighty man has stumbled against the mighty, and both are
fallen together."[1]

The disaster was utter, complete, not to be remedied
—the only thing to be done was to " fly apace," to put
the desert and the Nile between the vanquished and the
victors, and to deprecate the conqueror's anger by submission. Neco gave up the contest, evacuated Syria and
Palestine, and hastily sought the shelter of his own land,
whither Nebuchadnezzar would probably have speedily
followed him, had not news arrived of his father's, Nabopolassar's, death. To secure the succession, he had to
return, as quickly as he could, to Babylon, and to allow
the Egyptian monarch, at any rate, a breathing space.

Thus ended the dream of the recovery of an Asiatic
Empire, which Psamatik may have cherished, and of
which Neco attempted the realization. The defeat of
Carchemish shattered the unsubstantial fabric into
atoms, and gave a death-blow to hopes which no
Pharaoh ever entertained afterwards.

[1] Jeremiah xlvi. 3-12.

XXIII.

THE LATER SAITE KINGS.—PSAMATIK II., APRIES, AND AMASIS.

THE Saïtic revival in art and architecture, in commercial and general prosperity, which Psamatik the First inaugurated, continued under his successors. To the short reign of Psamatik II. belong a considerable number of inscriptions, some good bas-reliefs at Abydos and Philæ, and a large number of statues. One of these, in the collection of the Vatican, is remarkable for its beauty. Apries erected numerous *stelæ*, and at least one pair of obelisks, wherewith he adorned the Temple of Neith at Saïs. Amasis afforded great encouragement to art and architecture. He added a court of entrance to the above temple, with propylæa of unusual dimensions, adorned the dromos conducting to it with numerous androsphinxes, erected colossal statues within the temple precincts, and conveyed thither from Elephantine a monolithic shrine or chamber of extraordinary dimensions. Traces of his architectural activity are also found at Memphis, Thebes, Abydos, Bubastis, and Thmuïs or Leontopolis. Statuary flourished during his reign. Even portrait-painting was attempted; and Amasis sent a likeness of himself, painted on panel, as a present to the people of Cyrene. It was maintained by the Egyptians of a century later that the reign of Amasis was the most prosperous time which Egypt had ever seen, the land being more productive, the cities more numerous, and the entire people more happy than either previously or subsequently. Amasis certainly gave a fresh impulse to commerce, since he held frequent communication with the Greek states of Asia Minor, as well as with the settlers at Cyrene, and gave increased privileges to the trading community of Naucratis.

Even in a military point of view, there was to some extent a recovery from the disaster of Carchemish. The Babylonian empire was not sufficiently established or consolidated at the accession of Nebuchadnezzar for that monarch to form at once extensive schemes of conquest. There was much to be done in Elam, in Asia Minor, in Phœnicia, and in Palestine, before his hands could be free to occupy themselves in the subjugation of more distant regions. Within three years after the battle of Carchemish Judæa threw off the yoke of Babylon, and a few years later Phœnicia rebelled under the hegemony of Tyre. Nebuchadnezzar had not much difficulty in crushing the Jewish outbreak ; but Tyre resisted his arms with extreme obstinacy, and it was not till thirteen years after the revolt took place that Phœnicia was re-conquered. Even then the position of Judæa was insecure : she was known to be thoroughly disaffected, and only waiting an opportunity to rebel a second time. Thus Nebuchadnezzar was fully occupied with troubles within his own dominions, and left Egypt undisturbed to repair her losses, and recover her military prestige, as she best might.

Neco outlived his defeat about eight or nine years, during which he nursed his strength, and abstained from all warlike enterprises. His son, Psamatik II., who succeeded him B.C. 596, made an attack on the Ethiopians, and seems to have penetrated deep into Nubia, where a monument was set up by two of his generals, Apollonius, a Greek, and Amasis, an Egyptian, which may still be seen on the rocks of Abu-Simbel, and is the earliest known Greek inscription. The following is a fac-simile, only reduced in size :—

ΒΑSIΛΕΟSΕΛΘΟΝΤΟSΕSΕΛΕΦΑΝΤΙΝΑΝΨΑΜΑΤΙΧΟ
ΤΑΥΤΑΕΓΡΑΨΑΝΤΟΙSΥΝΨΑΜΜΑΤΙΧΟΙΤΟΙΘΕΟΚΛΟS
ΕΓΛΕΟΝΘΑΘΟΝΔΕΚΕΡΚΙΟSΚΑΤΥΓΕΔΘΕΥΙSΟΓΟΤΑΜΟS
ΑΝΙΒΑΓΟΛΛΟSΟSΟΒΧΕΓΟΤΑSΙΜΤΟΑΙΓΥΓΤΙΟSΔΒΑΜΑSΙS
ΕΛΡΑΦΕΔΑΜΕΑΡ+ΟΝΑΜΟΙΒΙ+ΟΚΑΙΓΕΛΕΟSΟΥΔΑΜΟ

Apries, the son of Neco, brought this war to an end in the first year of his reign (B.C. 590) by the arms of one of his generals; and, finding that Nebuchadnezzar was still unable to reduce Phoenicia to subjection, he ventured, in B.C. 588, to conclude a treaty with Zedekiah, king of Judah, and to promise him assistance, if he would join him against the Babylonians. This Zedekiah consented to do, and the war followed which terminated in the capture and destruction of Jerusalem, and the transfer of the Jewish people to Babylonia.

It is uncertain what exact part Apries took in this war. We know that he called out the full force of the empire, and marched into Palestine, with the object of relieving Zedekiah, as soon as he knew that that monarch's safety was threatened. We know that he marched towards Jerusalem, and took up such a threatening attitude that Nebuchadnezzar at one time actually raised the siege (Jer. xxxvii. 5). We do not know what followed. Whether Apries, on finding that the whole Chaldæan force had broken up from before Jerusalem and was marching against himself, took fright at the danger which he had affronted, and made a sudden inglorious retreat; or whether he boldly met the Babylonian host and contended with them in a pitched battle, wherein he was worsted, and from which he was forced to fly into his own land, is uncertain. Josephus positively declares that he took the braver and more honourable course: the silence of Scripture as to any battle is thought to imply that he showed the white feather. In either case, the result was the same. Egypt recoiled before Babylon; Palestine was evacuated; and Zedekiah was left to himself. In B.C. 586 Jerusalem fell; Zedekiah was made a prisoner and cruelly deprived of sight; the Temple and city were burnt, and the bulk of the people carried into captivity. Babylon rounded off her dominion in this quarter by the absorption of the last state upon her south-western border that had maintained the shadow of independence: and the two great powers of these parts, hitherto prevented from coming into contact by the intervention of a sort of political "buffer," became conterminous, and were thus brought into a position in which it was not possible that a collision should for any considerable time be avoided.

Recognizing the certainty of the impending collision, Apries sought to strengthen his power for resistance by attaching to his own empire the Phœnician towns of the Syrian coast, whose adhesion to his side would secure him, at any rate, the maritime superiority. He made an expedition against Tyre and Sidon both by land and sea, defeated the combined fleet of Phœnicia and Cyprus in a great engagement, besieged Sidon, and after a time compelled it to surrender. He then endeavoured further to strengthen himself on the land side by bringing under subjection the Greek city of Cyrene, which had now become a flourishing community; but here his good fortune forsook him; the Cyrenæan forces defeated the army which he sent against them, with great slaughter; and the event brought Apries into disfavour with his subjects, who imagined that he had, of malice prepense, sent his troops into the jaws of destruction. According to Herodotus, the immediate result was a revolt, which cost Apries his throne, and, within a short time, his life; but the entire narrative of Herodotus is in the highest degree improbable, and some recent discoveries suggest a wholly different termination to the reign of this remarkable king.

It is certain that in B.C. 568 Nebuchadnezzar made an expedition into Egypt. According to all accounts this date fell into the lifetime of Apries. Amasis, however, the successor of Apries, appears to have been Nebuchadnezzar's direct antagonist, and to have resisted him in the field, while Apries remained in the palace at Saïs. The two were joint kings from

B.C. 571 to B.C. 565. Nebuchadnezzar, at first, neglected Saïs, and proceeded, by way of Heliopolis and Bubastis (Ezek. xxx. 17), against the old capitals, Memphis and Thebes. Having taken these, and "destroyed the idols and made the images to cease," he advanced up the Nile valley to Elephantine, which he took, and then endeavoured to penetrate into Nubia. A check, however, was inflicted on his army by Nes-Hor, the Governor of the South, whereupon he gave up his idea of Nubian conquest. Returning down the valley, he completed that ravage of Egypt which is described by Jeremiah and Ezekiel. It is probable that in B.C. 565, three years after his first invasion, he took Saïs and put the aged Apries to death.[1] Amasis he allowed still to reign, but only as a tributary king, and thus Egypt became "a base kingdom" (Ezek. xxix. 14), "the basest of the kingdoms" (ibid. verse 15), if its former exaltation were taken into account.

The "base kingdom" was, however, materially, as flourishing as ever. The sense of security from foreign attack was a great encouragement to private industry and commercial enterprise. The discontinuances of lavish expenditure on military expeditions improved the state finances, and enabled those at the head of the government to employ the money, that would otherwise have been wasted, in reproductive undertakings. The agricultural system of Egypt was never better organized or better managed than under Amasis. Nature seemed to conspire with man to make the time one of joy and delight, for the inundation was scarcely ever before so regularly

[1] Josephus, *Ant. Jud.* x. 9, 97.

abundant, nor were the crops ever before so plentiful. The "twenty thousand cities," which Herodotus assigns to the time, may be a myth; but, beyond all doubt, the tradition which told of them was based upon the fact of a period of unexampled prosperity. Amasis's law, that each Egyptian should appear once each year before the governor of his canton, and show the means by which he was getting an honest living, may have done something towards making industry general; but his example, his active habits, and his encouragement of art and architecture, probably did more. His architectural works must have given constant employment to large numbers of persons as quarrymen, boatmen, bricklayers, plasterers, masons, carpenters, and master builders; his patronage of art not only gave direct occupation to a multitude of artists, but set a fashion to the more wealthy among his subjects by which the demand for objects of art was multiplied a hundredfold. Sculptors and painters had a happy time under a king who was always building temples, erecting colossi, or sending statues or paintings of himself as presents to foreign states or foreign shrines.

The external aspect of Egypt under the reign of Amasis is thus as bright and flourishing as that which she ever wore at any former time; but, as M. Lenormant observes, this apparent prosperity did but ill conceal the decay of patriotism and the decline of all the institutions of the nation. The kings of the Saïte dynasty had thought to re-vivify Egypt, and infuse a little new blood into the old monarchy founded by Menes, by allowing the great stream of liberal ideas, whereof Greece had already made herself the propagator, to expand itself in her midst. Without knowing it, they had by these means introduced on the banks of the Nile a new element of decline. Constructed exclusively for continuance, for preserving its own traditions in defiance of the flight of centuries, the civilization of Egypt could only maintain itself by remaining unmoved. From the day on which it found itself in contact with the spirit of progress, personified in the Grecian civilization and in the Greek race, it was under the absolute necessity of perishing. It could neither launch itself upon a wholly new path, one which was the direct negation of its own genius, nor continue on without change its own existence. Thus, as soon as it began to be penetrated by Greek influence, it fell at once into complete dissolution, and sank into a state of decrepitude, that already resembled death. We shall see, in the next section, how suddenly and completely the Egyptian power collapsed when the moment of trial came, and how little support the surface prosperity which marked the reign of Amasis was able to render to the Empire in the hour of need and distress.

XXIV.

THE PERSIAN CONQUEST.

THE subjection of Egypt to Babylon, which commenced in B.C. 565, was of that light and almost nominal character, which a nation that is not very sensitive, or very jealous of its honour, does not care to shake off. A small tribute was probably paid by the subject state to her suzerain, but otherwise the yoke was unfelt. There was no interference with the internal government, or the religion of the Egyptians; no appointment of Babylonian satraps, or tax-collectors; not even, so far as appears, any demands for contingents of troops. Thus, although Nebuchadnezzar died within seven years of his conquest of Egypt, and though a time of disturbance and confusion followed his death, four kings occupying the Babylonian throne within little more than six years, two of whom met with a violent end, yet Amasis seems to have continued quiescent and contented, in the enjoyment of a life somewhat more merry and amusing than that of most monarchs, without making any effort to throw off the Babylonian supremacy or reassert the independence of his country. It was not till his self-indulgent apathy was intruded upon from without, and he received an appeal from a foreign nation, to which he was compelled to return an answer, that he looked the situation in the face, and came to the conclusion that he might declare himself independent without much risk. He had at this time patiently borne his subject position for the space of above twenty years, though he might easily have reasserted himself at the end of seven.

The circumstances under which the appeal was made were the following. A new power had suddenly risen up in Asia. About B.C. 558, ten years after Nebuchadnezzar's subjection of Egypt, Cyrus, son of Cambyses, the tributary monarch of Persia under the Medes, assumed an independent position and began a career of conquest. Having made himself master of a large portion of the country of Elam, he assumed the title of "King of Ansan," and engaged in a long war with Astyages (Istivegu), his former suzerain, which terminated (in B.C. 549) in his taking the Median monarch prisoner and succeeding to his dominions. It was at once recognized through Asia that a new peril had arisen. The Medes, a mountain people of great physical strength and remarkable bravery, had for about a century been regarded as the most powerful people of Western Asia. They had now been overthrown and conquered by a still more powerful mountain race. That race had at its head an energetic and enterprising prince, who was in the full vigour of youth, and fired evidently with a high ambition. His position was naturally felt as a direct menace by the neighbouring states of Babylon and Lydia, whose royal families were interconnected. Crœsus of Lydia was the first to take alarm and to devise measures for his own security. He formed the conception of a grand league between the principal powers whom the rise of Persia threatened, for mutual defence against the common enemy; and, in furtherance of this design, sent, in B.C. 547, an embassy to Egypt, and another to Babylon, proposing a close alliance between the three countries. Amasis had to determine whether he would maintain his subjection to Babylon and refuse the offer; or, by accepting it, declare himself a wholly independent monarch. He learnt by the embassy, if he did not know it before, that Nabonadius, the Babylonian monarch, was in difficulties, and could not resent his action. He might probably think that, under the circumstances, Nabonadius would regard his joining the league as a friendly, rather than an unfriendly, proceeding. At any rate, the balance of advantage seemed to him on the side of complying with the request of Crœsus. Crœsus was lord of Asia Minor, and it was only by his permission that the Ionian and Carian mercenaries, on whom the throne of the Pharaohs now mainly depended, could be recruited and maintained at their proper strength. It would not do to offend so important a personage; and accordingly Amasis came into the proposed alliance, and pledged himself to send assistance to whichever of his two confederates should be first attacked. Conversely, they no doubt pledged themselves to him; but the remote position of Egypt rendered it extremely improbable that they would be called upon to redeem their pledges.

Nor was even Amasis called upon actually to redeem the pledges which he had given. In B.C. 546,

ALLIANCE OF EGYPT, BABYLON, AND LYDIA. 371

Crœsus, without summoning any contingents from his allies, precipitated the war with Persia by crossing the river Halys, and invading Cappadocia, which was included in the dominions of Cyrus. Having suffered a severe defeat at Pteria, a Cappadocian city, he returned to his capital and hastily sent messengers to Egypt and elsewhere, begging for immediate assistance. What steps Amasis took upon this, or intended to take, is uncertain; but it must have been before any troops could have been dispatched, that news reached Egypt which rendered it useless to send out an expedition. Crœsus had scarcely reached his capital when he found himself attacked by Cyrus in his turn; his army suffered a second defeat in the plain before Sardis; the city was besieged, stormed, and taken within fourteen days. Crœsus fell, alive, into the hands of his enemy, and was kindly treated; but his kingdom had passed away. It was evidently too late for Amasis to attempt to send him succour. The tripartite alliance had, by the force of circumstances, come to an end, and Amasis was an independent monarch, no longer bound by any engagements.

Shortly afterwards, in B.C. 538, the conquering monarchy of Persia absorbed another victim. Nabonadius was attacked, Babylon taken, and the Chaldæan monarchy, which had lasted nearly two thousand years, brought to an end. The contest had been prolonged, and in the course of it some disintegration of the empire had taken place. Phœnicia had asserted her independence; and Cyprus, which was to a large extent Phœnician, had followed the example of the mother-country. Under these circumstances, Amasis thought he saw an opportunity of gaining some cheap laurels, and accordingly made a naval expedition against the unfortunate islanders, who were taken unawares and forced to become his tributaries. It was unwise of the Egyptian monarch to remind Cyrus that he had still an open enemy unchastised, one who had entered into a league against him ten years previously, and was now anxious to prevent him from reaping the full benefit of his conquests. We may be sure that the Persian monarch noted and resented the interference with territories which he had some right to consider his own ; whether he took any steps to revenge himself is doubtful. According to some, he required Amasis to send him one of his daughters as a concubine, an insult which the Egyptian king escaped by *finesse* while he appeared to submit to it.

It can only have been on account of the other wars which pressed upon him and occupied him during his remaining years, that Cyrus did not march in person against Amasis. First, the conquest of the nations between the Caspian and the Indian Ocean detained him ; and after this, a danger showed itself on his north-eastern frontier which required all his attention, and in meeting which he lost his life. The independent tribes beyond the Oxus and the Jaxartes have through all history been an annoyance and a peril to the power which rules over the Iranian plateau, and it was in repelling an attack in this quarter that Cyrus fell. Amasis, perhaps, congratulated himself on the defeat and death of the great warrior king ; but Egypt would, perhaps, have suffered less had the invasion, which was sure to come, been conducted by the noble, magnanimous, and merciful Cyrus, than she actually endured at the hands of the impulsive, tyrannical, and half-mad Cambyses.

The first step taken by Cambyses, who succeeded his father Cyrus in B.C. 529, was to reduce Phœnicia under his power. The support of a fleet was of immense importance to an army about to attack Egypt, both for the purpose of conveying water and stores, and of giving command over the mouths of the Nile, so that the great cities, Pelusium, Tanis, Saïs, Bubastis, Memphis, might be blockaded both by land and water. Persia, up to the accession of Cambyses, had (so to speak) no fleet. Cambyses, by threatening the Phœnician cities on the land side, succeeded in inducing them to submit to him ; he then, with their aid, detached Cyprus from her Egyptian masters, and obtained the further assistance of a Cypriote squadron. Some Greek ships also gave their services, and the result was that he had the entire command of the sea, and was able to hold possession of all the Nile mouths, and to bring his fleet up the river to the very walls of Memphis.

Still, there were difficulties to overcome in respect of the passage of an army. Egypt is separated from Palestine by a considerable tract of waterless desert, and it was necessary to convey by sea, or on the backs of camels, all the water required for the troops, for the camp-followers, and for the baggage animals. A numerous camel corps was indispensable for the conveyance, and the Persians, though employing camels on their expeditions, are not likely to have possessed any very considerable number of these beasts. At any rate, it was extremely convenient to find a fresh and abundant supply of camels on the spot, together with abundant water-skins. This good fortune befell the Persian monarch, who was able to make an alliance with the sheikh of the most powerful Bedouin tribe of the region, who undertook the entire responsibility of the water supply. He thus crossed the desert without disaster or suffering, and brought his entire force intact to the Pelusiac branch of the Nile, near the point where it poured its waters into the Mediterranean Sea.

At this point he found a mixed Egyptian and Græco-Carian army prepared to resist his further progress. Amasis had died about six months previously, leaving his throne to his son, Psamatik the Third. This young prince, notwithstanding his inexperience, had taken all the measures that were possible to protect his kingdom from the invader. He had gathered together his Greek and Carian mercenaries, and having also levied a large native army, had posted the entire force not far from Pelusium, in an advantageous position. On his Greeks and Carians he could thoroughly depend, though they had lately seen but little service; his native levies, on the contrary, were of scarcely any value; they were jealous of the mercenaries, who had superseded them as the ordinary land force, and they had had little practice in warfare for the last forty years. At no time, probably, would an Egyptian army composed of native troops have been a match for such soldiers as Cambyses brought with him into

PSAMATIK III. DEFEATED AT PELUSIUM. 375

Egypt — Persians, Medes, Hyrcanians, Mardians, Greeks—trained in the school of Cyrus, inured to arms, and confident of victory. But the native soldiery of the time of Psamatik III. fell far below the average Egyptian type; it had little patriotism, it had no experience, it was smarting under a sense of injury and ill-treatment at the hands of the Saïte kings. The engagement between the two armies at Pelusium was thus not so much a battle as a carnage. No doubt the mercenaries made a stout resistance, but they were vastly outnumbered, and were not much better troops than their adversaries. The Egyptians must have been slaughtered like sheep. According to Ctesias, fifty thousand of them fell, whereas the entire loss on the Persian side was only six thousand. After a short struggle, the troops of Psamatik fled, and in a little time the retreat became a complete rout. The fugitives did not stop till they reached Memphis, where they shut themselves up within the walls.

It is the lot of Egypt to have its fate decided by a single battle. The country offers no strong positions, that are strategically more defensible than others. The whole Delta is one alluvial flat, with no elevation that has not been raised by man. The valley of the Nile is so wide as to furnish everywhere an ample plain, wherein the largest armies may contend without having their movements cramped or hindered. An army that takes to the hills on either side of the valley is not worth following : it is self-destroyed, since it can find no sustenance and no water. Thus the sole question, when a foreign host invades Egypt, is this : Can it, or can it not, defeat the full force of Egypt in an open battle ? If it gains one battle, there is no reason why it should not gain fifty ; and this is so evident, and so well known, that on Egyptian soil one defeat has almost always been accepted as decisive of the military supremacy. A beaten army may, of course, protract its resistance behind walls, and honour, fame, patriotism, may seem sometimes to require such a line of conduct ; but, unless there is a reasonable expectation of relief arriving from without, protracted resistance is useless, and, from a military point of view, indefensible. Defeated commanders have not, however, always seen this, or, seeing it, they have allowed prudence to be overpowered by other considerations. Psamatik, like many another ruler of Egypt, though defeated in the field, determined to defend his capital to the best of his power. He threw himself, with the remnant of his beaten army, into Memphis, and there stood at bay, awaiting the further attack of his adversary.

It was not long before the Persian army drew up under the walls, and invested the city by land, while the fleet blockaded the river. A single Greek vessel, having received orders to summon the defenders of the place to surrender it, had the boldness to enter the town, whereupon it was set upon by the Egyptians, captured, and destroyed. Contrarily to the law of nations, which protects ambassadors and their escort, the crew was torn limb from limb, and an outrage thus committed which Cambyses was justified in punishing with extreme severity. Upon the fall of the city, which followed soon after its investment, the

FALL OF MEMPHIS.

offended monarch avenged the crime which had been committed by publicly executing two thousand of the principal citizens, including (it is said) a son of the fallen king. The king himself was at first spared, and might perhaps have been allowed to rule Egypt as a tributary monarch, had he not been detected in a design to rebel and renew the war. For this offence he, too, was condemned to death, and executed by Cambyses' order.

The defeat had been foretold by the prophet Ezekiel, who had said:—

"Woe worth the day! For the day is near,
Even the day of the Lord is near, a day of clouds;
It shall be the time of the heathen.
And a sword shall come upon Egypt, and anguish shall be in Ethiopia;
When the slain shall fall in Egypt; and they shall take away her multitude,
And her foundations shall be broken down.
Ethiopia and Phut and Lud, and all the mingled people, and Chub,
And the children of the land that is in league, shall fall with them by the sword. . . .
I will put a fear in the land of Egypt.
And I will make Pathros desolate,
And will set a fire in Zoan, and will execute judgments in No. . . .
Sin [Pelusium] shall be in great anguish,
And No shall be broken up, and Noph shall have adversaries in the daytime.
The young men of Aven and of Pi-beseth shall fall by the sword:
And these cities shall go into captivity.
At Tehaphnehes also the day shall withdraw itself,
When I shall break there the yokes of Egypt;
And the pride of her power shall cease."[1]

According to Herodotus, Cambyses was not content with the above-mentioned severities, which were per-

[1] Ezekiel xxx. 3-18.

haps justifiable under the circumstances, but proceeded further to exercise his rights as conqueror in a most violent and tyrannical way. He tore from its tomb the mummy of the late king, Amasis, and subjected it to the grossest indignities. He stabbed in the thigh an Apis-Bull, recently inaugurated at the capital with joyful ceremonies, suspecting that the occasion was feigned, and that the rejoicings were really over the ill-success of expeditions carried out by his orders against the oasis of Ammon, and against Ethiopia. He exhumed numerous mummies for the mere purpose of examining them. He entered the grand temple of Phthah at Memphis, and made sport of the image. He burnt the statues of the Cabeiri, which he found in another temple. He scourged the priests of Apis, and massacred in the streets those Egyptians who were keeping the festival. Altogether, his object was, if the informants of Herodotus are to be believed, to pour contempt and contumely on the Egyptian religion, and to insult the religious feelings of the entire people.

On the other hand, we learn from a contemporary inscription, that Cambyses so far conformed to Egyptian usages as to take a "throne-name," after the pattern of the ancient Pharaohs; that he cleared the temple of Neith at Saïs of the foreigners who had taken possession of it; that he entrusted the care of the temple to an Egyptian officer of high standing; and that he was actually himself initiated into the mysteries of the goddess. Perhaps we ought not to be greatly surprised at these contradictions. Cambyses had the iconoclastic spirit strong in him, and, under excitement, took a pleasure in showing his abhorrence of Egyptian superstitions. But he was not always under excitement—he enjoyed lucid intervals, during which he was actuated by the spirit of an administrator and a statesman. Having in many ways greatly exasperated the Egyptians against his rule, he thought it prudent, ere he quitted the country, to soothe the feelings which he had so deeply wounded, and conciliate the priest-class, to which he had given such dire offence. Hence his politic concessions to public feeling at Saïs, his initiation into the mysteries of Neith, his assumption of a throne-name, and his restoration of the temple of Saïs to religious uses. And the policy of conciliation, which he thus inaugurated, was continued by his successor, Darius. Darius built, or repaired, the temple of Ammon, in the oasis of El Khargeh, and made many acknowledgments of the deities of Egypt; when an Apis-Bull died early in his reign, he offered a reward of a hundred talents for the discovery of a new Apis; and he proposed to adorn the temple of Ammon at Thebes with a new obelisk. At the same time, in his administration he carefully considered the interests of Egypt, which he entrusted to a certain Aryandes as satrap; he re-opened the canal between the Nile and the Red Sea, for the encouragement of Egyptian commerce; he kept up the numbers of the Egyptian fleet; in his arrangement of the satrapies, he placed no greater burthen on Egypt than it was well able to bear; and he seems to have honoured Egypt by his occasional presence. He failed, however, to allay the discontent, and even hatred, which the outrages of Cambyses had aroused; they still remained indelibly impressed on the Egyptian mind; the Persian rule was detested; and in sullen dissatisfaction the entire nation awaited an opportunity of reclaiming its independence and flinging off the accursed yoke.

XXV.

THREE DESPERATE REVOLTS.

THE first revolt of the Egyptians against their conquerors, appears to have been provoked by the news of the battle of Marathon. Egypt heard, in B.C. 490, that the arms of the oppressor, as she ever determined to consider Darius, had met with a reverse in European Greece, where 200,000 Medes and Persians had been completely defeated by 20,000 Athenians and Platæans. Darius, it was understood, had taken greatly to heart this reverse, and was bent on avenging it. The strength of the Persian Empire was about to be employed towards the West, and an excellent opportunity seemed to have arisen for a defection on the South. Accordingly Egypt, after making secret preparations for three years, in B.C. 487 broke out in open revolt. She probably overpowered and massacred the Persian garrison in Memphis, which is said to have numbered 120,000 men, and, proclaiming herself independent, set up a native sovereign.

The Egyptian monuments suggest that this monarch bore the foreign-sounding name of Khabash. He fortified the coast of Egypt against attempts which might be made upon it by the Persian fleet, and doubtless prepared himself also to resist an invasion by land. But he was quite unable to do anything effectual. Though Darius died in the year after the revolt, B.C. 486, yet its suppression was immediately undertaken by his son and successor, Xerxes, who invaded Egypt in the next year, easily crushed all resistance, and placed the province under a severer rule than any that it had previously experienced. Achæmenes, his brother, was made satrap.

Twenty-five years of tranquillity followed, during which the Egyptians were submissive subjects of the Persian crown, and even showed remarkable courage and skill in the Persian military expeditions. Egypt furnished as many as two hundred triremes to the fleet which was brought against Greece by Xerxes, and the squadron particularly distinguished itself in the sea-fights off Artemisium, where they actually captured five Grecian vessels with their crews. Mardonius, moreover, set so high a value on the marines who fought on board the Egyptian ships, that he retained them as land-troops when the Persian fleet returned to Asia after Salamis.

No further defection took place during the reign of Xerxes; but in B.C. 460, after the throne had been occupied for about five years by Xerxes' son, Artaxerxes, a second rebellion broke out, which led to a long and terrible struggle. A certain Inarus, who bore rule over some of the African tribes on the western border of Egypt, and who may have been a descendant of the Psamatiks, headed the insurrection, and in conjunction with an Egyptian, named Amyrtæus, suddenly attacked the Persian garrison stationed in Egypt, the ordinary strength of which was 120,000 men. A great battle was fought at Papremis, in the Delta, wherein the Persians were completely defeated, and their leader, Achæmenes, perished by the hand of Inarus himself. Memphis, however, the capital, still resisted, and the struggle thus remained doubtful. Inarus and Amyrtæus implored the assistance of Athens, which had the most powerful navy of the time, and could lend most important aid by taking possession of the river. Athens, which was under the influence of the farsighted Pericles, cheerfully responded to the call, and sent two hundred triremes, manned by at least forty thousand men, to assist the rebels, and to do as much injury as possible to the Persians. On sailing up the Nile, the Athenian fleet found a Persian squadron already moored in the Nile waters, but it swept this obstacle from its path without any difficulty. Memphis was then blockaded both by land and water; the city was taken, and only the citadel, Leucon-Teichos, or "the White Fortress," held out. A formal siege of the citadel was commenced, and the allies lay before it for months, but without result. Meanwhile, Artaxerxes was not idle. Having collected an army of 300,000 men, he gave the command of it to Megabyzus, one of his best generals, and sent him to Egypt against the rebels. Megabyzus marched upon Memphis, defeated the Egyptians and their allies in a great battle under the walls of the town, relieved the Persian garrison which held the citadel, and recovered possession of the place. The Athenians retreated to the tract called Prosopitis, a sort of island in the Delta, surrounded by two of the branch streams of the Nile, which they held with their ships. Here Megabyzus besieged them without success for eighteen months; but at last he bethought himself of a stratagem like that whereby Cyrus is said to have captured Babylon, and adapted it to his purpose. Having blocked the course of one of the branch streams, and diverted its waters into a new channel, he laid bare the river-bed, captured the triremes that were stuck fast in the soft ooze, marched his men into the island, and overwhelmed the unhappy Greeks by sheer force of numbers. A few only escaped, and made their way to Cyrene. The entire fleet of two hundred vessels fell into the hands of the conqueror; and fifty others, sent as a reinforcement, having soon afterwards entered the river, were attacked unawares and defeated, with the loss of more than half their number. Inarus, the Libyan monarch, became a fugitive, but was betrayed by some of his followers, surrendered, and crucified. Amyrtæus, who had been recognized as king of Egypt during the six years that the struggle lasted, took refuge in the Nile marshes, where he dragged out a miserable existence for another term of six years. The Egyptians offered no further resistance; and Egypt became once more a Persian satrapy (B.C. 455).

It was at about this time that Herodotus, the earliest Greek historian, the Father of History, as he has been called, visited Egypt in pursuance of his plan of gathering information for his great work. He was a young man, probably not far from thirty years of age (for he was born between the dates of the battles of Marathon and Thermopylæ). He travelled through the land as far as Elephantine, viewing with his observant eyes the wonders with which the "Story of Egypt" has been so much occupied ; and he described them with the enthusiasm that we have occasionally noted. He saw the battle-field on which Inarus had just been defeated—the ground strewn with the skulls and other bones of the slain ; he made his longest stay at Memphis, then at the acme of its greatness ; he visited the quarries on the east of the Nile whence the stone had been dug for the pyramids, and he gazed upon the great monuments themselves, on the opposite side of the stream. We have seen that he visited Lake Mœris, and examined the famous Labyrinth, which he thought even more wonderful than the pyramids themselves. Finally, he sailed away for Tyre, and Egypt was again closed to travellers from Greece.

A second period of tranquillity followed, which covered the space of about half a century. Nothing is known of Egypt during this interval ; and it might have been thought that she had grown contented with her lot, and that her aspirations after independence were over. For fifty years she had made no sign. Even the troubled time between the death of Artaxerxes I. and the accession of Darius II. had not tempted her to strike a blow for freedom. But still she was, in reality, irreconcilable. She was biding her time, and preparing herself for a last desperate effort.

In B.C. 406 or 405, towards the close of the reign of Darius Nothus, the third rebellion of Egypt against Persia broke out. A native of Mendes, by name

Nepheritis, or more properly Nefaa-rut, raised the banner of independence, and commenced a war, which must have lasted for some years, but which terminated n the expulsion of the Persian garrison, and the re-establishment of the throne of the Pharaohs. It is unfortunate that no ancient authority gives any account of the struggle. We only know that, after a time, the power of Nefaa-rut was established; that Persia left him in undisturbed possession of Egypt, and that he reigned quietly for the space of six years, employing himself in the repair and restoration of the temple of Ammon at Karnak. Nothing that can be called a revival, or *renaissance*, distinguished his reign; and we must view his success rather as the result of Persian weakness, than of his own energy. His revolt, however, inaugurated a period of independence, which lasted about sixty years, and which threw over the last years of the doomed monarchy a gleam of sunshine, that for a brief space recalled the glories of earlier and happier ages.

XXVI.

A LAST GLEAM OF SUNSHINE—NECTANEBO I.

A TROUBLED time followed the reign of Nefaa-rut. The Greek mercenary soldiery, on whom the monarchs depended, were fickle in their temperament, and easily took offence, if their inclinations were in any way thwarted. Their displeasure commonly led to the dethronement of the king who had provoked it ; and we have thus, at this period of the history, five reigns in twenty-five years. No monarch had time to distinguish himself by a re-organization of the kingdom, or even by undertaking buildings on a large scale— each was forced to live from hand to mouth, meeting as he best might the immediate difficulties of his position, without providing for a future, which he might never live to see. Fear of re-conquest was also perpetual ; and the monarchs had therefore constantly to be courting alliances with foreign states, and subjecting themselves thereby to risks which it might have been more prudent to have avoided.

With the accession of Nectanebo I. (Nekht-Horheb), about B.C. 385, an improvement in the state of affairs set in. Nekht-hor-heb was a vigorous prince, who held the mercenaries well under control, and, having raised a considerable Egyptian army, set himself to place Egypt in such a state of defence, that she might confidently rely on her own strength, and be under no need of entangling herself with foreign alliances. He strongly fortified all the seven mouths of the Nile, guarding each by two forts, one on either side of each stream, and establishing a connection between each pair of forts by a bridge. At Pelusium, where the danger of hostile attack was always the greatest, he multiplied his precautions, guarding it on the side of the east by a deep ditch, and carefully obstructing all the approaches to the town, whether by land or sea, by forts and dykes and embankments, and contrivances for laying the neighbouring territory under water. No doubt these precautions were taken with special reference to an expected attack on the part of Persia, which was preparing, about B.C. 376, to make a great effort to bring Egypt once more into subjection.

The expected attack came in the next year. Having obtained the services of the Athenian general, Iphicrates, and hired Greek mercenaries to the number of twenty thousand, Artaxerxes Mnemon, in B.C. 375, sent a huge armament against Egypt, consisting of 220,000 men, 500 ships of war, and a countless number of other vessels carrying stores and provisions. Pharnabazus commanded the Persian soldiery, Iphicrates the mercenaries. Having rendezvoused at Acre in the spring of the year, they set out early in the summer, and proceeded in a leisurely manner through Philistia and the desert, the fleet accompanying them along the coast. This route brought them to Pelusium, which they found so strongly fortified that they despaired of being able to force the defences, and felt it necessary to make a complete change in their plan of attack. Putting to sea with a portion of the fleet, and with troops to the number of three thousand, and sailing northward till they could no longer be seen from the shore, they then, probably at nightfall, changed their course, and steering southwest, made for the Mendesian mouth of the Nile, which was only guarded by the twin forts with their connecting bridge. Here they landed without opposition, and proceeded to reconnoitre the forts. The garrison gave them battle outside the walls, but was defeated with great loss; and the forts themselves were taken. The remainder of the force conveyed by the ships, was then landed without difficulty; and the invaders, having the complete mastery of one of the Nile mouths, had it in their power to direct their attack to any point that might seem to them at once most important and most vulnerable.

Under these circumstances the Athenian general, Iphicrates, strongly recommended a dash at Memphis. The main strength of the Egyptian army had been concentrated at Pelusium. Strong detachments held the other mouths of the Nile. Memphis, he felt sure, must be denuded of troops, and could probably be carried by a *coup de main;* but the advice of the rapid Greek was little to the taste of the slow-moving and cautious Persian. Pharnabazus declined to sanction any rash enterprise—he would proceed according to the rules of art. He had the advantage of numbers— why was he to throw it away? No, a thousand times no. He would wait till his army was once more collected together, and would then march on Memphis, without exposing himself or his troops to any danger. The city would be sure to fall, and the object of the expedition would be accomplished. In vain did Iphicrates offer to run the whole risk himself—to take no troops with him besides his own mercenaries, and attack the city with them. As the Greek grew more hot and reckless, the Persian became more cool and wary. What might not be behind this foolhardiness? Might it not be possible that the Greek was looking to his own interests, and designing, if he got possession of Memphis, to set himself up as king of Egypt? There was no knowing what his intention might be; and at any rate it was safest to wait the arrival of the troops. So Pharnabazus once more coolly declined his subordinate's offer.

Nectanebo, on his side, having thrown a strong garrison into Memphis, moved his army across the Delta from the Pelusiac to the Mendesian branch of the Nile, and having concentrated it in the neighbourhood of the captured forts, proceeded to operate against the invaders. His troops harassed the enemy in a number of petty engagements, and in the course of time inflicted on them considerable loss. In this way midsummer was reached—the Etesian winds began to blow, and the Nile to rise. Gradually the abounding stream spread itself over the broad Delta; roads were overflowed, river-courses obliterated; the season for military operations was clearly past. There was no possible course but to return to Asia. Iphicrates and Pharnabazus took their departure amid mutual recriminations, each accusing the other of having caused the expedition to be a complete failure.

The repulse of this huge host was felt by the Egyptians almost as the repulse of the host of Xerxes was felt by the Greeks. Nectanebo was looked upon as a hero and a demigod ; his throne was assured ; it was felt that he had redeemed all the failures of the past, and had restored Egypt to the full possession of all her ancient dignity and glory. Nectanebo continued to rule over "the Two Lands" for nine years longer in uninterrupted peace, honour, and prosperity. During this time he applied himself, with considerable success, to the revival of Egyptian art and architecture. At Thebes he made additions to the great temple of Karnak, restored the temple of Khonsu, and adorned with reliefs a shrine originally erected by Ramesses XII. At Memphis he was extraordinarily active : he built a small temple in the neighbourhood of the Serapeum, set up inscriptions in the Apis repository in honour of the sacred bulls, erected two small obelisks in black granite, and left his name inscribed more than once in the quarries of Toora. Traces of his activity are also found at Edfu, at Abydos, at Bubastis, at Rosetta in the Delta, and at Tel-el-Maskoutah. The art of his time is said to have all the elegance of that produced under the twenty-sixth (Psamatik) dynasty, but to have been somewhat more florid. The two black obelisks above-mentioned, which are now in the British Museum, show the admirable finish which prevailed at this period. The sarcophagus which Nectanebo prepared for himself, which adorns the same collection, is also of great beauty.

We cannot be surprised to find that Nectanebo

was worshipped after his death as a divine being. A priesthood was constituted in his honour, which handed down his cult to later times, and bore witness to the impression made on the Egyptian mind by his character and his successes.

XXVII.

THE LIGHT GOES OUT IN DARKNESS.

NECTANEBO'S successors had neither his foresight nor his energy. Te-her, the Tachos or Teos of the Greeks, who followed him on the throne in B.C. 366, went out of his way to provoke the Persians' by fomenting the war of the satraps against Artaxerxes Mnemon, and, having obtained the services of Agesilaüs and Chabrias, even ventured to invade Phœnicia and attempt its reduction. His own hold upon Egypt was, however, far too weak to justify so bold a proceeding. Scarcely had he reached Syria, when revolt broke out behind him. The Regent, to whom he had entrusted the direction of affairs during his absence, proved unfaithful, and incited his son, Nekht-nebf, to become a candidate for the crown, and to take up arms against his father. The young prince was seduced by the offers made him, and Egypt became plunged in a civil war. But for the courage and conduct of Agesilaüs, which were conspicuously displayed, Tacho would have yielded to despair and have given up the contest. In two decisive battles the Spartan general completely defeated the army of the rebels, which far outnumbered that of Tacho, and replaced the king on his tottering throne.

However, it was not long before the party of the rebels recovered from their defeats. Agesilaüs either joined them, or withdrew from the struggle, and removing to Cyrene died there at an advanced age. Tacho, deserted by his followers, quitted Egypt and fled to Sidon, whence he made his way across the desert to the court of the Great King. Ochus, who had by this time succeeded Mnemon, received him favourably, and professed an intention of embracing his cause; but nothing came of this expression of good-will. Tacho lived a considerable time at the court of Ochus, without any steps being taken to restore him to his former position. At last a dysentery carried him off, and legitimated the position of the usurper who had driven him into exile.

The end now drew nigh. Nekht-nebf, whom the Greeks called Nectanebo II., having after a time established himself firmly upon the throne, and got rid of pretenders, resumed the ambitious policy of his predecessor, and entered into an alliance with the people of Sidon and their neighbours, who were in revolt against Persia. He had the excuse that Ochus, some time previously, had sent an expedition against Egypt, which he had repulsed by the assistance of two Greek generals, Diophantus of Athens and Lamius of Sparta. But this expedition was a thing of the past; it had inflicted no injury on Egypt, and it demanded no revenge. Nekht-nebf was in no way called upon to join the rebel confederacy, which (in B.C. 346) raised the flag of revolt from Persia, and sought to enrol in its ranks as many allies as possible. But he rashly gave in his name, and sent to Sidon.

as his contingent towards the army that was being raised, four thousand of his Greek mercenaries, under the command of Mentor of Rhodes. With their aid, Tennes, the Sidonian king, completely defeated the troops which Ochus had sent against him, and drove the Persians out of Phœnicia.

The success, however, which was thus gained by the rebels only exasperated the Persian king, and made him resolve all the more on a desperate effort. The time had gone by, he felt, for committing wars to satraps, or sending out generals, with a few thousand troops, to put down this or that troublesome chieftain. The conjuncture called for measures of no ordinary character. The Great King must conduct an expedition in person. Every sort of preparation must be made; arms and provisions and stores of all kinds must be accumulated; the best troops must be collected from all parts of the empire; a sufficient fleet must be manned; and such an armament must go forth under the royal banner as would crush all opposition. Ochus succeeded in gathering together from the nations under his direct rule 300,000 foot, 30,000 horse, 300 triremes, and 500 transports or provision-ships. He then directed his efforts towards obtaining efficient assistance from the Greeks. Though refused aid by Athens and Sparta, he succeeded in obtaining a thousand Theban heavy-armed under Lacrates, three thousand Argives under Nicostratus, and six thousand Æolians, Ionians, and Dorians from the Greek cities of Asia Minor. The assistance thus secured was numerically small, amounting to no more than ten thousand men—not a thirtieth part of his native force;

but it formed, together with the Greek mercenaries from Egypt—who went over to him afterwards—the force on which he placed his chief reliance, and to which the ultimate success of his expedition was mainly due.

The overwhelming strength of the armament which Ochus had brought with him into Syria alarmed the chiefs of the rebel confederacy. Tennes, especially, the Sidonian monarch, despaired of a successful resistance, and made up his mind that his only chance of safety lay in his appeasing the anger of Ochus by the betrayal of his confederates and followers. He opened his designs to Mentor of Rhodes, the commander of the Greek mercenaries furnished by Egypt, and found him quite ready to come into his plans. The two in conjunction betrayed Sidon into the hands of Persia, by the admission of a detachment within the walls; after which the defence became impracticable. The Sidonians, having experienced the unrelenting temper and sanguinary spirit of the Persian king, who had transfixed with javelins six hundred of their principal citizens, came to the desperate resolution of setting fire to their houses, and so destroying themselves with their town. One is glad to learn that the cowardly traitor, Tennes, who had brought about these terrible calamities, did not derive any profit from them, but was executed by the command of Ochus, as soon as Sidon had fallen.

The reduction of Sidon was followed closely by the invasion of Egypt. Ochus, besides his 330,000 Asiatics, had now a force of 14,000 Greeks, the mercenaries under Mentor having joined him. Marshalling his army in four divisions, he proceeded to the attack.

The first, second, and third divisions contained, each of them, a contingent of Greeks and a contingent of Asiatics, commanded respectively by a Greek and a Persian leader. The Greeks of the first division, consisting mainly of Bœotians, were under the orders of Lacrates, a Theban of enormous strength, who regarded himself as a second Hercules, and adopted the traditional costume of that hero, a lion's skin and a club. His Persian colleague was Rhosaces, satrap of Ionia and Lydia, who claimed descent from one of " the Seven " that put down the conspiracy of the Magi. In the second division, where the Argive mercenaries served, the Greek leader was Nicostratus, the Persian Aristazanes, a court usher, and one of the most trusted friends of the king. Mentor and the eunuch Bagoas, Ochus's chief minister in his later years, were at the head of the third division, Mentor commanding his own mercenaries, and Bagoas the Greeks whom Ochus had levied in his own dominions, together with a large body of Asiatics. The king himself was sole commander of the fourth division, as well as commander-in-chief of the entire host. Nekht-nebf, on his side, was only able to oppose to this vast array an army less than one-third of the size. He had enrolled as many as sixty thousand of the Egyptian warrior class, and had the services of twenty thousand Greek mercenaries, and of about the same number of Libyan troops.

Pelusium, as usual, was the first point of attack. Nekht-nebf had taken advantage of the long delay of Ochus in Syria to see that the defences of Egypt were in good order ; he had made preparations for resistance at all the seven mouths of the Nile, and had guarded Pelusium with especial care. Ochus, as he had expected, advanced along the coast route which led to this place. Part of his army traversed the narrow spit of land which separated the Lake Serbonis from the Mediterranean, and in doing so met with a disaster. A strong wind setting in from the north, as the troops were passing, brought the waters of the Mediterranean over the low strip of sand which is ordinarily dry, and confounding sea and shore and lake together, caused the destruction of a large detachment; but the main army, which had probably kept Lake Serbonis on the right, reached its destination intact. A skirmish followed between the Theban troops of the first division under Lacrates and the garrison of Pelusium under Philophron; but this first engagement was without definite result.

The two armies lay now for a while on the Pelusiac branch of the Nile, which was well protected by forts, fortified towns, and a network of canals on either side of it. There was every reason to expect that Nekht-nebf, by warily guarding his frontier, and making full use of his resources, might baffle for a considerable time, if not wholly frustrate, the Persian attack. But his combined self-conceit and timidity ruined his cause. Taking the direction of affairs wholly upon himself and asking no advice from his Greek captains, he failed to show any of the qualities of a great commander, and was speedily involved in difficulties with which he was quite incapable of dealing. Having had his first line of defence partially forced by a bold movement on the part of the Argives under Nicostratus, instead of trying to redeem the misfortune by a counter-movement, or a concentration of troops, he hastily abandoned to his generals the task of continuing the resistance on this outer line, and retiring to Memphis, concentrated all his efforts on making preparations to resist a siege.

Meantime, the Persians were advancing. Lacrates the Theban set himself to reduce Pelusium, and, having drained dry one of the ditches, brought his military engines up to the walls of the place. In vain, however, did he batter down a portion of the wall—the garrison had erected another wall behind it; in vain did he advance his towers—they had movable towers ready prepared to resist him. No progress had been made by the besiegers, when on a sudden the resistance of the besieged slackened. Intelligence had reached them of Nekht-nebf's hasty retreat. If the king gave up hope, why should they pour out their blood to no purpose? Accordingly they ma1e overtures to Lacrates for a surrender upon terms, and it was agreed that they should be allowed to evacuate the place and return to Greece, with all the goods and chattels that they could carry with them. Bagoas demurred to the terms; but Ochus confirmed them, and Pelusium passed into the possession of the Persians without further fighting.

About the same time Mentor had proceeded southwards and laid siege to Bubastis. Having invested the town, he caused intelligence to reach the besieged that Ochus had determined to spare all who should surrender their cities to him without resistance, and to treat with the utmost severity all who should fight strenuously in their defence. By these means he introduced dissension within the walls of the towns, since the native Egyptians and their Greek allies naturally distrusted and suspected each other. At Bubastis the Egyptians were the first to move. The siege had only just begun when they sent an envoy to Mentor's colleague, Bagoas, to offer to surrender the town to him. But this proceeding did not suit the Greeks, who caught the messenger, extracted from him his message, and then attacked the Egyptian portion of the garrison and slew great numbers of them. The Egyptians, however, though beaten, persisted, established communication with Bagoas, and fixed a day on which they would receive his forces into the town. Mentor, who wished to secure to himself the credit of the surrender, hereupon exhorted his Greek friends to be on the watch, and, when the time came, to resist the movement. This they did with such success that they not only frustrated the attempt, but captured Bagoas himself, who had ventured within the walls. Bagoas had to implore the interference of his colleague on his behalf, and was obliged to promise that henceforth he would attempt nothing without Mentor's knowledge and consent. Mentor gained his ends, had the credit of being the person to whom the town surrendered itself, and at the same time established his ascendancy over Bagoas. It is clear that had the Egyptians possessed an active and able commander, advantage might have been taken of the jealousies which divided the Persian generals from their Greek colleagues, to bring the expedition into difficulties.

Unfortunately, the Egyptian monarch, alike pusillanimous and incapable, was so far from making any offensive effort, that he was not prepared even to defend his capital against the invaders. When he found that Pelusium and Bubastis had both fallen, and that the way lay open for the Persians to march upon Memphis and invest it, he left the city with all the wealth on which he could lay his hands, and fled away into Ethiopia. Ochus did not pursue him. He was content to have regained a valuable province, which for above fifty years had been lost to the Persian crown, without even having had to fight a single pitched battle, or to engage in one difficult siege. According to the Greek writers, he showed his contempt of the Egyptian religion after his conquest by stabbing an Apis-Bull, and violating the sanctity of a number of the most holy shrines ; but the story of the Apis-Bull is probably a fiction, and it was to obtain the plunder of the temples, not to insult the Egyptian gods, that he violated the shrines. There is no trace of his having treated the conquered people with cruelty, or even with severity. Prudence induced him to destroy the walls and other fortifications of the chief Egyptian towns ; and cupidity led him to carry off into Persia all the treasures that Nekht-nebf had left behind. Even the sacred books, of which he is said to have robbed the temples, may have been taken on account of their value. We do not hear of his having dragged off any prisoners, or inflicted any punishment on the country for its rebellion. Even the tribute is not said to have been increased.

There is nothing surprising in the fact that, when once Persia took resolutely in hand the subjugation of the revolted province, a few months sufficed for its accomplishment. The resources of Persia were out of all comparison with those of Egypt; alike in respect of men and of money, there was an extreme disparity. What had protected Egypt so long was the multiplicity of Persia's enemies, the large number of wars that were continually being waged and the want of a bold, energetic, and warlike monarch. As soon as the full power of the vast empire of the Achæmenidæ was directed against the little country which had detached itself, and pretended to a separate existence, the result was certain. Egypt could no more maintain a struggle against Persia in full force than a lynx could contend with a lion. But while all this is indubitably true, the end of Egypt might have been more dignified and more honourable than it was. Nekht-nebf, the last king, was a poor specimen of the Pharaonic type of monarch. He had none of the qualities of a great king. He did not even know how to fall with dignity. Had he gathered together all the troops that he could anyhow muster, and met Ochus in the open field, and fallen fighting for his crown, or had he even defended Memphis to the last, and only yielded himself when he could resist no longer, a certain halo of glory would have surrounded him. As it was, Egypt sank ingloriously at the last—her art, her literature, her national spirit decayed and almost extinct—paying, by her early disappearance from among the nations of the earth, the penalty of her extraordinarily precocious greatness.

INDEX.

A

Aahmes I., 152
"Aa-khepr-ka-ra, Abode of," 168
"Abode of Aa-khepr-ka-ra," 168
Abraham, deceit of, 127, 129
Abraham in Egypt, 125
Abyssinia, rainfall in, 113
Alliance with Babylon and Lydia, 371
Amasis, prosperity under, 367
Amenemhat I., 101
Amenemhat I., hunting prowess of, 103
Amenemhat III., 109
"Amenemhat the Good," 116
Amenemhat's Labyrinth, 121
Amenemhat's Reservoir, 118
Amenhotep II., conquests of, 206
Amenhotep II., cruelty of, 207
Amenhotep III., colossi of, 208
Amenhotep III., lion-hunting of, 220
Amenhotep III., personal appearance of, 222
Amenhotep III., wars of, 219
Amenhotep IV., accession of, 223
Ammon, High Priest of, 289
Ammon, restoration of temple of, 290
Ammon, temple of, 105, 167, 173, 186
Amon-mes, or Amomneses, pretender to crown, 265
Animal worship, 31
Animals, sacred, 31
Antef I., 97

Antef II.'s dogs, 98
Antiquities of Egypt, 45
Apé, or Apiu, city of, 96
Apepi and Joseph, 145
Apepi, rule of, 144
Apis, sacred bull, 32
Apries offends Nebuchadnezzar, 363
Architecture, 21, 245, 267
Art and literature, decline of, 285, 311
Art and literature, revival of, 350
Asa, Judæa revolts under, 307
Asa, victory of, 309
Asia, invasion of, 167, 195
Asshur-bani-pal, accession of, 336
Asshur-bani-pal, death of, 338
Asshur-bani-pal, defeat of Tehrak by, 336
Assyria, 11
Assyrian gifts to Thothmes III., 194
Athor cow, 33
Auaris, siege of, 152

B

Babylon, revolt of, 345
Bacis, sacred bull, 32
Bahr Yousouf, 1
Bastinado, 45
Bek-en-ranf, burning of, 323
Builders, the Pyramid, 82
Buildings of Thothmes III., 199, 201
Bulls, sacred, 32

404 INDEX.

C

Cairo, Modern, 52, 95
Cambyses, indignities by, 378
Campaigns of Thothmes III., 191
Chaldean Monarchy, end of, 371
Character, Egyptian, 24
Character, types of, 27
Colossi of Amenhotep III., 208
Condition, social, 60
Corrupting influences, 353
Costume, early, 60
Costume of Women, 62
Crocodile, mode of hunting, 104
Crœsus, 370
Cushites, the, 154
Cyprus, 197
Cyrene, death of, 394
Cyrus, death of, 372

D

Darius, death of, 382
Darius, revolt against, 381
David and Solomon, empire of, 295
Decline, 244, 269, 283
Decline of art and literature, 285, 311
Decline of morals, 286
Defeat, double, of invaders, 277
Defeat of Neco by Nebuchadnezzar, 358
Deities, Egyptian, 30
Deities, evil, 36, 37
Delta, the, 1, 95, 102
Disaster of the Red Sea, 264
Disintegration, 311, 317
Disk worship, 223, 225, 230, 231
Drollery, Egyptian, 29
Dynasties, rival, established, 311

E

Egypt, monotony of, 19
Egypt, seasons of, 14
Egypt, shape of, 1
Egypt, situation of, 11
Egypt, size of, 9
Egypt, soil of, 10
Egyptian history, happiest age of, 100

Egyptian independence re-established, 389
Egyptian myths, 47
Egyptian physique, 25
Egyptians, nature of, 28
Elephant hunting, 194
El-Uksur, temple of, 217
Empire of David and Solomon, 295
Esarhaddon, accession of, 331
Esarhaddon's defeat of Tehrak, 333
Ethiopia and Syria, struggles between, 337
Ethiopia, Egyptian influence in, 315
Ethiopia, last efforts of, 339
Ethiopian rule firmly established, 323
Ethiopians, cruelty of, 338
Evil deities, 36, 37
Expeditions into Asia, 167, 195

F

Famines through deficient inundation, 115
Fayoum, obelisk at, 106
Fayoum, the, 4, 7
Fellahin, explanation of, 45
First sea-fight, 277
Fleet of Hatasu, 178
Flora of Egypt, 15
Foreigners, encouragement of, 351
Forests, incense, 183
Free Trade in Punt, 183

G

Geology of Egypt, 15
Great Pyramid, 72
Greece, trade with, 352
Ghizeh, three Pyramids at, 67
Ghizeh, tombs at, 56, 137
Gyges and Psamatik, 345

H

Hall at Karnak, 266
Hall of Seti, 245
Handicrafts, Egyptian, 44
Hapi, 32

INDEX. 405

Hapi, merchant fleet of, 178
Hapi regarded as a male, 178
Hapi regent for Thothmes II., 173
Hapi, Thothmes III.'s animosity against, 187
Hatasu actual queen, 177
Hatasu's fleet, return of, 184
Hebrew art, Egyptian influence in, 297
Heliopolis, temple at, 106
Her-hor, first high-priest king, 290
Herodotus, 384
Hittites, peace with, 242
Hittites, treaty with, 243
Hittites, war with, 233
Hosea, Shabak's dealings with, 325
Hostage, Thothmes III.'s system of, 195
Hyksôs conquered, 151
Hyksôs, religion of, 143
Hyksôs rule, 139

I

Immigrants, Semitic, 109, 130
Immortality of the soul, belief in, 39
Inarus, death of, 384
Inarus, revolt of, 383
Incense forests, 183
Industries, revival of, 350
Influences, corrupting, 353
Inundation, 13
Inundation, deficient, famines through, 115
Invasion, 396
Invasion by land and sea, 275
Invasion, Libyan, 255
Invasion, the great, 134
Israel's oppressor, 249

J

Jeroboam at Shishak's court, 301
Jerusalem, destruction of, 362
Joseph and Apepi, 145
Josiah, defeat of, by Nico, 357
Judæa insecure, 361
Judæa's conquest, record of, 305

K

Kadesh, battle of. 239
Karnak, hall at, 266
Karnak, temple at, 173, 198, 200, 304, 349, 386
Khabash, accession of, 381
Khartoum, 8
Khu-en-Aten, 227
Khu-en-Aten, personal appearance of, 229
Khufu, King, 82, 90
King, supposed first, 49
Kings in awe of priests, 288

L

Labouring class, condition of, 45
Labyrinth, Amenemhat's, 121
Legend of Osiris, 34
Libyan desert, battle in, 346
Libyan invasion, 255
Libyans, defeat of, 273
Libyans, slaughter of, 274
Literature and art, decline of, 311
Lower Egypt, 96
Lower orders, condition of, 45
Luxor, temple of, 217

M

Medes, the, 369
Medinet-Abou, temple at, 272
Megiddo, capture of, 191
Memphis, 51
Memphis, blockade and fall of, 377, 383
Memphis taken by Esarhaddon, 333
Menephthah I., accession of, 253
Menes, King, 50, 52
Men-kau-ra, King, 68, 82, 90
Men-khepr-ra, King, accession, of, 294
Mentu-hotep I., 97
Mertitefs, wife of Sneferu, 64
Meydoum, pyramid of, 58
Mi-Ammon-Nut, accession of, 338
Mi-Ammon-Nut, death of, 340
Mi-Ammon-Nut, Submission to, 340

Mnevis, sacred bull, 32
Mœris, lake, 120
Monuments, objects on, 196
Moral standard, 42
Morality, Egyptian, 41
Morals, decline of, 286
Myth, chief Egyptian, 34
Myths, Egyptian, 47

N

Naïri, war on the, 167
Napatra, Necropolis at, 316
Natural History of Egypt, 16
Naval power of Thothmes, III.
Navy of Nero, 354
Nebuchadnezzar and Neco, 358
Nebuchadnezzar overruns Egypt, 365
Neco, accession of, 354
Neco defeats Josiah, 357
Neco, navy of, 354
Neco, victories of, 358
Nectanebo I., accession of, 387
Nectanebo I., sarcophagus of 391
Nefer-mat, son of Sneferu, 64
Nekht-nebf, accession of, 394
Nile, navigation on, 13
Nile, rising of the, 113
Nile valley, 1, 95, 102, 117
Nineveh, 192

O

Obelisk of Usurtasen I., 137
Objects on monuments, 196
Ochus, expedition of, 394
Osiris, legend of, 34
Osorkon I., accession of, 306

P

Pacis, sacred bull, 32
Parihu, king of Punt, 182
Payment of tribute, 149
Pelusium, surrender of, 399
Persia, third rebellion against, 385
Persian conquest, 368
Persian power, rise of, 369
Persians, revolt against, 382
Pharnabazus, attack by, 388

Pharnabazus, repulse of, 390
Phœnicia, 11
Phthah, temple of, 51, 349
Piankhi, king of Napatra, 317
Piankhi, rebellion against, 318
Piankhi, submission of petty princes to, 320
Pinetum I., accession of, 293
Plagues of Egypt, the, 262
Polytheism, 31
Priest, High, of Ammon, 289
Priest-kings, last of the, 297
Priests, kings in awe of, 288
Prosopis, battle of, 260
Prosperity under Amasis, 367
Psamatik I. and Gyges, 345
Psamatik I., origin of, 343
Psamatik I., sole king, 347
Psamatik I., marriage of, 348
Psamatik I., victory of, 346
Psamatik II., architectural activity of, 361
Psamatik III., accession of, 374
Psamatik III., death of, 377
Psamatik III., defeat of, 375
Public schools, 45
Punt, free trade in, 183
Punt's, Queen of, visit to Hatasu, 182
Pyramid builders, Egypt under the, 91
Pyramid builders, the, 82
Pyramid, great, 72
Pyramid of Meydoum, 58
Pyramid of Saccarah, 59
Pyramids, Egyptian idea of, 66
Pyramids, three, at Ghizeh, 67

R

Ra-Sekenen III., Apepi's jealousy of, 150
Ra-Sekenen III., war forced upon, 151
Ramesses I., 232
Ramesses II., Hittite war of, 239
Ramesses II., Israel's oppressor, 249
Ramesses III., accession of, 271
Ramesses III., closing years of, 283

INDEX. 407

Ramesses III., plot to kill, 284
Ramesses III., temple of, 272
Red Sea, disaster of, 264
Rehoboam, submission of, 303
Religion, 35-41
Reservoir, Amenemhat's, 118
Revival of Arts and Industries, 350
Revolt against Darius, 381
Revolt against the Persians, 382
Rival dynasties, 311
Rut-Ammon, accession and death of, 338

S

Saccarah, Great Pyramid of, 59
Sacred animals, 31
Sacred bulls, 32
St. John Lateran, monument of, 202
Sankh-ka-ra, King, 99
Saplal, Hittite king, 232
Sargon, death of, 327
Sargon, founder of last Assyrian dynasty, 326
Schools, public, 45
Sea-fight, first, 277
Second cataract, 106, 111
Semetic immigrants, 130
Sennacherib, accession of, 327
Sennacherib, victories of, 328
Sennacherib's army, destruction of, 329, 331
Set, Egyptian deity, 143
Set the victorious, 269
Seti the Great, victories of, 234
Seti the Great, wars of, 236
Seti the Great, long wall of, 237
Seti the Great, Pillared Hall, 245
Seti the Great, tomb of, 246
Seti I., head of, 250
Seti I., images of, 248
Seti I., mummy of, 251
Shabak burns Bek-en-ranf, 323
Shabak, death of, 327
Shabak's conquest of Lower Nile, 324
Shabak's dealings with Hosea, 325
Shabatok, accession of, 327
Shafra, King, 82, 90, 92
Shasu, campaign against the, 273

Shepherds, Egypt under, 139
Sheshonk dynasty, defeat of, 309
Shishak, accession of, 300
Shishak, dominion of, 304
Shishak, foreign origin of, 298
Shishak invades Judæa, 303
Shishak's reception of Jeroboam, 301
Sidon, capture of, 396
Siege of Memphis, 376
Signs on tombs, 57
Slave-hunting lucrative, 220
Sneferu, first certain king, 54
Social condition, 60
Social ranks, 43
Society, divisions of, 43
Song of Egyptians, 26
Song of victory, 198
Soul, belief in immortality of, 39
Sphinx, the, 92
Standard, moral, 42
Suez, Isthmus of, 11
Syria and Ethiopia, struggle between, 337
Syria evacuated by Neco, 359

T

Tachos, accession of, 393
Taxation, heavy, 45
Tehrak, death of, 337
Tehrak defeated by Asshur-banipal, 336
Tehrak defeated by Esarhaddon, 333
Tel-el-Bahiri, 185
Tel-Mouf, 51
Temple of Ammon, 167, 173, 186, 290
Temple of Karnak, 198, 200, 304, 349, 386
Temple of Medinet-Abou, 272
Temple of Phthah, 349
Temple of Tel-el-Bahiri, 185
Theban kings, 99
Thothmes I., accession of, 158
Thothmes I., greatness of, 168
Thothmes I., victories of, 159
Thothmes II., death of, 177
Thothmes III., animosity against Hatasu, 187

Thothmes III., buildings of, 199, 201
Thothmes III., campaigns of, 191
Thothmes III., conquests of, 204
Thothmes III., lost obelisks of, 201
Thothmes III., naval power of, 197
Thothmes III., personal appearance of, 204
Thothmes III.'s system of tribute, 195
Thothmes III., tributes of, 196
Tinæus, King, 135
Tombs at Ghizeh, 56, 137
Tombs, description of, 57
Tombs, signs on, 57
Trade with Greece, 352
Trade with the Jews, 295
Transport, difficulty of, 12
Treaty with the Hittites, 243
Tribute, payment of, 49

U

Usurtasen I., obelisk of, 137
Usurtasen I., son of Amenemhat, 104
Usurtasen I., statue of, 105
Usurtasen II., 109
Usurtasen III., conquest of, 111

V

Victoria, lake, 8
Victory, song of, 198
Vocal Memnon, the, 212

W

Wady Halfa, 106
Wady Magharah, 54, 106
Water, modes of storing, 117
Western Asia, history of, 162
Western Asia, topography of, 155
" Wilderness of the Wanderings," 164
Women, costume of, 62
Women held in high estimation, 170
Worship, animal, 31

Z

Zabara, Mount, 15
Zerah, defeat of, 308

The Story of the Nations.

MESSRS. G. P. PUTNAM'S SONS take pleasure in announcing that they have in course of publication a series of historical studies, intended to present in a graphic manner the stories of the different nations that have attained prominence in history.

In the story form the current of each national life will be distinctly indicated, and its picturesque and noteworthy periods and episodes will be presented for the reader in their philosophical relation to each other as well as to universal history.

It is the plan of the writers of the different volumes to enter into the real life of the peoples, and to bring them before the reader as they actually lived, labored, and struggled—as they studied and wrote, and as they amused themselves. In carrying out this plan, the myths, with which the history of all lands begins, will not be overlooked, though these will be carefully distinguished from the actual history, so far as the labors of the accepted historical authorities have resulted in definite conclusions.

The subjects of the different volumes will be planned to cover connecting and, as far as possible, consecutive epochs or periods, so that the set when completed will present in a comprehensive narrative the chief events in the great STORY OF THE NATIONS; but it will, of. course not always prove practicable to issue the several volumes in their chronological order.

The "Stories" are printed in good readable type, and in handsome 12mo form. They are adequately illustrated and furnished with maps and indexes. They are sold separately at a price of $1.50 each.

The following is a partial list of the subjects thus far determined upon:

THE STORY OF *ANCIENT EGYPT. Prof. GEORGE RAWLINSON.
" " " *CHALDEA. Z. A. RAGOZIN.
" " " *GREECE. Prof. JAMES A. HARRISON,
       Washington and Lee University.
" " " *ROME. ARTHUR GILMAN.
" " " *THE JEWS. Prof. JAMES K. HOSMER,
       Washington University of St. Louis.
" " " *CARTHAGE. Prof. ALFRED J. CHURCH,
       University College, London.
" " " BYZANTIUM.
" " " THE GOTHS. HENRY BRADLEY.
" " " *THE NORMANS. SARAH O. JEWETT.
" " " *PERSIA. S. G. W. BENJAMIN.
" " " *SPAIN. Rev. E. E. and SUSAN HALE.
" " " *GERMANY. S. BARING-GOULD.
" " " THE ITALIAN REPUBLICS.
" " " HOLLAND. Prof. C. E. THOROLD ROGERS.
" " " *NORWAY. HJALMAR H. BOYESEN.
" " " *THE MOORS IN SPAIN. STANLEY LANE-POOLE.
" " " *HUNGARY. Prof. A. VÁMBÉRY.
" " " THE ITALIAN KINGDOM. W. L. ALDEN.
" " " EARLY FRANCE. Prof. GUSTAVE MASSON.
" " " *ALEXANDER'S EMPIRE. Prof. J. P. MAHAFFY.
" " " THE HANSE TOWNS. HELEN ZIMMERN.
" " " *ASSYRIA. Z. A. RAGOZIN.
" " " *THE SARACENS. ARTHUR GILMAN.
" " " TURKEY. STANLEY LANE-POOLE.
" " " PORTUGAL. H. MORSE STEPHENS.
" " " MEXICO. SUSAN HALE.
" " " *IRELAND. Hon. EMILY LAWLESS.
" " " PHŒNICIA.
" " " SWITZERLAND.
" " " RUSSIA.
" " " WALES.
" " " SCOTLAND.

* (The volumes starred are now ready, January, 1888.)

G. P. PUTNAM'S SONS
NEW YORK   LONDON
27 AND 29 WEST TWENTY-THIRD STREET   27 KING WILLIAM STREET, STRAND

www.ingramcontent.com/pod-product-compliance
Lightning Source LLC
Chambersburg PA
CBHW051734300426
44115CB00007B/563